MODERN LETTER WRITING MADE EASY

Lillian Eichler Watson shows you how to write correct, effective and gracious letters for all occasions. Using hundreds of sample letters, Mrs. Watson helps you solve every letter-writing problem—effective sales letters, formal social occasions, condolences, club correspondence, love letters, bread-and-butter notes, and the lively, personal "visit on paper."

THE BANTAM BOOK OF CORRECT LETTER WRITING

COMPLETE • INFORMATIVE • EASY TO USE

THE BANTAM BOOK OF CORRECT LETTER WRITING

·

An abridgment based on
LILLIAN EICHLER WATSON'S
STANDARD BOOK OF LETTER WRITING

BANTAM BOOKS
TORONTO · NEW YORK · LONDON · SYDNEY · AUCKLAND

RL 7, IL age 12 and up

THE BANTAM BOOK OF CORRECT LETTER WRITING
An abridgment based on Lillian Eichler Watson's
STANDARD BOOK OF LETTER WRITING.
Copyright, 1948, by Lillian Eichler Watson.

*A Bantam Book / published by arrangement with
Prentice-Hall, Inc.*

*Bantam edition / April 1958
29 printings through September 1983*

Library of Congress Catalog Card Number: 58-5993

ISBN 0-553-24145-1

Published simultaneously in the United States and Canada

PRINTED IN THE UNITED STATES OF AMERICA

H   38 37 36 35 34 33 32 31

Acknowledgment

The author wishes to thank the following for permission to use material in this book:

Printers' Ink: H. D. Shaw, "How to Write an Effective Letter."

Victor O. Schwab: *How to Write a Good Advertisement.*

John B. Opdycke: *Take a Letter, Please!*

Thomas Y. Crowell Company: Curtis Gentry, *Fifty Famous Letters of History.*

Doubleday and Company, Inc.: Captain Robert E. Lee, *Recollections and Letters of General Robert E. Lee.*

Simon and Schuster, Inc.: M. Lincoln Schuster, *A Treasury of the World's Great Letters.*

Latham Ovens: "Letter to a Soldier."

Pantheon Books Inc.: G. Selden-Goth, *Felix Mendelssohn-Bartholdy Letters.*

Charles Scribner's Sons: Elliot Merrick, *Northern Nurse.*

R. H. Morris Associates: "How to Pre-judge the Effectiveness of Your Letter."

Table of Contents

BOOK III

YOUR PERSONAL CORRESPONDENCE

BOOK IV

YOUR BUSINESS AND CLUB CORRESPONDENCE

BOOK V

CHILDREN'S CORRESPONDENCE

As long as there are postmen, life will have zest.

—WILLIAM JAMES

THE BANTAM BOOK OF

CORRECT
LETTER
WRITING

Book I

*

The Basic Rules
of
Successful Letter Writing

* * *

1. Letter Writing as a Social Asset

There's an old familiar saying that you must have heard many times: "To have a friend, you must be a friend."

It's equally true that to receive interesting letters, you must *write* interesting letters. If you write only when absolutely necessary, when duty or responsibility demands, you are missing out on what can be one of the greatest personal enjoyments of life.

But apart from the pleasure and satisfaction that a wide correspondence with friends can mean to you, letter writing is an important social asset. The ability to write good letters can be as useful to you socially as the ability to talk well or entertain successfully. In some ways letter writing can be even more useful to you, for it helps facilitate all social activities—often saves you much time, trouble and inconvenience.

The letter you write is your personal representative. It takes your place when circumstances make it impossible for you to be there in person. It goes to the hospital to cheer a sick friend. It goes to your hostess to thank her for entertaining you. It conveys your best wishes, congratulations, condolences—when you are not able to do so in person.

WHAT THE ABILITY TO WRITE
GOOD LETTERS CAN MEAN TO YOU

Letters can be one of the most powerful and far-reaching influences in your life, if you let them be. They can do amazing

1

things—can help you in more ways than you may realize. In fact, few accomplishments can serve you so well, in so many varied ways, all through life, as the ability to write good letters.

We are not here concerned with the great *practical* value of letter writing, which is discussed in a later chapter. Everybody knows and realizes the tremendous importance of letter writing as a business asset. Everybody knows that good convincing letters win more jobs and influence more people than dull, stereotyped, rubber-stamp letters.

But what is not so well-known and well-realized is the importance of letter writing as a personal asset. Letters can add in every way, and in very great measure, to the enjoyment of life. They can bridge any distance . . . bring friends closer in intimacy and understanding . . . enrich social relationships . . . increase personal popularity . . . win affection . . . inspire love . . . provide a most satisfying means of self-expression!

A LETTER IS LIKE A
VISIT ON PAPER

If you "hate to write letters," it's simply because you have not yet discovered the fun it can be to write and receive letters that are *good talk* on paper. Do you hate to visit your friends and talk with them face to face? Then why hate to write a letter which is—or should be—a pleasant "visit" on paper?

Many people actually disregard letters from family and friends, deliberately neglecting to answer them. Others put off answering until the person who wrote has every reason to feel slighted and hurt. To leave a letter unanswered is like saying, "I can't be bothered writing! I don't think you're worth the time and effort it takes to write a letter."

Surely you wouldn't dream of saying that directly to anyone! Then don't imply it by leaving letters unanswered, or by putting off your answer for too long a time. Courtesy demands that every letter you receive be answered . . . and answered promptly.

This is especially true of family letters. It is not only a discourtesy but an unkindness to ignore letters from relatives who are concerned about your welfare, or the welfare of members of your immediate family. Few things can give a greater lift to the spirit, a greater boost to morale, than a cheerful, newsy letter . . . an intimate visit on paper with someone near and dear.

The late General Smedley D. Butler said, "Give our fighting men bullets and biscuits and a letter from home and they'll lick the world!"

He rated letters from home right up at the top with ammunition and food . . . the three most vital elements for a fighting man's well-being and morale.

How eagerly, in all times and all places, have people waited for mail from home! How wistfully have they repeated, over and over again, that old familiar question: "Any mail for me?"

"I wonder what letter was ever received with such thankfulness!" wrote Thomas Carlyle's wife, thanking him for a letter that arrived on her birthday.

"I long for a letter from you!" wrote Princess Alice of England—happily married to Prince Louis of Hesse and living with him in Darmstadt—but lonely for her mother, Queen Victoria, as any child might be lonely for a parent.

"Your letter and mother's have come at last! I was so glad to get them I cried," wrote Anne Sullivan Macy to Helen Keller, her beloved pupil and lifelong friend.

HOW LETTERS CAN ENRICH LIFE— CREATE MORE ENDURING FRIENDSHIPS

There's a lot of truth in the old saying, "Out of sight, out of mind!" But letters keep your influence and personality alive— keep you in the hearts and minds of those far removed from you. Through an appreciation and understanding of the best uses of letter writing, you can not only maintain your friendships uninterrupted over long periods of separation, but you can lay the foundations for much real pleasure and enjoyment in future years. Letter writing brings its own great rewards; and not the least of these are more enduring friendships and far less likelihood of ever being lonely or bored.

History tells us of many beautiful and inspiring friendships built on letters alone. A hundred years ago, Elizabeth Barrett, a lonely invalid, published a volume of poems which brought a friendly letter of praise from Robert Browning. Miss Barrett, in her own words, "pounced upon the opportunity of corresponding with the poet" . . . and the whole world knows the result of that correspondence.

George Bernard Shaw and Ellen Terry carried on a fascinating correspondence for more than twenty-five years—a delightful romance on paper that enriched the lives of both.

Charles Lamb, Horace Walpole, Madame de Sévigné, Madame de Staël, John Keats, Robert Louis Stevenson are only a few of the notable letter writers of the past.

THE BUSIEST PEOPLE MAKE THE BEST LETTER WRITERS

So don't ever say, "I haven't the time to write!" Everyone has exactly twenty-four hours a day—no more, no less. The time is there; it's up to you to use some part of it for writing interesting letters *if you want to receive interesting letters in return.*

After all, it's the busiest people who usually make the best letter writers! They have so much more to write about.

Washington, Hamilton, Emerson, Mark Twain—all were conscientious letter writers who took time from their busy careers to correspond regularly with family and friends.

Lincoln was often too busy to eat or sleep, but never too busy to write the letters he wanted to write. Some of the most human and touching letters in existence are from his pen, written when he was most oppressed and most obsessed by the state of the Union.

But by far one of the most brilliant and prodigious correspondents of all time was Benjamin Franklin. Scientist, statesman, philosopher, editor, printer, inventor—Frankin had so many busy careers, you would think he had no time at all for personal correspondence. Yet he wrote regularly to friends on both sides of the Atlantic. He thoroughly *enjoyed* letter writing. He looked upon it as a pleasant relaxation and as an enrichment of life rather than a dull, time-consuming duty.

The busiest woman in Labrador, one bitter cold Christmas not very long ago, was an Australian nurse by the name of Kate Austen. But Nurse Austen was not too busy to acknowledge with a long, friendly letter every gift of food or clothing received for distribution to the natives in that bleak and barren outpost of the north. Among the gifts was a box of knitted things for children, made and sent by a woman in Toronto. Nurse Austen, busy, harassed, and not too well that winter, could have written just an ordinary routine note of thanks, cold and informal. But that was not her way. She sat down and wrote a *real* letter telling all about the village, and the names of the children who were wearing the knitted gloves and caps, and what they said when they got them, and how they looked when they wore them. She wanted the woman who had made and sent all those lovely knitted things "to see how much happiness and warmth she had created."

Here is the answer Nurse Austen received. It illustrates perfectly what I said at the very beginning of this chapter: that to *receive* interesting letters, you must *write* interesting letters!

Dear Miss Austen,

Your letter made me happy. I did not expect such a full return. I am eighty years old, and I am blind. There is little I can do except knit, and that is why I make so many caps and sweaters and scarves. Of course I cannot write this, so my daughter-in-law is doing it for me. She also sewed the seams and made the button-holes for the knitted things.

I know something of the work you are doing. At the age of nineteen I married a man who was going to China to be a missionary. For forty years, with an occasional year at home in America, we worked in China, and during that time our two sons and a daughter were born to us, of whom only one son survives. After forty years, my husband's health began to fail. We returned to the States where he took charge of a settlement house in Brooklyn, New York. A surprising number of the problems we faced there were similar to problems we had met in China. When my husband died, I came to Toronto to live with my son and daughter-in-law. They are very good to me, and I pride myself that I am little trouble to them, though it is hard for a blind old lady to be sure of anything.

What I most wanted to say, my dear, is this. For sixty years I have been making up missionary packages of such clothing or food or medicine or books as I could collect. In various parts of the world and to various parts of the world I have sent them. Sometimes I have received a printed slip of acknowledgement from the headquarters depot or mission board, sometimes nothing. Occasionally I have been informed that my contribution was destined for Syria or Armenia or the upper Yangtze. But never before in all that time have I had a personal letter picturing the village and telling me who is wearing the clothing and what they said. I did not suppose that ever in my lifetime I should receive a letter like that. May God bless you.

> Sincerely yours,
> Laura N. Russell

WRITE THE LETTERS THAT
DON'T NEED TO BE WRITTEN

Comparatively few of us ever discover the joy of writing the letters *we do not need to write.* How long has it been since you sat down to write a letter for no other purpose than to give someone pleasure? Why not form the habit of writing little notes now and then to those you like, and whose friendship you value? Try to make opportunities to write, instead of waiting for some logical reason or excuse to come up.

For example, you might write a friendly little note of encouragement to someone just entering college . . . or someone just starting out in business. You might write a few words of cheer to an invalid . . . a shut-in . . . or someone you know is lonely, worried or unhappy. Or you might try a letter of congratulation to someone who has just had a promotion, wishing him or her success in the new job. Such notes are always received with gratitude, and often remembered a lifetime.

SEND PERSONAL LETTERS INSTEAD
OF GREETING CARDS WHENEVER YOU CAN

A good time to write personal notes to your friends is on birthdays and holidays, instead of sending the customary greeting cards. A personal message is more gracious, and means so much more than a printed sentiment. Even the old traditional "Happy New Year!" has more meaning—sounds more eloquent and sincere—when it's in your own handwriting.

But perhaps you are thinking, "I *must* send greetings cards—they save time! I couldn't possibly write personal notes to all my friends at Christmas."

That's true, of course, if you have a great many friends and acquaintances. It would be too big a job to write letters to all of them; and a needless waste of time and energy when greeting cards are so universally used.

But among those many friends, aren't there a few who would deeply appreciate a personal message? Isn't it worth a little extra effort for the intense satisfaction that an unexpected "visit on paper" can mean to them . . . and to you?

IF YOU "DON'T KNOW WHAT TO SAY"
IN A LETTER

If you complain that you never know what to say in a letter, it's only because you still think of writing as somehow different from talking. It isn't! Talking is an expression of thoughts and ideas in spoken words. Writing is, or should be, those same words on paper.

The only person who can truthfully say he has nothing interesting to write about is the person who sits alone in an empty room twenty-four hours a day—seeing no one, doing nothing—just sitting and staring. And even he could write an interesting letter telling his impressions of complete solitude!

So don't ever say that you don't know what to write in a letter! It's an admission that you are leading a dull and empty life. Write about the things you see, and hear and do—and plan to do! Write to share good news or relate an interesting experience. Write to express your thoughts and ideas on whatever subjects are mutually interesting to you and your correspondent.

Has he been ill? *Ask how he's feeling!* Has he been worried about his job? *Ask how he's getting along!* Is he interested in gardening? *Tell him about some recent experience—successful or otherwise—that you have had with flowers!* Does he like to read? *Tell him about the interesting book you've just read, and why you think he may enjoy it!*

In other words, write about the very same things you'd talk about if you were together.

2. Personality in Letter Writing

You may not have thought of it just this way, but the letter you write is part of *you,* an expression of your personality. Therefore to write letters that are mere patterns of form is to present a *colorless* personality.

Letters, by their very nature, are too individual to be standardized. A letter may be absolutely perfect according to the standards of good taste and good form; but unless it also expresses something of the writer's personality, it is not a good letter.

In other words, don't be satisfied to write letters that are just *correct* and nothing more. Try to write letters that are *correct for you* . . . letters that are warm and alive with reflections of your own personality.

And if this sounds like a platitude, stop for a moment and think back over your recent correspondence. What was the most interesting letter you received? Was it a letter anyone could have written? Or was it a letter that instantly "came alive" as you read it—that brought the personality of the sender right into the room with you, as though you were face to face, *listening* instead of *reading?*

The fault with too many letters, today as in the past—the reason so many letters are dull and lifeless, and often fail to accomplish the purpose for which they are written, is simply this: *They sound exactly like the letters everyone else writes.* They are neither exciting to receive nor stimulating to read.

MAKE YOUR LETTERS SOUND
THE WAY YOU DO

By all the approved standards of today, the most natural letters are the best letters.

Therefore the very first thing you should strive for in letter writing is a natural, spontaneous sincerity. The first and most important rule is *"Be yourself!"*

The whole secret is to write in an easy, natural way—without self-consciousness—like one friendly human being talking to another. Make your letters sound as much as possible like your conversation. Make your letters sound the way *you* sound . . . and they'll take on your personality.

So few people write naturally and without constraint that letters so written are bound to be outstanding. The trouble is that most of us try to compose letters instead of just writing as we speak. We try to sound literary and impressive.

There is no reason why you should write to your friends any differently than you speak to them—except, of course, in a strictly formal communication. To talk one way and write another is an affectation that betrays itself in the forced and insincere language of your letters.

The ideal is to write *without awareness of writing*—to let the words flow from your pen as they flow from your lips. The person who receives your letter should be almost able to see and hear you while reading it. That's the final test. That's what tells whether or not your letter has *personality*.

VISUALIZE THE PERSON TO WHOM YOU ARE WRITING

Before you start a letter, always try to visualize the person to whom you are writing. It will help you express yourself in an easier and more natural style.

Think of his interests, his likes and dislikes, his activities, his hobbies. Imagine yourself seated in a room with that person, talking of things that are mutually interesting. What information would you volunteer? What questions would you ask? Or what questions would *he* ask, and how would you answer them? Map out in your mind what you would be most likely to say to that person if you were with him . . . and say it. Say it out loud, and listen to the sound of it.

Then write your letter!

JUST WRITE AS YOU SPEAK— THAT'S THE WHOLE SECRET

You'll find that writing letters is easier, and a lot more fun, when you get on to the knack of writing as you speak. There's really no great trick to it. Just keep thinking of what you want to say, not the way to say it. Remember that the important thing is the message, not the words. If you keep thinking of what you want to say, the words will take care of themselves. The *first* way of saying it that comes to your mind is usually the best way for you. It's your way; it gives *your personality* to the letter. The more you keep thinking about *how* to say it, the more stilted and involved its expression is likely to become.

This is not an original idea. William Cobbett, a vigorous and terse writer of the early nineteenth century—and William Hazlitt, a contemporary—are two of many who advised a style of writing "as natural as effortless conversation." The advice applies to letter writing as it does to all other forms of writing; and is as sound and workable today as it was then. Here are Cobbett's words—a source of inspiration to some of our best-known modern writers:

> Sit down to write what you have thought, and not to think what you shall write! Use the first words that occur to you, and never attempt to alter a thought; for that which has come of itself into your mind is likely to pass into that of another more readily and with more effect than anything which you can, by reflection, invent.

Many people become "tongue-tied" when they sit down to write a letter. They find it difficult to express themselves in a simple, natural way—because, for some reason, they think they must write "better" than they speak. Usually, though, they succeed only in writing less interestingly. Their sentences creak with the mechanics of construction; and their letters sound labored and forced . . . and what is worse, insincere.

As you know, people always talk best when they don't stop to think about it. And the same is true of letter writing. The best letters are lively, smooth-flowing "talk," put down on paper without too much thought to the actual mechanics of writing. It's the letter written with *least difficulty*—the letter written without the distressing "labor pains" of construction—that sounds most natural and sincere.

Your aim, therefore, should be to write with ease. And that is best accomplished by writing as you speak: by using the identical words and phrases—even the very slang and the familiar patter—of your ordinary everyday speech.

USE YOUR CUSTOMARY
WORDS AND PATTER

The more closely your letter follows your own characteristic patter, the more engagingly it reflects the color and warmth of your personality.

So don't grope for flowery words that just make you sound affected! Don't try to write any differently than you speak!

For example, if you would ordinarily say to a friend: "Guess what? The most wonderful thing has happened! We're going to California to live!" . . . don't get tangled up in pompous rhetoric when you sit down to write! It will sound delightfully vivid and alive if you write it just that way in your letter. It will sound like *you*.

There is nothing actually wrong about the following letter of thanks. It's typical of the usual letter of this kind, written by the average person:

> Thanks for a most delightful evening. The dinner was superb and we enjoyed it very much. We look forward to reciprocating in the near future.

But it is not the purpose of this book to teach you the "average" or "typical" way of writing letters! That destroys the very quality we believe most desirable: an easy, natural sincerity. Surely if you met your hostess in the street, you wouldn't thank her in such careful, studied words! You would be yourself. You would let your personality shine through. You would sound cordial and enthusiastic. You would let her see that you really enjoyed and appreciated her hospitality.

If the following is approximately what you would say to your hostess in person, write it exactly that way in your letters:

> We had real fun at your house last night, Jane! And the dinner was tops, as usual. Jim is still raving about that luscious dessert. (I wish *I* could make it!) Thanks a million for a really swell evening. It will be our turn next—soon, I hope.

That's *you* talking! That's not "fine English"—nor studied form—nor cut-and-dried, run-of-the-mill phraseology! It's just YOU: *your* words, *your* patter, *your* personality. And that's why it has a freshness and charm that are lacking in the first letter.

Naturally, you must consider the person to whom you are writing. You do not speak to a dignified public official, a visiting celebrity, nor the principal of your daughter's school on the same intimate, carefree basis that you speak to an old friend. Nor do you *write* to everyone on the same basis.

Ask yourself, "For whom am I writing?"—then make your letter fit that person.

Ask yourself, "What would I say in conversation with that

person?"—then say those same things, in the same way, in your letter.

Keep your correspondent in mind. Read your letter through his eyes. Does it ring true? Does it sound natural and sincere? Is that what you would say in conversation with him?

SOME EASY WAYS TO MAKE YOUR LETTERS SOUND CONVERSATIONAL

You have probably noticed that in conversation with people you rarely say "I am," or "you have" or "they are." Such careful enunciation of each word sounds stilted and formal. You almost always contract the two words into one. "I'm going to the park" is the way you'd say it. Or "You've been away so long!" Or "They're coming for the week end." Try writing it that way; you'll find it adds a more amiable and informal touch to your letters.

Another good idea is to put occasional "asides" in your letters, the way you do in conversation. They provide an interesting change of pace. For example, if you were talking to someone, you might say: "I went to see Mary's new house yesterday. Remember she told us about it last Christmas? It's a beauty!" Merely by changing the pitch of your voice, you can easily change from one subject to another in conversation. And here's how you can do the same thing in a letter:

> I went to see Mary's new house yesterday. (Remember she told us about it last Christmas?) It's a beauty! It's exactly the kind of house Bill and I would like to have some day (if we ever have a house of our own!).

Still another good trick is to address the person by name occasionally, just as you do in conversation. "Bob, it's so beautiful here!" is more intimate and personal than the flat statement, "This is a beautiful place." And "I'd love to see you soon, Eileen," is not only more conversational, but more flattering than "I hope to have the pleasure of seeing you before long." There's nothing a person enjoys more in a letter than the frequent repetition of his own name!

You know that you can always hold a person's interest in conversation by telling a story or relating an incident that has some bearing on the subject under discussion. The same principle applies to letter writing. Any letter is more enjoyable if it contains at least one interesting personal anecdote. For example, you might be writing about a mutual friend who is planning a first air flight, and is excited by the prospect. In telling about it in your letter, you might say:

> That reminds me of the first flight *I* made, years ago!
> It was on the *Bermuda Clipper;* and although I've
> made hundreds of flights since, I'll never forget the
> thrill of that first one. Imagine! About an hour out
> we flew into a sudden storm. To avoid it, etc. . . ."

Surely such personal anecdotes make for more fascinating reading than the mere blunt statement of fact! "Bill is flying to California next week. He's very excited about it." Don't let it go at that! Add something out of your own experience— something only *you* can write—something that makes your letter *individual*.

When you are talking with people, you give emphasis to important words and ideas by the inflections of your voice. In letter writing you can achieve the same effect by *underlining* the important words and ideas. For example, read this paragraph:

> I'm so disappointed I could cry. I had another letter
> from Bob and now he says it looks as though he can not
> be back in time for your wedding. He says he's fright-
> fully sorry, but there's just nothing he can do about
> it. Oh, Anne—isn't it awful!

Now see how underlining gives emphasis where needed, and makes the paragraph come to life:

> I'm so disappointed I could <u>cry</u>. I had another letter
> from Bob and <u>now</u> he says it looks as though he can <u>not</u>
> be back in time for your wedding. He says he's fright-
> fully sorry, but there's just <u>nothing he can do about it.</u>
> Oh, Anne—isn't it <u>awful!</u>

An occasional word of slang, or a favorite phrase or colloquialism, adds spice to your letters—as it does to your conversation. But don't overdo it! Such phrases as "It's raining cats and dogs!" . . . "Was my face red!" . . . "I'm pleased as Punch!" . . . "Thanks a million!" if you used them in your speech—add a pleasantly characteristic tang to your letters. *But only if used once!* A "pet" phrase used over and over again in a letter soon becomes boring—and even irritating.

Above all, avoid those stuffy, stereotyped, rubber-stamp, be-whiskered words and phrases that belong to the past! No letter can possibly sound conversational if it's full of such overworked phrases as "in regard to" . . . "on the other hand" . . . "in accordance with" . . . "as a matter of fact" . . . "along the lines of" . . . "at my earliest convenience." It's true that such antiquated phraseology is more likely to be found in business letters than in social and personal correspondence. But there are still too many pompous, old-fashioned words and phrases in general use; and your letters will have more sparkle and personality if you avoid them.

KEEP YOUR LANGUAGE SIMPLE— SHORT WORDS ARE THE BEST

One of the most important factors in producing interesting letters—letters with a pleasant, conversational tone to them—is the use of simple, understandable language. Plain, familiar words are the best. Short, rugged words—the simple, home-spun words of everyday speech—are usually more vivid and expressive than the bookish, important-sounding words many people like to use in their letters.

So keep your language simple! *Write as you speak.* Don't use formal, high-sounding words that you wouldn't think of using in conversation. Remember that the finest English in the world is *simple* English.

do	is a better word than	*accomplish*
write	is a better word than	*correspond*
often	is a better word than	*frequently*
find	is a better word than	*locate*
go	is a better word than	*attend*

And whenever you can, use a single vigorous word instead of an elaborate, complicated phrase. Why use two or three words when *one* will do?

please	is better than	*will you be good enough to*
now	is better than	*at the present time*
like	is better than	*along the lines of*
since	is better than	*inasmuch as*

Writing *simply* does not mean writing *obviously*, without beauty or style. Your simple words should have meaning, sub-stance an. life. They should be colorful and expressive . . . words tha have force and vigor . . . *words that say some-thing*.

Use lots of verbs, for verbs are the busy little motors that give movement and action to your writing. A simple sentence in which somebody *does* something, or *goes* somewhere, is more forceful and effective than a long, involved sentence with a lot of adverbs, participles and infinitives. And keep your verbs *short!* Keep them rugged and expressive. Make them say what you have to say crisply and to the point. Verbs like come, go, run, walk, do, fly, jump, send, meet, buy, cry, coax, break, give force and action to your sentences.

HOW TO WRITE WITH GREATER
EASE AND CLARITY

In writing a letter, always be sure that you present your thoughts or ideas in logical order. Keep in mind what you want to say . . . develop it along lines of clear, simple reasoning . . . and let each idea suggest the one that follows. Don't jump around from one thing to another. Always complete what you have to say before going on to something else; and be sure to use a new paragraph for every new thought or idea.

Often the last sentence of a paragraph will suggest the first sentence of the next one. For example, if you are writing about a trip you plan to make, and the last sentence of the paragraph reads: "We are leaving at the end of this month, after Robert returns to school"—that gives you a perfect lead for the next paragraph: "We are quite pleased with Robert's first report from Andover. He is apparently doing very well in all his subjects" . . . and so on.

Try to avoid long, rambling sentences and long involved paragraphs. A letter composed of short sentences and short paragraphs is not only more inviting to the eye, but reads more easily and delivers your message or idea with greater speed. If a reader is obliged to wade through long sentences, and a lot of competing ideas all jumbled up in a single paragraph—perhaps going back once or twice to "pick up the threads"—he is likely to miss what you mean entirely.

Two or three short sentences are always better than one long one. Here, for example, is a long, involved sentence which the average person would have to read at least twice to understand:

> Married to a former war correspondent who is now writing fiction, she is living with him and his family in New York and studying voice and dancing—prior to going to Hollywood in the Spring for a screen test.

See what a tremendous increase in force and clarity there is when this long sentence becomes three short ones:

She is married to a former war correspondent who is now writing fiction. They are currently living with his family in New York. She is studying voice and dancing, and will go to Hollywood in the Spring for a screen test.

Another way to give your letters sharpness and clarity is to use concrete, specific words whenever possible. For example, when you say "I am going abroad next month," the word "abroad" is vague and indefinite. The sentence instantly takes on more life and vitality when you say, "I am going to England next month." "She has a child" isn't nearly as expressive as "She has a two-year-old son." "He sent me flowers for my birthday" isn't as interesting as the specific "He sent me yellow tea roses for my birthday."

PEOPLE JUDGE YOU BY YOUR LETTERS

Every letter you write creates either a *good* or *bad* impression on the person who receives it.

So be as well-groomed in your letters as you are in your dress—as well-mannered as you are in your personal contacts! Don't ever say anything in a letter you wouldn't say to a person's face. Don't spread rumors, or repeat unkind gossip, or write anything that is confidential and shouldn't be revealed . . . for such letter-writing conduct is in bad taste.

If you can't be proud of the letter you have written—if you wouldn't be willing to have strangers judge you by its appearance, and its contents—*don't mail it.* Even if it's a letter to a relative or close friend who will understand—*don't mail it!* There's no guarantee your letter won't be seen by outsiders; you can't be sure your thoughtlessly or carelessly written letter won't show up some day to cause you embarrassment and regret.

Don't let any letter go out under your name unless you feel that it does you justice, that it's a credit to you in every way. Don't let any letter go out under your name unless you feel it will create a *good impression* on the person who receives it. It's far better not to send any letter at all than to send one that stamps you a thoughtless or ill-bred person.

Remember—*your letter represents you.* Be sure it represents you to best advantage!

AVOID CARELESS REMARKS
THAT MAY BE MISUNDERSTOOD

There is this important difference between conversation and letter writing: What is spoken is done with and gone. It may or may not be remembered. A careless or thoughtless remark can be retracted . . . or explained . . . or made to seem unimportant by the friendliness of a gesture or a smile.

But not so with a careless or thoughtless "remark" in a letter! It's there in black and white, and there it remains, repeating itself with every reading. It may have been meant as a jest. It may not have been meant at all the way it sounds. But you aren't there to explain it!

So *think before you write!* Don't say anything that can be misunderstood, that can be construed as curt or unkind . . . as unfriendly . . . as ungracious or rude.

Never mail a letter without reading it over from beginning to end. It's a good idea to read it aloud and listen to the sound of it. Listen through the ears of the person who is to receive it. Make sure that he will not get any implications or shades of meaning that you do not intend. If there's even one word or phrase that can be misinterpreted, it's better to write the letter over.

DON'T WRITE ANYTHING
YOU MAY LATER REGRET

Often it's a great emotional relief to sit down and write someone a letter when you are worried, angry or annoyed. But watch out! That's exactly when you are most likely to write something you may be sorry about later—something you'd wish very much you *hadn't* said.

Make it a practice never to send out a letter written in anger, or in a mood of depression or despair. Write it, by all means! Pour out your heart on paper. It's a wonderful way to get rid of the "blues" . . . to rid your system of the poisons of worry, bitterness or fear. *But don't mail it.* Even if you want to very much, *don't mail it.* Put it aside for a while; then take it out and read it over in a day or so when your anger has cooled or you see the bright side of things again. You may thank your lucky stars you didn't mail it!

THE LETTER EVERYONE
LOVES TO RECEIVE

The most *welcome* letter—the letter that is received with joy and read with satisfaction—is the letter written from the *reader's* point of view, with the reader's interests and problems in mind. It's the letter with an amiable *"you"* attitude, rather than a self-centered *"I"* attitude, that everyone loves to receive.

So try to acquire the knack of putting yourself in the

reader's place, of trying to see things from the reader's point of view! Failure to recognize and fully appreciate this human element in letter writing . . . failure to see things from the other person's point of view . . . is the cause of most of the dull, tactless, uninteresting and *unwelcome* letters that get into the mail.

It's always best to write your letters when you feel especially friendly and kindly disposed toward the person to whom you are writing. And start off with a compliment or word of praise, if you can! It will win attention and influence your reader as nothing else can! But be sure you *mean* what you say—that your compliment is honest and sincere—otherwise it won't ring true.

People like to feel important, and they resent very much any implication that they are *not* important. Bear that in mind when writing letters! Don't boast about your accomplishments. Don't try to impress the reader with *your* knowledge, *your* importance. The one sure way to a person's heart is to let him know you consider him rather superior, that you recognize and respect his knowledge and judgment. In other words, *make your reader feel important.*

And watch the tone of your letter! No one ever really enjoys a letter that is filled with "peeves" and complaints—a letter that is gloomy and pessimistic. Remember that in letters, as in personal contact, people respond most eagerly to enthusiasm and good cheer.

So try not to pour all your worries and troubles into your letters! Don't write of ill-health . . . of servant problems . . . of domestic difficulties . . . of business reverses. Don't write bad news in a letter, if you can help it. Don't write of disagreeable or unpleasant things . . . of shocking or disturbing things . . . that is, of course, if you want your letter to be read with enjoyment.

The letter everyone loves to receive is *friendly.* It's like a smile . . . a handclasp . . . a warm and cherry "Hello!"

3. The Physical Characteristics of Your Letter

What you write in your letter—its message, the tone and spirit of its contents, the news you tell and the friendliness and cheer you radiate—*these are of first importance.*

But almost equally important is the *appearance* of your letter. It should not only be interesting to read, but attractive and inviting to the eye. For the appearance of your letter reveals character and personality as surely as the clothes you wear and the language you use.

A letter full of blots and erasures, written on shoddy paper with a violent shade of ink, and with no regard for margins, punctuation or sequence of pages, is as offensive in its way as bad table manners. It's no pleasure . . . and certainly no compliment! . . . to receive such a letter.

And yet, evident as this must be to almost everyone, people in general are surprisingly *careless* about the appearance of their letters. Most people pay little or no attention to those few simple, but extremely important fundamentals, dictated by good manners and good taste.

After all, no one but a complete boor would dream of making a social call in tennis shoes—a business call in dungarees! People *dress up* when they go to make a call, in order to make the best possible impression. And for that very same reason you should "dress up" your letters!

Remember—the letter you write is your personal representative. *Be sure it represents you to best advantage.* Be sure that every letter you send out makes as good an impression as you would in a face-to-face visit. That means a neat, clean letter . . . a pleasant-looking and prepossessing letter. It means a letter that in no way repels nor offends by its physical characteristics.

So be as individual as you like in the contents of your letter; be as original as the limits of your imagination permit! But in regard to those fundamentals of good taste which govern the *appearance* of your letter—be guided by the rules! There are just a few of them. By following the suggestions in this chapter, you can be sure your letters will always make a good appearance . . . and therefore a good impression.

THE CORRECT STATIONERY FOR
SOCIAL AND PERSONAL CORRESPONDENCE

The first thing to consider is the choice of stationery.

Always use the best texture and quality of paper you can afford—not only because it makes a better impression, but because it's more practical. It's easier to write on good paper, easier to produce a neat, attractive-looking letter. Paper of inferior quality generally absorbs ink and gives a rough, feathery edge to the writing. Then, too, paper of good quality stands up better under the rough treatment it may receive on its way through the mail; it isn't likely to arrive in a battered or untidy condition. That's important if your letter is going a long way—perhaps to another country.

For your *formal* correspondence—such as invitations, acknowledgments, formal notes of thanks, condolence, and so forth—plain white unruled paper, of standard size and shape, is always the best. It should be a double sheet that folds once into its envelope; and be sure the envelope matches. Mismatched stationery is never desirable; but it's particularly bad taste when used for formal social correspondence.

For *informal* correspondence—such as friendly letters, family letters, informal notes of thanks, congratulations and the like—there is a much wider scope for personal choice. The only limitations are those of good taste. In stationery, as in everything else, there are now styles almost every season, and you may indulge your fancy as you like. There are no inflexible rules; just be sure to avoid extremes of size, shape, color of style. Any extreme that makes your letter conspicuously different from others is in poor taste—like loud and flashy clothing.

The use of vivid, highly colored stationery is an example. Avoid the use of such striking shades as red, green and purple, which instantly call attention to themselves. If you like color in your stationery, choose a delicate, subdued shade such as ivory, tan or gray. Avoid loud, gaudy shades. And remember, white is always acceptable, always in good form, for every type of correspondence.

Giddy borders and decorations on letter paper are for the very young only (or for the immature in taste). Keep *your* stationery simple and dignified. Envelope linings of contrasting color may be used provided they are not too vivid and conspicuous.

Folded sheets are widely used, particularly for feminine correspondence. However, if you like long letters, if your handwriting is bold and large, or if you use a typewriter for your personal correspondence, you may find single sheets more convenient. Today, both types are considered equally correct for all letters.

Don't use ruled stationery for your letters. Ruled paper is only for children learning how to write! If you can't keep your lines straight, use one of those handy dark-lined guides which are usually furnished with stationery. You just slip it under the page and let it guide you while you are writing.

Try to use stationery that fits the letter. For example, if you are writing a long, chatty letter with all the accumulated news of the past month, use fairly large sheets of paper. But if you are writing a short message, perhaps just a few words, use smaller-size stationery. It's not advisable to use correspondence cards or tiny sheets that fit into very small envelopes. Under-size letters are discouraged by the postal authorities because they present difficulty in handling and are easily lost or misplaced. A letter is assured quicker and safer delivery if it's more nearly regular size.

It's not considered good form to use *postal cards* for personal or social correspondence. This does not refer to the picture post cards on which travelers send greetings back home (a good old custom, dear to our hearts!). It refers to the stamped postal cards issued by the government and intended primarily for business use. It is certainly not the best of taste to air one's private affairs on the back of a card for everyone to see and read.

The use of office or hotel stationery for personal correspond-ence is not recommended, except in an emergency. The use of a sheet of paper from a child's school tablet, and any stray en-velope that happens to be around, is *never* recommended under any circumstances! If you don't have suitable stationery avail-able, put off writing the letter until you can get some . . . or if the message can't wait, telephone.

Many people like to have their personal stationery engraved with their name and address. Others like to have an attractive engraved monogram on their letter paper. Either is correct . . . but never use *both* on the same stationery. That's osten-tatious—like wearing too much jewelry. If you use a mono-gram, be sure it's a *simple* one. An elaborate, highly colored monogram shows as poor taste as the choice of loud paper.

Don't use a crest, unless such distinction rightfully belongs to your family. The use of a crest that doesn't belong to you is not far removed in principle from the use of a "phony" title.

If you are planning engraved writing paper—or engraved invitations or announcements of any kind—it's best to consult a reputable stationer. He can show you samples of paper and engraving, and help you make a correct and satisfactory choice.

SHORT NOTES SHOULD
BE HANDWRITTEN

Although the typewriter is being used more and more gener-ally for personal correspondence, there can be no denying the fact that a handwritten note is more intimate and personal . . . and somehow, more sincere. Therefore it is best to write short notes, especially notes of thanks, congratulation, sympathy and so forth, by hand.

But be sure to write *plainly!* Nobody likes to puzzle over words, trying to figure them out. A poor handwriting—an illegible hard-to-read handwriting—is usually just *careless, indifferent writing.*

You can greatly improve your penmanship if you want to. It may take a little time, and it may take a lot of practice; but it's certainly worth it! Try copying a style of writing you admire. Copy the words over and over again, until they look the way you want them to. You may be surprised at the great difference in your writing in a very short time, if you make a real effort to improve it and make it more legible. Experiment with types of pens, too. Often the type of point used makes a difference in the smoothness and legibility of your writing.

Remember—no letter can present a pleasing, attractive appearance if it's poorly written. So don't scribble! Don't scrawl! Write with deliberation and care, taking time to complete every word—to dot every *i* and cross every *t*. Only in that way can you improve your penmanship to the point where clear and legible writing becomes habitual with you.

Don't use very brightly colored ink to write your letters. Black is the best; though dark blue and dark green are also acceptable. Violet, bright green and red are not good taste.

You know, of course, that only pen and ink will do for your handwritten correspondence. Never write in pencil unless you are ill, or are in a moving vehicle like a train or plane. Writing a letter in pencil is a rudeness to the person who receives your letter, unless circumstances make it unavoidable (in which case you should be sure to explain).

USE OF THE TYPEWRITER

The use of the typewriter is so convenient, and such a great timesaver, that any prejudice against its use for social correspondence which may have existed in the past is now completely gone.

There are probably more personal letters written on the typewriter today than are written by hand. And the use of the typewriter for social correspondence has also increased enormously. In fact, it's now good form to type practically every kind of letter—the only important exceptions being *formal* invitations, acknowledgments and the like. Also, as mentioned before, short notes of thanks, congratulation and sympathy are best written in long hand, as they seem more personal and sincere when they are in your own handwriting.

So type your personal correspondence and your informal social notes, if you want to! Just be sure you *know how* to type—that your letters are clean and neat and well-spaced, without errors or erasures—as pleasing to the eye as though you had carefully written them by hand. In fact, they should be even more pleasing to the eye . . . for typing adds a special neatness and precise legibility of its own.

Of course that neatness and legibility depend to a great extent upon the condition of your typewriter; so be sure it's in *good* condition. Change the ribbon as soon as the impressions begin to look light and faded. And keep the type faces sharp and clean.

All typewritten letters *must be signed by hand*, with pen and ink. A typed signature is discourteous.

THE SPACING AND ARRANGEMENT
OF A LETTER

Whether your letter is typed or written by hand, it should "sit nicely" on the page. That means it should be well-spaced and well-balanced, with reasonably wide and straight margins.

When writing with pen and ink, leave adequate space *between* the lines as well as generous margins at the sides. A well-spaced letter is more inviting to the eye and easier to read.

If your letter is to be typewritten, give some thought beforehand to the approximate length of it, so you can plan its spacing. A letter that is typed grotesquely off-center on a page does not make a good impression. The final appearance of your letter, handwritten or typed, should be of a picture set neatly in a frame.

Don't use folded stationery for typing letters; it's neither convenient nor practical. Special paper for typing personal correspondence is available wherever stationery is sold. It comes in single sheets, of course; and is about 7½ x 10 inches in size. That's slightly smaller than commercial letterheads which are 8½ x 11 inches. For a long letter that fills the page, there should be a margin of at least an inch and a half at the top, bottom and left-hand side—and approximately the same margin on the right-hand side. For short notes, the margins are proportionately wider—so that the letter looks well-spaced on the page.

It is not advisable to type on both sides of a sheet of paper.

If you cannot get your letter on one sheet, use a second sheet to complete it.

SEQUENCE OF PAGES AND
FOLDING THE LETTER

The sequence of pages depends upon the length of the letter. Social notes— like informal invitations, notes of thanks, condolence, and so forth—should be short enough to go on the first page. Personal letters that carry over to a second page of a folded sheet should be written on pages *one* and *three*. A long letter should follow the natural page order, and not skip around from *one* to *three*, from *two* to *four*. Skipping around in a letter confuses the reader, and can be very irritating. Even when you write in the natural order of pages, it's a good idea to *number* them as it makes reading easier. Writing sideways or crosswise in a letter is bad taste and should be avoided.

Most letter paper folds once into its envelope, although large-size sheets for typewriter use may require two folds. Take the little time necessary to fold your letter *neatly,* with the *edges even.* A carelessly folded letter implies indifference toward the person to whom the letter is sent.

A double sheet is folded evenly from the lower to the top edge, and inserted in the envelope fold first.

A single sheet is also folded evenly from the lower to the top edge, and is also inserted in the envelope fold first.

A sheet too large to go in the envelope with a single fold should be folded in three equal sections, and placed in the envelope with the closed end first.

HOW TO AVOID MISTAKES
IN SPELLING AND GRAMMAR

A misspelled word in a letter is like a mispronounced word in conversation. It certainly doesn't show you to good advantage.

So watch your spelling! When you are in doubt as to the meaning, spelling or plural form of a word, *look it up in your dictionary!* And once you look up a word and learn to spell it correctly, continue to *use* that word. Use it frequently enough to impress it on your memory.

Watch your grammar as you watch your spelling; and make a conscientious effort to avoid grammatical errors. Add a good grammar to your dictionary, and you'll be well-fortified for any problem in the use of words or in sentence structure that may present itself.

THE USE OF PUNCTUATION

Your letter should look interesting and inviting to the eye . . . it should look readable, *exciting*. And the way to achieve that effect . . . the way to avoid an unbroken, forbidding look that bores the reader before he even begins to read! . . . is by the proper use of punctuation.

If you want to see the difference that punctuation can make, look first at this "anemic" paragraph:

> I have just heard the good news. Congratulations. I think it's wonderful, simply wonderful, that you have at last received the recognition you deserve. Tell me how does it feel to be president of the company where you were once an office boy. I can just imagine how happy and proud Edith is. The best of luck to you Jim in your new job.

Now look at it, and see how punctuation has given it new life and sparkle, new *meaning!*

> I have just heard the good news. Congratulations! I think it's wonderful—simply wonderful—that you have at last received the recognition you deserve! Tell me: how does it feel to be president of the company where you were once an office boy? I can just imagine how happy and proud Edith is. . . . The best of luck to you, Jim, in your new job!

Punctuation is a device for making things easier to read and interpret. It gives the emphasis and expression to *writing* that pauses, gestures and the raising and lowering of the voice give to *speech*. If you are in doubt about the use of punctuation, consult your dictionary or grammar.

4. The Parts of a Letter

Every well-constructed letter is made up of five essential parts. They comprise the structure, or framework, of your letter. You don't need to follow exactly all details within each part; but you *must* follow the general form if you want to produce a correct and acceptable letter. All letters—social, personal and business*—should conform to this basic outline:

1. THE HEADING
   which is your address and the date

2. THE SALUTATION
   which is your complimentary greeting

3. THE BODY OF THE LETTER
   which is your message

4. THE CLOSE
   which is your complimentary "good-by"

5. THE SIGNATURE
   which should be in pen and ink, and *legible!*

In addition to these five basic parts there is also the *superscription*—which is not, strictly speaking, a part of the letter. The superscription is the outside address, written on the envelope . . . and it must be very carefully and correctly written, if the letter is not to go astray!

But let us discuss individually and in detail each of the five parts which go to make up a well-written, well-integrated letter.

THE HEADING

The very first thing you write in a letter is the heading, which is simply your address and the date. Of course, if the stationery used has a printed or engraved address already inscribed, the heading consists of the date only.

Place the heading at least one inch from the top edge of

* For specific information on the form, structure and content of business letters, see Book IV, beginning on page 223.

the sheet. Start writing approximately in the center, so that the heading ends three-quarters of an inch or so from the right margin. Here is the way the heading should look at the top of your letter:

> *250 Park Avenue*
> *New York, N.Y.*
> *July 6, 19—*

You can indent the lines if you like. But a straight edge is considered more modern and better form. Notice that there are no commas at the ends of the lines; and no period after the date. The names of cities—even long names like Philadelphia, San Francisco, Minneapolis, Cincinnati—should be written out completely. But the names of states may be abbreviated if you like . . . especially if the abbreviations are well-known and familiar like N.Y., N.J., Mass., Cal., and so forth. In general it's best *not* to abbreviate the names of places.

Don't ever write a letter without a heading. It's curt . . . like pushing open a door without knocking. And it's best to write the *complete* heading, even though your letter is going to an intimate friend who knows your address. It's a courtesy—a custom—and if you omit it, the person who receives your letter has the right to assume (1) that you don't know any better or (2) that you know better but are indifferent and just don't care.

Of course, in any communication requiring acknowledgment —such as a letter of condolence—it's not only a rudeness but a distinct inconvenience to omit the address. For in that case the person may be required to look up your address; and with dozens of other letters to be acknowledged, that can be a nuisance—and even a hardship.

The date, too, is important and should never be omitted. It goes immediately below the address—never above it, or on the same line with it. Don't abbreviate the month . . . like Jan., Feb., Apr. Write it out; it looks much better. And you don't need an *st* or *rd* or *th* after the day of the month—like April 1st, 3rd, 10th. The correct form is:

> April 1, 19—
> April 3, 19—
> April 10, 19—

Always put a comma between the day of the month and the year, to separate the numerals and prevent confusion.

THE SALUTATION

The salutation of a letter is the complimentary greeting to the person to whom the letter is written. It's like saying, *"Hello."*

You write the salutation at the left-hand side of the sheet, about half an inch below the heading. The point at which you start the salutation will be your left-hand margin; the rest of the letter will be in a straight line with it. So the salutation should start at whatever point you want the margin to be . . . anywhere from one to two inches, or more, from the edge of the paper.

Long use and familiar custom have made "Dear John" or "Dear Mary" the popular form of address in letters. But that doesn't mean you cannot say "Dearest" or "Darling" or "My own precious Anne" in an intimate letter to someone you love. Just bear in mind that in routine everyday correspondence, standard forms of salutation are best . . . and any sharp deviation from the customary and familiar should be avoided.

"My dear" is considered more formal than "Dear"—so if you are writing a friendly, informal letter to someone, the salutation should be "Dear Frank" or "Dear Mr. Smith." But if you are writing a formal note—or if you are writing to someone you don't know very well, perhaps a new acquaintance, the salutation should be "My dear Mr. Smith."

Some forms of address are looked upon as bad taste and should be avoided. For example, never use "Dear Friend" or "My dear Friend," as your salutation. Equally undesirable are "Madame," "Dear Miss" and "Friend Jack." The use of the name alone as a salutation is rude and incorrect. So never start a letter like this:

Mr. Frank Smith:

This is to inform you that the tickets which you sent me . . . and so on.

Conform to standard familiar styles of salutation—except in intimate family letters, or in love letters, where you use your own private endearments.

THE BODY OF THE LETTER

The body of a letter is naturally the most important part of it. It's what you write in the letter . . . what you say . . . your message.

And that's strictly *your* department! No one can tell you what to say in your letters. The most we can do is make suggestions; and that's what all the remaining chapters of this book are about.

You may write to cheer a sick friend . . . to share good news with a distant relative . . . to express sympathy, thanks or regret . . . to accept an invitation or explain why you cannot accept it.

In writing the body of your letter, start a new paragraph every time you change to a new subject. Begin each sentence with a capital and end it with a period or other punctuation. Watch your spelling. Watch your grammar. Keep your letter cheerful, concise and correct. Keep it *conversational*.

The length of your letter is not important. It may be just a short note, or it may be a long, chatty letter, full of news. Just be sure that your short letter doesn't sound abrupt; that your long letter doesn't ramble on and on until the reader becomes confused and bored. It's a wonderful quality in letter writing to know what you want to say—to say it—and *to stop*.

THE CLOSE

The close of a letter is the "good-by"—the complimentary greeting before you sign your name and slip the letter into its envelope.

You write this closing phrase two or three spaces below the body of the letter, beginning about in the center of the page. Only the first word should be capitalized; and there should be a comma at the end.

The wording varies according to the type of letter, and according to the degree of friendship and intimacy with the

THE PARTS OF A LETTER

HEADING

SALUTATION:

BODY

COMPLIMENTARY CLOSE,

SIGNATURE

person addressed. You wouldn't write "Devotedly yours," or "With deepest affection," to someone who is little more than a casual acquaintance. Nor would you write a cold and impersonal "Very truly yours," to an old and well-loved friend. Your closing phrase should be neither flowery nor curt, but friendly to the degree that you are friendly with your correspondent.

Business letters, letters to professional people, and very formal social notes generally close with "Yours truly," or "Very truly yours."

For informal social notes, and for the general run of friendly correspondence, the forms most frequently used are:

> Sincerely yours,
> Yours very sincerely,
> Always sincerely yours,
> Yours cordially,
> Most cordially yours,
> Faithfully yours,

Letters to intimate friends or relatives might close with any of these familiar forms:

> Yours affectionately,
> Always affectionately yours,
> Lovingly yours,
> Your loving sister,
> Lovingly, your sister,
> With love,

As for love letters, the wording is whatever the degree of affection inspires . . . from a simple "Fondly yours," to a fervent "Yours with the utmost devotion."

Though it's best to conform to conventional closings in business and social letters, you can "let yourself go"—if you like—in your personal and family correspondence. Here you can use your own pet expressions, your favorite phrases of endearment. You can even eliminate formal openings and closings entirely, if that is your preference. So if you want to start your letter, "I've been thinking of you all day, Kate darling!"—and if you want to close your letter, "Good-by, my dearest one!"—by all means write it just that way.

Mark Twain frequently signed his letters, "Yrs Affy, Sam." His family loved the quaint, familiar phrase . . . and his friends considered it a compliment when he so signed his letters to them.

To an old comrade he loved but rarely saw, Lincoln signed himself, "Your friend forever, A. Lincoln."

To his nine-year-old boy away at school, Alexander Hamilton usually wrote, "A good night to you, my darling son!"

To people he especially liked, William H. Page closed his letters with, "Always heartily yours."

The position of the word "yours" in a formal complimentary closing may be either at the beginning or the end of the phrase, as you prefer. There's not the slightest shade of difference in meaning between "Yours sincerely," and "Sincerely yours." Strictly speaking, the use of an adverb ending in *ly* (like truly, cordially, lovingly) calls for the use of the accompanying pronoun "yours" to complete the phrase. Therefore, it's always better to include it in your very formal correspondence. But in your friendly and informal correspondence, you may omit the pronoun if you like—closing with a simple "Sincerely," or "Cordially."

It is not advisable to use the word "yours" alone—except, perhaps, at the close of a love letter where the word takes on special meaning and eloquence. But "Yours, John Smith" at the close of a business or social letter sounds hurried and abrupt, and is not especially complimentary.

Always be sure that the salutation and the close of your letter conform. For example, a letter that begins with "Tom, my beloved," should certainly close with the same warmth of feeling—not with a cold and formal "Very truly yours." A letter that expresses no warmth of feeling all the way through should not end with a sudden protestation of love or affection, like an afterthought tacked on at the end. "With loads of love," is just such an overworked appendage, gushy and insincere.

"Warmly yours," is bad form and should be avoided. "Hastily yours," and "Yours in haste," are rude and unflattering.

The phrase, "Respectfully yours," should be used only by a tradesman to a customer, or by an employee to an employer. It is frequently used when writing to church dignitaries or to high public officials; but "Faithfully yours," is considered a more acceptable form for that purpose.

"Gratefully yours," should be used only when a benefit has been received. You might use it, for example, in a letter to a surgeon who has successfully operated on someone dear to you . . . or a lawyer who has won a difficult case . . . or a teacher who has given special attention to your child.

"Fraternally yours," is often used between members of the same society, but the phrase is stodgy and old-fashioned. "Faithfully yours," or "Cordially yours," sounds more sincere—and certainly more up-to-date!

"Believe me, Sincerely yours," is an old English form still

used by many people to express formality in the closing of a note. But it's a timeworn and cumbersome phrase and should be avoided, along with such other stilted expressions as "I beg to remain," . . . "I have the honor to remain," . . . "I remain, Your humble servant," . . . "I am, Yours obediently." It is surprising to find that some comparatively recent books on the subject still accept these clumsy, antiquated forms; but they have no place whatever in modern letter writing and are not recommended even in the most formal correspondence.

Less offensive ornaments of expression are "With best wishes," and "With kindest regards,"—though these, too, date back to a more flowery age of letter writing than our own. Use them if you like; but bear in mind that the trend today is more and more toward simple, unadorned expression—natural and sincere.

THE SIGNATURE

The signature of a letter is written below the complimentary close and somewhat to the right, so that it ends just about in line with the right-hand margin of the letter. There are three basic rules to observe:

1. Always sign by hand, in ink.
2. Write *legibly*, so there can be no doubt as to the exact spelling of your name.
3. Sign your name without any accompanying title.

Your name is your own, of course, to sign as you choose. If "Chuck" is the name by which you are most fondly and familiarly known to your correspondent—then "Chuck" it should be in your letter! Signing a sedate "Edgar" or "Thomas" to someone who always calls you "Chuck" destroys the friendly tone of your letter.

But for your less intimate correspondence, you will want to know these few simple rules of good form:

A gentleman does not write "Mr." before his name when signing a letter. He signs all formal social correspondence—and all business letters, unless the business associate is also a personal friend*—with his full name but no title: "Thomas Matthew Benton." Informal social notes and letters to friends are signed simply "Thomas" or "Tom."

A married woman does not sign letters with "Mrs." preceding the name. In social correspondence, she uses her given name alone (Elizabeth) . . . or the nickname by which she is affectionately known to her friends (Betty) . . . or her full

---

* For detailed information on business signatures, see pages 232-4.

name (Elizabeth Kingsley Benton), depending upon the degree of intimacy between her and her correspondent. Under no circumstances does she sign a letter "Mrs. Thomas M. Benton." However, in a business letter or a letter to a complete stranger, she may wish to indicate how the reply to her should be addressed. In that case she adds her married name, *in parentheses,* either directly below the signature or over toward the left—in line with the left-hand margin. For example:

> Yours very truly,
> Elizabeth Kingsley Benton
> (Mrs. Thomas Matthew Benton)

or

> Yours very truly,
> Elizabeth K. Benton

(Mrs. Thomas M. Benton)

In a letter to a tradesman or servant, a married woman may not wish to use her first name. In that case she signs "E. K. Benton" (for Elizabeth Kingsley Benton) . . . and in the lower left-hand corner of her letter, in parentheses, she writes her married name.

An unmarried woman signs her social correspondence "Anita" or "Anita Benton." In business letters she may use the form "(Miss) Anita Benton."

A widow signs her social correspondence exactly as she did before her husband's death. Her business letters may also be signed as before, with "Mrs. Thomas M. Benton" in parentheses below the signature. Or if she prefers, she may just put "Mrs." in parentheses before her own name:

> Yours very truly,
> (Mrs.) Elizabeth Kingsley Benton

A divorced woman, unless she legally resumes her maiden name, signs her social letters as before . . . with her own first name and surname, and her former husband's surname: "Elizabeth Kingsley Benton." In business correspondence, instead of her former husband's name in parentheses below the signature, she uses her own—as follows:

> Yours very truly,
> Elizabeth Kingsley Benton
> (Mrs. Elizabeth K. Benton)

A doctor signs his letters, "Thomas Matthew Benton" or "Thomas Matthew Benton, M.D."—*never* "Dr. Thomas Matthew Benton."

A minister signs his letters "John Francis Pratt" or "John Francis Pratt, D.D.—*never* Rev. John Francis Pratt.

Whether a man is a college professor, a justice of the Supreme Court, or President of the United States, he signs his letters without any title or "handle" attached to his name. Of course in a business letter, a letter to an editor or colleague, or a letter of a professional or scientific nature, a man's title, position, affiliations and so forth may be required—to give substance and authority to his communication. In that case, the essential data are written *below the name,* not as a part of it. For example, a physicist who writes a paper on atomic energy and sends it to the editor of a scientific journal for publication, would sign his covering letter:

Edward T. Hill, Ph.D.
Professor, Department of Physics
University of Maine

If the letter is written on University of Maine stationery, as it is very likely to be, that part of the data need not be included under the signature.

A degree following the name is not in the same category as a title, and is entirely acceptable. But it should be used only when the nature of the communication calls for it: when it has some definite bearing on the subject of the letter and denotes authority to discuss that subject. Naturally one doesn't tack a degree to one's name when writing a letter of sympathy or acknowledging a dinner invitation!

In a letter to a stranger, a degree following the name is often helpful in indicating how the reply should be addressed. For example, earned degrees such as Ph.D., M.D., D.D. and D.D.S. entitle the person to be addressed as "Doctor." But holders of honorary degrees such as LL.D. and Litt.D. are *not* ordinarily addressed as "Doctor." A bachelor of arts or science (B.A. or B.S.) or a master of arts or science (M.A. or M.S.) is addressed simply as "Mr."

In all correspondence—business or social—it is important to avoid confusion due to incomplete or misleading signatures. While there are no hard and fast rules against the use of initials or abbreviations (such as "T. M. Jones" or "Mac"), it is always advisable to write out the full name if there is any possibility of being mistaken for someone else.

The use of "Junior" and similar terms helps to prevent confusion when two or more people in the same family have the same name. "Jr." should be used only by a son whose signature is identically the same as that of his father . . . as, for example, "John D. Rockefeller, Jr." But if a man is named for a grandfather or an uncle, he is "James Carter, 2nd"—*not* "James Carter, Jr." If he, his father and grandfather *all* have the same name, he is "James Carter, 3rd."

As a rule, the "Jr." is dropped on the death of the father, and the son becomes simply "James Carter." But it is often desirable to retain the "Jr." for business reasons. This is especially true if a man has achieved prominence in some field, and is known to many people by name and by reputation. In that case the "Jr." must be regarded as a permanent part of his signature, and he should continue to use it indefinitely in correspondence—even though the need to distinguish son from father has ceased to exist.

No special problem of signature is involved when a daughter's name is identically the same as her mother's. In intimate correspondence, the contents of the letter naturally tell whether it's "Jane Keith" the daughter, or "Jane Keith" the mother writing. And in all other correspondence, the daughter uses "Miss" in parentheses before her name—the mother uses "Mrs. Henry Keith" in parentheses below *her* name—to differentiate between them and avoid confusion. There is no term similar to "Jr." that a woman can use; and since "Jr." is as masculine as "Mr.," it should certainly never be borrowed for that purpose! "Mary Blake, Jr." must be regarded as contradictory and incorrect, even though we see it occasionally in the letters of prominent people.

And now, just one thing more before we leave the subject of signatures: When you sign your name, *your letter is completed.* It is, or should be, ready to slip into its envelope and send on its way. To add postscripts after signing your name is like standing at the open door after saying good-by and remembering a number of things you wanted to say but didn't. Try to put everything you want to say in your letter before signing your name, for postscripts are unsightly and unnecessary. But if you *must* add something you forgot to say, do so without the use of the "P.S." Just add another paragraph to your letter, below the signature, making it as brief as possible.

HOW TO ADDRESS
THE ENVELOPE

If you want to insure swift, accurate delivery of your letter —and at the same time make a good impression on the person who receives it—be sure to address the envelope clearly . . . correctly . . . *completely*.

Begin writing the address slightly below the middle of the envelope, far enough to the left to permit the name to be written without crowding. If you are not using a typewriter, take enough time to write the name and address as legibly and precisely as you can. Give all the necessary data: name, number, street, town or city, state—*and be sure you're right!* If there's even the slightest doubt in your mind as to the name of the street, the number of the house, or the spelling of the town—look it up! Don't take a chance, unless you want to risk having your letter returned . . . or perhaps end up in the Dead Letter Office where thousands of letters are sent every day because of careless, incomplete or incorrect names and addresses.

Try to arrange the writing on the envelope so that it "sits well"—looks balanced and inviting to the eye. Avoid crowding the name and address too high against the top of the envelope, or too low against the bottom edge. When completed, the block of writing or typing should tend toward the right-hand side of the envelope, slightly below the middle—and with at least a little white space to the right and below.

In writing the name and address, you may either use a straight margin, one line directly below the other—or you may indent each line in "step" fashion. Postal authorities prefer the slanting arrangement as it's easier to read.

Here is the way a properly addressed envelope should look:

Mrs. Thomas Matthew Benton

250 Park Avenue

New York, 23, N.Y.

Punctuation is not generally used on an envelope, except when is helps to prevent confusion or misdirection. For example, commas at the end of each line are not necessary and are now rarely used. But a dash between a house number and a street number is always advisable (341—85th Street); and commas separating the zone number from the name of the city and state make for greater legibility and easier reading (New York, 23, N.Y.). So use whatever punctuation helps the postman read the name and address correctly—but omit punctuation that serves no useful purpose.

The name of the person to whom you are writing should be given in full on the envelope, whenever possible. If it's a very long name—like Roger Delvin Keyes de Bruf—you would naturally find it more practical to use middle initials, addressing the envelope: "Mr. Roger D. K. de Bruf." But Mrs. John Price Hunt should be addressed as such—not as "Mrs. Hunt" or "Mrs. J. P. Hunt."

If you are writing to a new acquaintance, or to a stranger, give particular attention to the spelling of the name. Some people deeply resent a mistake in the spelling of their name—look upon it almost as a personal affront. So check and make sure! *Spell it right.* Don't address Mr. Wolfe as "Mr. Wolf"—or Mrs. Rumpel as "Mrs. Rumple." That's not the way to win friends and influence people!

If there is something unusual about the spelling of a name—like "Alys" for Alice, or "Ffrida" for Freda—try to remember that fact, and write it so on the envelope. But don't use nicknames like "Sid" or "Gert" in an outside address—unless, of course, the nickname is inseparably associated with the person's identity and he is widely known by it, socially and professionally (like Bing Crosby).

A married woman is ordinarily addressed in social correspondence by her husband's name: "Mrs. Thomas Matthew Benton."

A widow remains "Mrs. Thomas Benton." She is not addressed socially as Mrs. Elizabeth Benton." unless, due to business or professional activities, that is the name by which she is best known to her associates and friends.

A divorced woman continues to be addressed in correspondence by her former husband's name; unless she has indicated, in her own correspondence, that she prefers to be addressed as "Mrs. Elizabeth Kingsley Benton" or "Mrs. Kingsley Benton" (*Kingsley* having been her maiden name). The way she indicates this preference is to write it in parentheses in the lower left corner of her letters.

Always bear in mind that the way a woman writes her name in parentheses below her signature, or in the lower left corner of her letter, is the way she wants to be addressed. But if you receive a letter from a woman who is a stranger to you, and she signs herself "Mary Brown" without any other name in parentheses below it, you can assume she is unmarried and address her on the envelope as "Miss."

A woman is never addressed by her husband's title—as, for example, "Mrs. Dr. Thomas M. Benton" or "Mrs. Professor Edward T. Hill."

Until recently, a married woman with the title of "Doctor" was addressed only professionally by her professional name. Socially, she was addressed by her husband's name. But a woman who has earned a doctor's degree has certainly earned the right to be addressed by her title, socially as well as professionally. Therefore she should be addressed *either* by her professional name (Dr. Margaret Johnson Symonds) *or* by her married name (Mrs. Frank Symonds)—based upon the judgment and discretion of the person writing to her.

A delicate situation arises when a woman who is a doctor, and her husband who is a layman, are both addressed on one envelope. In the past the form "Mr. and Mrs. Frank Symonds" was always recommended for social use; and that form may still be used if, under the circumstances and in one's best judgment, it is the most desirable procedure. But if Dr. Margaret Johnson Symonds is a woman of great prominence and distinction in her profession, surely it would be more gracious to address her by her title. In that case the form to use would be: "Mr. Frank Symonds and Dr. Margaret J. Symonds." Though this is a departure from long-established usage, it is common practice today . . . and certainly common sense.

A husband and wife who are *both* doctors may be addressed socially *either* as "Dr. and Mrs. Charles F. Schiller" *or* as "Drs. Charles and Katherine Schiller."

A married woman who has a professional name but no professional title, like a writer or singer, is addressed by whatever name she is known to her correspondent. In her work, of course, it would be impractical to use any name but the one under which she functions and by which she is known. But in social life, she is customarily addressed by her married name.

A man is always addressed as "Mr.," unless he has some other title—*in which case that title should be used.* A list giving correct forms of address for public officials, church dignitaries, army and navy officers, etc. will be found on pages 311-31.

"Esquire" following a man's name originally denoted a *gentleman*—a person of education and social importance, as distinguished from an ordinary shopkeeper or clerk. In time it lost this significance, and came to be just an ordinary courtesy title or form of address—like "Mr." It was never used in conjunction *with* "Mr." but *instead* of it—as, "John Barrow, Esq." However, the use of "Esq." is no longer common practice and is not recommended, though one does still see it occasionally on a letter.

The use of "Jr." following a man's name does not eliminate the need for "Mr." preceding it. "Mr." and "Jr." do not mean the same thing (like "Mr." and "Esq.")—therefore the use of both is not a duplication. In other words, you would not address your letter to "John Barrow, Jr." but to "Mr. John Barrow, Jr."

Always be sure to write the proper title before a man's name, as it is highly uncomplimentary to address him without it. But do *not* use both title and degree at the same time. For example, a doctor is addressed *either* "Dr. Thomas M. Benton" *or* "Thomas M. Benton, M.D." The title is usually abbreviated; but in very formal social communications, such as engraved invitations and announcements, it is often spelled out (Doctor Thomas M. Benton).

A letter to a small boy is addressed "Master Robert Whitney." His young sister is addressed "Miss Marcia Whitney" regardless of age. (And don't put a period after the "Miss"— it's not an abbreviation!)

A letter to a servant was formerly addressed (very rudely, I think!) by name alone—as, for example, "Bertha Miller" or "Carl Lindstrom." But today most people prefer to address servants more graciously as "Miss Bertha Miller," "Mr. Carl Lindstrom."

Two or more men are usually addressed as "Messrs.," which is an abbreviation of "Messieurs" and means "Misters." Thus unmarried brothers living at the same address and invited to the same function, or perhaps thanked jointly for a gift sent by both, might be addressed as "Messrs. John and Stephen Howell."

A father and son, however, should not be lumped together as "Messrs." in social correspondence. They should be addressed individually, with separate invitations or notes of thanks sent to each. Or if they are addressed jointly, it should be as follows—with the name of the father at the top:

> Mr. Courtney Howell
> Mr. Stephen Howell
> 10 Hilltop Drive
> Ellsworth, Maine

Sisters living together may be addressed individually or jointly, depending upon the occasion and the circumstances.

For example, when sisters are invited to an important dinner or reception, *separate* invitations are more desirable for they imply a greater personal compliment to each. But it would be silly to send two identical announcements of a birth or marriage . . . or even two similar notes of thanks for a joint gift, or for hospitality received . . . to sisters living at the same address. One announcement, one letter of thanks, to both is the usual procedure. The envelope may be addressed simply to "Misses Mary and Joan Howell." Or, if you prefer, the full name of each may be written out—one below the other on the envelope, with the name of the older sister at the top.

Holiday greetings, such as Easter or Christmas cards, may be sent to "Mr. and Mrs. Frank North and family." But the phrase "and family" should never be used when addressing invitations . . . for it's no compliment to be tacked on unceremoniously, like an afterthought! Invitations should be addressed specifically to all members of a family who are invited. That doesn't necessarily mean *separate* invitations for every member of the family. Today even formal invitations may be addressed to "Mr. and Mrs. Frank North," with "Miss Barbara North" written below the names of her parents. If the Norths have two daughters, the names of both may be added. Or *two* invitations may be sent: one to "Mr. and Mrs. Frank North"—another to "Misses Barbara and Sandra North." If there is also a small son in the family, either a separate invitation is sent to him—or "Master Robert North" is written below the other names on the envelope.

Now as to the remainder of the address on the envelope: Bear in mind that the *name of the city* should never be abbreviated or contracted. For example, don't write "Frisco" for "San Francisco"—or "Philly" for "Philadelphia"—however familiar that abbreviated form may be in its own immediate territory. "L.A." may be dear to the hearts of those who live in Los Angeles and fondly refer to their city in that fashion; but it's a first-class nuisance to the postal authorities who must stop and figure out what it means. So always spell out the name of the city or town in full, and spell it *correctly*. Your letter will get to its destination more promptly if you do.

The *name of the state* may be abbreviated, especially if it's a long name like "Massachusetts" or "Pennsylvania" . . . or if the abbreviation is well-known and familiar like "N.Y." or "N.J."

If you are not using stationery with your name and address already printed or engraved on the envelope, be sure to include this important information. It makes it possible for your letter to be returned to you if for some reason it cannot be delivered. Give your *complete* name and address; and though the writing may be small, it should be legible. Postal authorities like to see the sender's name and address on the *face* of the envelope, in the upper left corner. But in letters of a social nature, it's customary to put the return address on the back of the envelope.

The stamp is placed in the upper right corner of the envelope—not on a slant, and never upside down—but neatly, please! There should be a narrow edge of envelope showing at the top and to the right of the stamp.

If there is any special instruction you want to add, such as "Personal" or "Please Forward," put it in the lower left corner of the envelope. But don't ever write a message on the envelope! Save that afterthought for your next letter; or if it's too urgent to put off, open up the envelope, take out your letter, and add what you forgot to say. An envelope with a message scribbled on it is in bad taste, and certainly doesn't represent you to best advantage.

Book II

*

Your Social Correspondence

* * *

1. The General Rules of Social Correspondence

A large part of everyone's correspondence is made up of what might be called the "letters of etiquette." These are the little notes of congratulation and condolence . . . the thank-you's . . . the bread-and-butter letters . . . the invitations and announcements . . . the acceptances and regrets.

It is with these so-called "duty" letters—these many and varied communications of social life—that most people are concerned. For here *correct form* counts more than it does in any other kind of correspondence. Here problems frequently present themselves; it's possible to make glaring errors; and one is likely to be judged more sternly than by ordinary correspondence.

So naturally, it's in writing these "letters of etiquette" that people want most to feel sure of themselves, to know what forms are acceptable according to the best current standards. A friendly letter may be gay and lighthearted as the writer's own personality, as original and different as one pleases. A business letter may be keyed to the special problem at hand, may go so far as to ignore form and precedent entirely to secure the results desired. But a social communication *must be correct*. Whether it's a brief note inviting friends to dinner, or an engraved invitation to an elaborate wedding reception, it must conform to the general rules.

This is simpler than may appear on the surface. Actually, there need never be any problem concerning social correspondence; for the forms are more or less fixed, and are easy to follow. Though these forms may be varied within the limits of good taste, and according to your own particular needs or preferences, it's better to follow them closely than try to be different just for the sake of being different. So confine your originality and unusual ideas to intimate, informal letters to friends. But in social correspondence, be guided by the fixed forms in general use today . . . and by the few simple, basic rules that follow.

ALL SOCIAL CORRESPONDENCE
HAS A SPECIFIC PURPOSE

The first thing to bear in mind is that all social communications are for a definite, specific purpose. The important thing is to keep that purpose in mind . . . to let nothing else obtrude . . . to convey your message graciously and to the point.

For example, if it's a letter of thanks, don't write about Aunt Tilly's tulips.

If it's a letter of condolence, don't write even briefly about some unrelated subject.

If it's an invitation, give only the essential facts: the time, the place, the occasion.

Many people make the mistake of combining business and social matters in one letter. That's something you should never do, however much you may be tempted to save time and trouble. *Always keep the specific purpose of the letter in mind, and stay with it.*

THE DIFFERENCE BETWEEN
FORMAL AND INFORMAL CORRESPONDENCE

All social correspondence falls into two general classifications: *formal* and *informal*.

Informal communications are simply handwritten notes, in the *first* person . . . like any little note you might write to an acquaintance or friend. They include the many brief notes of congratulation, appreciation, condolence and so forth that we are all called upon to write. They also include notes of invitation, acceptance and regret for simple, informal social affairs like bridge parties, small dinners and luncheons.

A formal invitation implies a large or elaborate social function . . . like a church wedding, a ceremonious dinner, an important reception or dance. Formal invitations are usually, but not necessarily, engraved. They are not written in the first person ("I would like you to come to dinner next Wednesday . . .) but in the *third* person ("Mr. and Mrs. Frank B. Hawes cordially invite you to dinner . . .). They are not written like ordinary letters, but are arranged in a decorative, irregularly indented form on the page.

EXAMPLE OF INFORMAL SOCIAL NOTE

Dear Mrs. Harris:

Will you come to luncheon on Wednesday, April twenty-seventh at one o'clock? My niece, Doris Fernell, is visiting us, and you have so often mentioned you would like to meet her.

I do hope you will be able to come!

Cordially yours,

Elizabeth K. Benton

EXAMPLE OF FORMAL SOCIAL COMMUNICATION

Dr. and Mrs. Thomas Matthew Benton
request the pleasure of your company
at a dinner dance for their niece
Miss Doris Fernell
Wednesday, the fourth of May
at eight o'clock
The Pierre

In the past it was permissible to use visiting cards for invitations, when one didn't wish to be formal or informal but somewhere midway between the two. The procedure was to write the occasion and the date in the lower left corner of the card, as follows:

Dinner at eight
May the fifth

The card was then slipped into an envelope and mailed, without further comment. Though one still occasionally sees this type of invitation, it is no longer generally used; and is, in fact, poor taste and should be avoided.

WHAT YOU SHOULD KNOW ABOUT INFORMAL CORRESPONDENCE

1. Don't be fooled by the word "informal." The stationery you used for your notes of invitation, acceptance, regret—

for your messages of condolence or congratulation —should be *important-looking*. Don't use tinted or decorated note paper; that's for your intimate, personal correspondence only. Don't use business or club stationery; that's definitely bad taste. Use only good quality plain white note paper of standard size. Double sheets are more impressive than single sheets for social use; and it's considered better form to get all the message on one page than to carry it over.

2. Informal social notes are usually brief, and should be handwritten. Some people prefer to type all their correspondence, including social notes; and although it's not actually incorrect to do so, it's more *gracious* to write a note of sympathy or thanks by hand. Invitations, of course, should not be typed; a handwritten invitation is much more personal and friendly.

3. Make it a point never to put off writing your necessary social correspondence. A message of sympathy or appreciation, long delayed, loses much of its effectiveness. So attend to your little "duty" notes promptly!

4. Be sure that any note of invitation you send out is explicit and *complete*. Don't leave anything to the imagination. Give the occasion, the place, the date, the time. For example don't say "I'd like you and Tom to come to dinner next Wednesday." Say "I'd like you and Tom to come to dinner on Wednesday, June tenth."

5. Evening invitations, whether formal or informal, must include both husband and wife—unless, of course, it's a "stag." An informal invitation is addressed to the wife alone, for herself and her husband. The envelope is addressed to "Mrs. Thomas M. Benton"—but the invitation makes specific mention of the husband. For example:

Dear Betty:

We are planning a little dinner to celebrate our tenth anniversary, and of course we want you and Tom to come. It's next Friday, June eighth, at seven o'clock.

I do hope you can make it, as Jim and I are looking forward with great pleasure to seeing you both.

Affectionately yours,
Rosalind

6. An informal note of invitation like the one above is answered the same way—by means of a brief, handwritten note. It's written by the wife, for her husband and herself; and though the envelope is addressed to the hostess alone, the names of *both* host and hostess should be mentioned in the acknowledgment.

7. Bear in mind that an invitation is a compliment and deserves a prompt and gracious reply. Always try to answer an informal note of invitation within twenty-four hours if you can—but certainly within three days at the most. Your hostess may want to make other arrangements if you can not accept. Always answer by note if you are invited by note. There are times, of course, when it may be necessary to telephone your acceptance or regret. But a note in your own handwriting is more courteous . . . and therefore more desirable.

8. Your response to an invitation should be a *definite* acceptance or regret. Don't keep your hostess in doubt with such vague comments as:

   "I'll try my best to come."
   "I'll come if I'm in town."

   State definitely that you are coming or that you are *not* coming, so your hostess can make her plans accordingly. She may want to invite someone else if you can't come.

9. When you write a note accepting an invitation, be sure to express pleasure at having been invited. It's the gracious thing to do. If you cannot accept the invitation, express your disappointment and regret . . . and give the reason for not accepting. Don't just say, "I'm sorry I can't come to your luncheon next Tuesday" . . . but "I'm sorry I can't come to your luncheon next Tuesday because that's the day Bob gets home from school." Make your note cordial and appreciative, but *stay with the subject:* discuss the matter of the luncheon invitation only. Don't be tempted to write about the fine marks your son got at school, or the way you had his room redecorated as a surprise.

10. In accepting an invitation, always repeat essential data such as the day of the week, the date, the hour and so forth. For example, don't just write "I'll be delighted to attend your luncheon . . ." but "I'll be delighted to attend your luncheon on Thursday, May tenth, at one o'clock." This enables the hostess to correct any mistake in date or time that either you or she may have made.

WHAT YOU SHOULD KNOW ABOUT
FORMAL CORRESPONDENCE

1. Formal correspondence may seem difficult and forbidding
   to the uninitiated; but actually it should present no real
   problems. For its very phraseology is standard and fixed,
   and entails less composition than the simplest little informal note. As a rule, formal invitations and announcements—issued only for elaborate and important affairs—
   are *engraved* on double sheets of fine quality white paper,
   in keeping with the dignity of the occasion. They may
   also be *handwritten,* in which case the wording, spacing
   and arrangement should follow the engraved forms exactly. Formal communications should *not* be printed;
   they should either be engraved in the traditional way,
   or written carefully by hand.

2. The style of lettering used in an engraved invitation is entirely a matter of personal choice. Script, gothic and
   shaded roman are the most popular choices; but this
   and other details of engraved forms are best decided in
   conjunction with your stationer or engraver. Either *plain*
   or *paneled* double sheets may be used; and though a
   family crest or coat of arms may be embossed without
   color at the top of the sheet, remember that here—as in *all*
   correspondence—simplicity is the keynote of good taste.
   The engraved form is decorative enough in itself without
   the use of monograms or other personal devices.

3. There are two distinct types of formal invitation. Both are
   correct, and either may be used . . . depending upon your
   own personal preference. The first is engraved *in full,*
   with the generalized phrase "request the pleasure of
   your company" instead of the specific name of the guest.
   Here is a typical example of such an invitation:

Dr. and Mrs. Thomas Matthew Benton
request the pleasure of your company
on the Twenty-fifth Anniversary of their marriage
on Thursday, the tenth of June
from four until seven o'clock
The Park Lane
New York

The second has a *blank space* in which the name of the
individual guest is written by hand. This fill-in type of
invitation is somewhat more personal, and therefore many
people prefer it:

Dr. and Mrs. Thomas Matthew Benton
request the pleasure of

Mr. and Mrs. Frank North's

company at a dance
on Friday, the twelfth of October
at ten o'clock
The Sherry-Netherland

4. No abbreviations, no nicknames, no informal phraseology of any kind are used in an engraved communication. Names should be spelled out in full, without the use of initials. The date, the time, even the year when it is given, are all spelled out instead of being written numerically. House numbers should be spelled out when short, but may be written numerically when long. Thus you would use "Ten Park Avenue" but "428 Ocean Drive." Telephone numbers are never used on engraved invitations.

5. The phrase "request the *honor of your presence*" is used for wedding invitations, and especially church weddings. "Request the *pleasure of your company*" is used for dinners, dances and similar functions. "Honour" and "favour" are British forms of spelling to which many still cling; but we prefer the American style of spelling, without the *u*, and recommend its use.

6. Formal invitations to dinners, dances, luncheons should be sent out three weeks in advance. This gives the hostess time to fill in, in case of regrets. Wedding invitations are generally mailed a month in advance. *Announcements* are sent out the day of the event or after it, not before.

7. A formal invitation should always include husband and wife; neither should be invited without the other unless it's a stag, or an afternoon function for ladies only (such as a luncheon or tea). If a daughter is included in the invitation, her name is written on the envelope below that of her parents. If two or more daughters are included, their names may either appear on the envelope below their parents' names; or they may be addressed separately—with individual invitations to each, or one invitation addressed jointly to "The Misses Howell" or "Misses Mary and Joan Howell." A young son may be included by adding his name to the envelope; but an adult male member of a family is invited by separate invitation. Brothers may be invited as "Messrs. John and Stephen Howell."

8. Surely it should not be necessary to have to ask for a

reply to an invitation! But in these hurried and careless times, it is often advisable to do so. If a reply is requested, one of the following forms should be used. Its proper position is in the lower left corner of the invitation, engraved in a somewhat smaller-size lettering than the rest of the message—or written in by hand if it is a hand-written communication:

> Please reply
> An answer is requested
> The favor of a reply is requested
> Please address reply to (address)
> Please send response to (address)
> Kindly reply to (address)

One of the most commonly used forms is "R.s.v.p." This is the abbreviation for *"Répondez s'il vous plaît"* which is French for "Reply if you please." The abbreviation frequently appears in capitals (R.S.V.P.), but to be strictly correct only the first letter should be a capital and the other letters should be small (R.s.v.p.). While this form of request for a reply is very popular and widely used, our own preference is for a simple English phrase like "Please reply."

9. The acceptance or regret of a formal invitation should be in *your own handwriting.* Don't use a printed form, to be filled in as the occasion requires. Such ready-made response to an invitation is in poor taste. Nor do we recommend the practice of sending a visiting card with "Accepts" or "Regrets" written in the corner—once good form, but now looked upon as a rudeness. Your reply should be written out carefully, in exactly the same phraseology as the invitation . . . and in the same irregularly indented form. It should be written on the first page of a double sheet of good quality plain white note paper, approximating as closely as possible the appearance of the invitation. Here, for example, is how the invitation of Dr. and Mrs. Benton on page 49 should be acknowledged.

> Mr. and Mrs. Frank North
> accept with pleasure
> Dr. and Mrs. Thomas M. Benton's
> invitation to a dance
> on Friday, the twelfth of October
> at ten o'clock
> The Sherry-Netherland

This would be in your own handwriting, of course—but placed and arranged as above, following the form of the engraved invitation. And no matter how well you know your hostess, or how eagerly you would prefer writing a cordial, friendly little note in reply . . . resist the temptation! For good social usage requires that a formal communication always be answered *in kind*.

10. Notice that the acknowledgment above is from both Mr. and Mrs. North—not Mrs. North alone. And notice also that the acknowledgment is made to *both* Dr. and Mrs. Benton. However, the envelope in which the acknowledgment is mailed should be addressed to Mrs. Benton only. When an invitation includes another member of the family, the acknowledgment should also include that person's name. For example, if the Norths' daughter, Sandra, was also invited to the Bentons' dance, the acknowledgment would read:

> Mr. and Mrs. Frank North
> Miss Sandra North
> accept with pleasure
> and so forth

11. If a husband and wife are invited to a formal dinner or reception, and the husband is unable to attend, the wife should send regrets for both. The reason for the regret is not always given in a formal acknowledgment; but it is more courteous to do so. For example, if Mr. North is out of town, Mrs. North might write as follows to Mrs. Benton . . . who could then invite her alone, or not, as she sees fit:

> Owing to Mr. North's
> absence from town on business
> Mrs. Frank North
> regrets she is unable to accept
> Dr. and Mrs. Thomas M. Benton's
> kind invitation
> for Friday, the twelfth of October

12. Occasionally an invitation must be recalled due to illness, a death in the family, or perhaps a broken engagement. Such recalls must go out as quickly as possible; and as there is no time to have them engraved, they should be carefully handwritten in formal phraseology—but in this case, not necessarily formal spacing. The reason for the recall of the invitation may or may not be given, at the

discretion of the persons most involved; but of course it's always more courteous to make an explanation. For example:

> Dr. and Mrs. Thomas Matthew
> Benton regret that, owing to the
> sudden illness of their son, they
> are obliged to recall their invita-
> tions for Friday, the twelfth of
> October.

2. Dinner Invitations and Acknowledgments

Engraved third-person invitations are a last lingering reminder of the extreme formality that once existed in social life. Comparatively few of us have occasion to issue such invitations today, except for certain special functions like weddings.

One occasion, however, that still calls for a strictly formal invitation is the elaborate, ceremonious dinner. This may be a dinner to honor a famous or special guest, to introduce a debutante daughter to society, or perhaps to celebrate a wedding anniversary. If the dinner is given at a club or hotel, the invitations are usually engraved. If given at home, the invitations may still be engraved; but frequently they are written by hand, especially when the dinner is a small one. But bear in mind that when formal invitations are written by hand, they do not deviate from the traditional form: they follow the wording and spacing of the engraved form exactly.

Now obviously, the type of invitation you send out does not determine the kind of dinner party you give. It's the other way around: the *type of dinner* determines the invitation. If you are planning a simple little dinner for a few friends—and you habitually call those friends on the telephone and say, "How about coming for dinner next Thursday"—that's the way to keep on doing it! But if you are planning a formal dinner, you must plan on formal invitations as well. Such invitations must be mailed two or three weeks in advance; and if you have them engraved, that takes another week or two—so you can see you need to make your plans well ahead of time. And be very sure you give the correct information to the engraver, for mistakes in spelling, in date, place, hour, etc. cannot be corrected once the form is run off.

ENGRAVED INVITATION
TO A FORMAL DINNER

Dr. and Mrs. Thomas Matthew Benton
request the pleasure of your company
at dinner
on Thursday, September the twentieth
at eight o'clock
250 Park Avenue

ENGRAVED FILL-IN TYPE
OF DINNER INVITATION

Dr. and Mrs. Thomas Matthew Benton
request the pleasure of

Mr. and Mrs. Roger B. Clark's

company at dinner
on Thursday, September the twentieth
at eight o'clock
250 Park Avenue

HANDWRITTEN INVITATION
TO A FORMAL DINNER

*Dr. and Mrs. Thomas Matthew Benton
request the pleasure of
Mr. and Mrs. Robert B. Clark's
company at dinner
on Thursday, September the twentieth
at eight o'clock.*

Handwritten invitations, as a rule, do not include the address . . . as most note paper used for social correspondence already has the address at the top. But cards or note paper to be engraved do *not* have the address at the top, and it must therefore be included in the body of the invitation.

Don't use "Mr. & Mrs." in social correspondence. Make it a point to spell out the word "and" and between "Mr. and Mrs." in all social correspondence. The symbol & is for business correspondence only.

ALWAYS RESPOND PROMPTLY
TO A DINNER INVITATION

A dinner invitation is one of the highest forms of social courtesy. It's a compliment to you and should be treated as such, being acknowledged promptly and with a definite acceptance or regret.

A formal invitation should be acknowledged within twenty-four hours, if possible. That gives the hostess time to make other arrangements if you send regrets. Don't reply with an informal note, as that suggests you are unfamiliar with good social usage. Follow the exact wording of the invitation, writing on the first page of your note paper only, and centering the message attractively so that it not only *reads* but *looks* formal. Here, for example, is the way an acceptance of the invitation above should look:

---

30 Sutton Place

Mr. and Mrs. Roger B. Clark
accept with pleasure
Dr. and Mrs. Thomas M. Benton's
kind invitation for dinner
on Thursday, September twentieth
at eight o'clock

There is a growing tendency nowadays to write formal acknowledgments without indented margins, following only the wording and not the arrangement of the invitation. There's no real objection to writing your acknowledgment this way, if you find the style more to your taste and liking. But the very best social usage still calls for decorative spacing; and though the following *may* be used, the form shown above is still preferred:

Mr. and Mrs. Roger B. Clark accept
with pleasure Dr. and Mrs. Thomas
M. Benton's kind invitation for
dinner on Thursday, September the
twentieth, at eight o'clock

If you cannot accept a dinner invitation, it's always courteous to give the reason why in your response. Formerly an acknowledgment was all that was required—no explanation. But that is now looked upon as rude and ungracious according to today's standards. The following are typical "regrets" to a formal dinner invitation—written by hand, of course, on your best white note paper:

Mr. and Mrs. Robert B. Clark
regret that a previous engagement
prevents their accepting
Dr. and Mrs. Thomas M. Benton's
kind invitation for dinner
on Thursday, September the twentieth

Mr. and Mrs. Robert B. Clark
regret exceedingly that they
are unable to accept
Dr. and Mrs. Thomas M. Benton's
kind invitation for dinner
on Thursday, September the twentieth
owing to illness in the family

An acceptance always requires the repetition of both the date and the hour to prevent the possibility of a misunderstanding. But a regret requires the repetition of the date only.

DINNER IN HONOR OF A
SPECIAL GUEST OR GUESTS

Invitation

Dr. and Mrs. Thomas Matthew Benton
request the pleasure of
Mr. and Mrs. Roger B. Clark's
company at dinner
on Thursday, September the twentieth
at eight o'clock
to meet Mr. John T. Alden

250 Park Avenue

Acceptance

Mr. and Mrs. Roger B. Clark
accept with pleasure
Dr. and Mrs. Thomas M. Benton's
kind invitation for dinner
on Thursday, September the twentieth
at eight o'clock
to meet Mr. John T. Alden

Regret

Mr. and Mrs. Roger B. Clark
regret that a previous engagement
prevents their accepting
Dr. and Mrs. Thomas M. Benton's
kind invitation for dinner
on Thursday, September the twentieth
to meet Mr. John T. Alden

Frequently, when the guests of honor are persons of particular importance or prominence, their names are placed at the top of the invitation. The words *"To meet"* may be used as shown; or the entire phrase, *"To meet General and Mrs. Wayne R. Pratt"* may be used as the first line.

Invitation

To meet
General and Mrs. Wayne R. Pratt

Dr. and Mrs. Thomas Matthew Benton
request the pleasure of your company
at dinner
at the Ritz-Carlton
on Thursday, September the twentieth
at half past seven o'clock

The acceptance follows the same wording. The regret reads:

Mr. and Mrs. Roger B. Clark
regret that owing to illness
they are unable to accept
Dr. and Mrs. Thomas M. Benton's
kind invitation for dinner
on Thursday, September the twentieth
to meet General and Mrs. Wayne R. Pratt

DINNER TO CELEBRATE
A SPECIAL OCCASION

When a dinner is given to celebrate some special occasion—like a wedding anniversary or a daughter's debut—that purpose is usually stated in the invitation.

Invitation

Mr. and Mrs. Paul Preston
request the pleasure of your company
at dinner
on the Twenty-fifth Anniversary of their marriage
Wednesday, the fifth of June
at seven o'clock
20 Lake Drive

or

Dr. and Mrs. Thomas Matthew Benton
request the pleasure of your companv
at dinner
in honor of their daughter
Miss Anita Benton
on Saturday, the fifteenth of November
at eight o'clock
The Waldorf-Astoria

Please send reply to
250 Park Avenue

The acceptance or regret follows the same wording. The regret should include the reason why.

DINNER FOLLOWED BY
CONCERT OR OPERA

Formal dinner invitations sometimes include an invitation to a play, opera, concert or lecture later on in the evening. As only a comparatively few guests can be invited to share such an evening, the invitations are almost always written by hand. For those who still cling to the old social traditions, and who like to entertain even small groups of friends occasionally with old-fashioned formality, we include these examples of correct invitations for "dinner and afterward."

Invitation

Dr. and Mrs. Thomas Matthew Benton
request the pleasure of
Mr. and Mrs. Peter Kenway's
company at dinner
on Wednesday, April the eighteenth
at seven o'clock
and at the Leonard Bernstein recital afterward

or

Dr. and Mrs. Thomas Matthew Benton
request the pleasure of
Mr. and Mrs. Peter Kenway's
company for dinner and the opera
on Wednesday, April the eigtheenth
at seven o'clock

Please reply to
250 Park Avenue

The acceptance or regret follows the same wording. The regret usually includes the reason why, as previously shown.

DINNER BY SONS AND DAUGHTERS IN HONOR OF PARENTS

When a group of children, married and unmarried, give a formal dinner in honor of their parents' silver or golden wedding anniversary, an invitation like the following is the most practical. It is issued in the names of all the sons and daughters, with a reply requested in the name of one person in the group selected to handle this part of the arrangements:

In honor of the
Fiftieth Wedding Anniversary of
Mr. and Mrs. James Gray
their sons and daughters
request the pleasure of

Mr. and Mrs. Thomas M. Benton's

company at dinner
on Friday, the sixth of June
at eight o'clock
The Hampshire House

Kindly send reply to
Miss Joyce Gray
Tuxedo Park, New York

A person receiving the invitation above is required to make formal acknowledgment to all the sons and daughters; but the envelope is addressd only to "Miss Joyce Gray," as requested. The acceptance or regret should be carefully written by hand, on good quality white note paper, and mailed within twenty-four hours after receipt of the invitation.

If you prefer to write your acknowledgment or regret without the indented margins, you may do so—as previously mentioned. But remember that to be socially correct, *the wording must follow the wording of the invitation and your regret should include your reason why.*

Those who are forced to decline the invitation and who are especially courteous and social-minded, send congratulations on the day of the dinner; and later write a note to the guests of honor (in this case, the parents)—explaining why they were unable to be present and how sorry they were to have missed it.

HOW TO POSTPONE OR CANCEL
FORMAL DINNER INVITATIONS

It frequently happens that a dinner party must be canceled or postponed, sometimes almost at the very last minute, due to illness or other circumstances. If there is time, the hostess writes a formal note . . . assuming, of course, that this was to have been a formal dinner and engraved invitations were sent out. If there isn't time for a note, the hostess (or someone representing her) should telephone or telegraph all guests at once.

The following examples show how formal dinner invitations are usually recalled or postponed. Because of the nature of the communication, these notes—though in the third person—are not, as a rule, written with indented spacing. It is considered somewhat better taste, in this particular instance, to eliminate the decorative arrangement—and write the notes as follows:

> Mr. and Mrs. Paul Preston regret that damages done to their house by a recent fire make it necessary to postpone the dinner arranged for April third until May fifth at the same time.

> Mr. and Mrs. James Carter, Jr. regret that they are obliged to recall their invitations for Thursday, the second of November, because of the death of their nephew, Mr. Henry Pierce Lowe.

Mr. and Mrs. Peter Kenway regret that
they are obliged to recall their invitations for next Thursday, due to
unavoidable circumstances.

The last of the above examples is the least courteous, for it
offers no explanation. Bear in mind that these are *formal*
notes, correct only when engraved invitations have been sent
out. For canceling or postponing a simple, informal dinner,
you would naturally write a more personal note of explanation.

HOW TO BREAK A FORMAL
DINNER ENGAGEMENT

Sometimes it's the *guest* and not the hostess who is obliged
to make a last-minute change of plans due to illness or other
circumstances. It goes without saying, of course, that a dinner
engagement should never be broken unless there is a very
good reason for it. And if there is such a reason, it calls for
prompt action—either by letter or telephone. The hostess
must be informed fully and at once of the circumstances which
prevent the guest from being present as planned.

Dear Mrs. Benton:

Mr. Carter has been called to Philadelphia on account of the sudden illness of his sister. We are very
anxious about her, and I am sure you will understand
why it is impossible for either of us to attend your dinner party next Tuesday.

We are both extremely sorry to break our engagement at this late date; and hope you and Dr. Benton
will forgive us.

Sincerely yours,
Florence Carter

INVITING A FRIEND TO FILL
AN EMPTY PLACE AT DINNER

When a hostess finds herself short one dinner guest, due
to the fact that someone was unable to come at the last minute, the usual thing is to call on a friend to fill in the gap.
If time is short, she telephones; otherwise she writes a note
frankly explaining the situation and asking the friend to fill
in as a special favor. It's not an easy letter to write. No one
likes to play "second fiddle"—to be invited only because
someone else was unable to come. But it's much better to put
it on this frank basis than to invite someone only a day or

two ahead of time *without* an explanation. That sort of last-minute invitation fools no one, and is much more likely to injure sensitive feelings than a straightforward note like the following:

Dear Frank:

If you have no other plans for this Thursday night, the twelfth, will you join my dinner party? One of my guests has just telephoned that he can't come because of illness.

So, you see, Frank, I'm putting it to you very honestly! I need another guest—and Jim and I can think of no one we'd rather have than you. Will you overlook the informality of this rather hurried invitation and make us both very happy by accepting?

Sincerely yours,
Laura Winston

There is usually no time to respond by letter to such an invitation. It's more likely to be acknowledged by telephone. But if there *is* time to write, the letter should be especially friendly and cordial. The invitation should either be accepted graciously . . . or a very good reason for not accepting it should be given.

Dear Laura:

I guess I should be sorry for that chap who is ill . . . but I'm not at all! I'm very glad of the opportunity to enjoy another of your delightful dinners.

So you and Jim can count me in, and thanks for asking me!

Yours sincerely,
Frank Lennon

Dear Laura:

I wish I could accept your invitation for Thursday night! I know I'd enjoy it as I have always enjoyed your charming dinner parties. But unfortunately I am leaving on a business trip tomorrow, and will be far from New York by Thursday.

My very best to you and Jim, and thanks for thinking of me!

Sincerely yours,
Frank Lennon

INFORMAL DINNER INVITATIONS
—AND HOW TO ANSWER THEM

The invitations and acknowledgments we have have been discussing up to this point are for elaborately formal and "special occasion" dinners only. But the average person today entertains *informally,* and has far more occasion to write simply little notes of invitation than to send out engraved social forms."

However, though informal notes provide much greater latitude than formal third-person invitations . . . they, too, follow a fairly fixed pattern. They are usually written in two brief paragraphs; and however the words may vary, the message always remains essentially this: "Will you come to dinner on a certain date, at a certain time?"

A note inviting people to dinner is always written by the hostess for her husband and herself. It is addressed to "Mrs." only, not to "Mr. and Mrs."—but the note should include mention of the husband, otherwise it is a discourtesy to him. For example:

> Dear Mrs. Jennings:
>
> Will you and Mr. Jennings have dinner with us on Tuesday, the fifth of May, at seven o'clock?
>
> It's a long time since we have had the pleasure of seeing you, and we do hope you can come.
>
> > Sincerely yours,
> > Elizabeth K. Benton

The person who receives such a note should answer it promptly, and with a *definite* acceptance or regret. It should not be a vague or conditional response that leaves the hostess "up a tree," so to speak. The answer should be a specific, "Yes, we'll be delighted to come!"—or "So sorry! We can't come because . . ."

The acceptance of any invitation, of course, should be an implied "Thank you"—graciously and unmistakably expressed. The words may say it any way you like; but the tone or spirit of your note must clearly convey the impression that you are pleased to have been invited . . . that you are glad to accept . . . and that you are looking forward to the occasion with eagerness.

Dear Mrs. Benton:

Mr. Jennings and I will be delighted to dine with you on Tuesday, the fifth of May, at seven o'clock. How very nice of you to ask us!

We are both looking forward with great pleasure to seeing you and Dr. Benton again.

Very sincerely yours,
Susan Jennings

If it's necessary to decline a dinner invitation, the note should be very carefully written to avoid giving offense. The reason for not being able to accept should be given; and it's always courteous to say how sorry you are, and to suggest how very hard you tried to overcome the obstacle that stood in the way. The tone of the letter should be one of sincere regret:

Dear Mrs. Benton:

I've been putting off this note until the last possible moment, hoping and hoping Mr. Jennings would get back from Baltimore in time for your dinner party. But now I must regretfully write that he'll still be out of town on Tuesday, the fifth; and we therefore cannot accept your kind invitation for dinner on that day.

It was sweet of you to ask us; and I know Mr. Jennings will be as sorry as I am to miss an evening with you and Dr. Benton. We know how delightful such evenings at your house usually are!

Sincerely yours,
Susan Jennings

The easiest way out of an invitation you do not care to accept is to plead a previous engagement. That is always an acceptable excuse. But be sure your note, however brief, sounds as though you are really sorry:

Dear Mrs. Benton:

I just can't tell you how sorry Mr. Jennings and I are that we cannot dine with you on Tuesday, the fifth of May. Unfortunately we already have an engagement for that evening.

Thank you for asking us, and we hope you will give us the opportunity to say "yes" some other time.

Sincerely yours,
Susan Jennings

Obviously the above invitations and acknowledgments are not intended for intimate friends. They are the kind of notes you would write to people you know *casually*, not closely . . . people you invite *occasionally*, for purely social reasons, not *frequently* because you love them and enjoy being with them.

But bear in mind that even to an intimate friend, an invitation should be an *invitation*—not a minor detail lost in a long account of local news, family gossip and other idle writing! An invitation seems much more important to the person who receives it when it's sent as a special and separate communication . . . instead of just part of a chatty letter.

Here, for example, is how you might invite a close friend to dinner . . . *correctly*, yet *cordially*:

Dear Ruth:

Tom and I are having some very special friends here for dinner on Thursday, October second. Naturally the party wouldn't be complete without you and Bill!

We hope you can come, as we are planning to show the movies we made in Nassau, and we know you and Bill are thinking of going there this winter.

Dinner is at seven, as usual. We'll be looking for you two charming people at that time, so don't disappoint us!

Affectionately yours,
Betty

Not even close friendship permits of laxity in the matter of response to a dinner invitation. A note like the above should be acknowledged promptly, and in kind. Although many people now prefer the convenience of telephoning a response, it's always better form to *answer by note when invited by note*.

Dear Betty:

How could we even *think* of turning down the prospect of another delightful evening with you and Tom? Of course we'll be there on Thursday, October second —promptly at seven!

Bill and I are both excited about seeing those Nassau pictures. We think that's where we're going for our vacation this winter; so it will be wonderful seeing your pictures and getting a "preview" of the island.

Thanks for asking us, Betty. . . . We're certainly looking forward to next Thursday!

Affectionately yours,
Ruth

There's an old familiar saying: "You never need to explain to a friend." But that doesn't apply to dinner invitations! If you refuse an invitation, you must explain why—even to a friend. Especially to a friend!

Dear Betty:

What a shame! We won't be able to come to your dinner party on Thursday because that's the day we're having the Gilmores *here* for dinner.

You remember I told you about Mr. Gilmore last week. He's one of Bill's most important clients. If it were anyone else, I'd alter my plans—even at the very last moment—rather than miss an evening with you and Tom! But I just can't do that with the Gilmores, Betty, I'm sure you understand.

Bill and I would certainly like to see those Nassau pictures, as we think that's where we're going this winter. Will you give us a private showing some time? Just say when and we'll be there!

Have a good time on Thursday. I certainly wish we could be with you!

Affectionately yours,
Ruth

INVITING FRIENDS TO
DINNER AND THE THEATER

Notes of invitation are often quite brief, these busy days, and no one thinks anything of it. An invitation for dinner and the theater is frequently just a hurried line or two from one friend to another. But that doesn't necessarily mean the note is curt or abrupt. It's just written fast, as so many things must be now.

Dear Ann:

We have four seats for the opening of the O'Neill play this Friday, the tenth. Will you and John join us here for dinner at seven sharp; and then go on with us later to the play? We'll be looking for you Friday night, so don't disappoint us!

Affectionately yours,
Doris

Acceptance

Dear Doris:

Delighted! We'll be there Friday at seven, and go with you afterward to the theater. How wonderful of you and Frank to ask us!

Affectionately yours,
Ann

Regret

Dear Doris:

I think you'd better ask some other couple for Friday. John's in Washington and won't be back for another week. Wait till he hears what a wonderful evening he missed with you and Frank! Thanks for asking us, Doris. I'm certainly sorry we can't say "yes"!

Affectionately yours,
Ann

WHEN A DAUGHTER ACTS
AS HOSTESS

In a motherless home, a young daughter is often required to act as hostess for her father. She does not send out dinner invitations in her own name, but always includes mention of her father and makes it clear that she is acting for him, at his request.

Dear Mrs. Everett:

Father wishes me to ask if you and Mr. Everett can dine with us on Monday, March the fifth, at seven o'clock.

We hope you can come, and look forward to seeing you.

Sincerely yours,
Marcia Curtis

The acceptance or regret must go to the *daughter,* not the father. The response to any invitation must go to the person who writes it.

NOTE TO RECALL AN INFORMAL DINNER INVITATION

Dear Mrs. Jennings:

I have just learned that my son, who is at school in Massachusetts, was injured in a basketball game. Although the injury is not serious, Dr. Benton and I feel we must go to him at once; and we are leaving tomorrow morning.

Under the circumstances, we must recall our dinner invitations for Tuesday, the fifth of May . . . and plan on a later date for our party.

I'm sure that you and Mr. Jennings will understand our anxiety, and will forgive this last-minute change in plans.

Sincerely yours,
Elizabeth K. Benton

NOTE TO BREAK AN INFORMAL DINNER ENGAGEMENT

Dear Mrs. Benton:

I'm so very sorry to have to write you this letter! After accepting your kind invitation for dinner on

Tuesday, May the fifth, I now find that we cannot be there after all.

Mr. Jennings has just been called to Chicago on business; and although he tried very hard to postpone the trip until after the fifth, he was unable to do so.

We had been looking forward with great pleasure to seeing you and Dr. Benton; and we both feel very badly about this unexpected development. We hope you understand, and that you will not be inconvenienced.

Sincerely yours,
Susan Jennings

NOTE TO AN INTIMATE FRIEND
RECALLING A DINNER INVITATION

Ruth, dear:

The dinner for Thursday, October the second, is off! Anita has the measles—of all things—and it looks as though I'll have to suspend all plans for entertaining for the time being.

Anita isn't very ill; but she demands a great deal of attention and I'm with her most of the time. Then, too, of course, the measles are contagious—so this is certainly no time to have friends at the house!

I'm sure you and Bill will understand, Ruth—and that you will forgive this last-minute change in plans. I'll write you as soon as the Benton household is back to normal again; and we'll plan another date for dinner.

My love to you both!

Betty

NOTE TO AN INTIMATE FRIEND
BREAKING A DINNER ENGAGEMENT

Dear Betty:

I'm so disappointed, I could *cry!* You know how I've been looking forward to your dinner next Thursday; and now, at almost the last moment, I find we can't make it after all.

As usual, Bill's been called out of town just when it's most inconvenient for us. He tried to postpone the trip for a few days, but couldn't do it. So here I am all alone again, Betty . . . with Bill on his way to Chicago . . . and both of us sorry as can be to break a dinner engagement with you at the last moment. I can't say I'd blame you if you stopped inviting us completely!

But you know it isn't our fault, darling. There's nothing we'd rather do than spend an evening with you and Tom. And we especially hate to miss those Nassau pictures! Will you let us come some evening and see them after Tom gets back?

> Affectionately yours,
> Ruth

A hostess who receives a note like the above should decide whether or not she wants her friend to come by herself. If she would rather not have an odd woman guest at the table, it's best not to answer the note at all; it doesn't actually require an acknowledgment. But if she wants her friend to come even without her husband, she telephones or writes at once and says in effect: "Never mind if Bill's out of town! Come to my dinner party anyway! I'm counting on you. . . ."

3. Luncheon and Supper Invitations and Acknowledgments

Luncheons and suppers are, by their very nature, gay and light-hearted—the informal, and often impromptu, gathering of friends for a good time. They represent a less serious type of entertaining than dinners; and are for the most part quite simple and unpretentious in character.

Invitations for such functions are informal, too. More often than not they are just telephoned; or they are given casually, without previous plan, when friends chance to meet. Any written invitations are in the form of friendly little notes. Formal third-person invitations are rarely used for either a luncheon or supper; and then, only when it's a large, elaborate affair planned for some special purpose or to honor some special guest.

For example, a large and ceremonious luncheon is sometimes given, at home or at a hotel, to announce an engagement . . . to celebrate a wedding anniversary . . . to present a debutante daughter . . . or for some similar purpose. Such socially important luncheons warrant the dignity and formality of engraved invitations. They are sent out two or three weeks in advance, and closely follow the phraseology of a dinner invitation:

Dr. and Mrs. Thomas Matthew Benton
request the pleasure of

Mr and Mrs. Frank North's

company at luncheon
in honor of their daughter
Miss Anita Benton
on Saturday, May the third
at one o'clock
250 Park Avenue

Please respond

The person who receives such an invitation should answer at once with a definite acceptance or regret, following the same formal wording as the invitation.

Another type of luncheon for which formal invitations are sometimes issued is the luncheon preceding an important sporting event such as a tennis match or football game. As only half a dozen people at the most are ordinarily invited to such a luncheon, invitations are rarely, if ever, engraved. They are carefully written by hand, following the decorative spacing and arrangement of engraved formal invitations.

Mr. and Mrs. Robert G. Scully
request the pleasure of your company
at luncheon
Saturday, the eighteenth of August
at one o'clock
at the Pickwick Club
before the tennis finals at Lynn Field

Please send reply to
10 Lake Drive

The above invitation includes the tennis match following luncheon, the host and hostess assuming responsibility for the tickets. Therefore an acceptance or regret should be written and mailed at once, so that other disposition can be made of the tickets if you are unable to accept the invitation. (Do not *telephone* your reply to a formal invitation unless you have been out of town and return too late to write . . . in which case you should explain the circumstances to the hostess.)

As a rule, luncheons are not given jointly by a husband and wife, except for special occasions like the above. Most men cannot attend social functions in the middle of the day; and luncheons are therefore generally planned for women alone, and invitations are issued in the name of the hostess alone. The name of the host never appears unless he is to be present at the luncheon and other men are to be invited as guests.

When a luncheon is given for a group of women—even a large, formal luncheon at a club or hotel—the invitations may be in the form of personal notes written by the hostess to her guests. But some women prefer formality even in their invitations, as they feel it gives more social significance to the occasion. Following is the standard form for an elaborate luncheon. It may be engraved for a large number of guests; but should be hand-written if only six or eight guests are invited.

Mrs. Thomas Matthew Benton
requests the pleasure of
your company at luncheon
on Friday, November the seventh
at one o'clock
250 Park Avenue

Please respond

The acceptance or regret should follow the wording of the invitation. It is not socially correct to write a personal note of explanation when declining a formal invitation. The regret should be as formal as the invitation itself, in the same wording and spacing. However, it is a courteous and friendly gesture to write a personal note to the hostess a week or so following the luncheon, to say how sorry you were to have missed it. This note would not be *instead* of the formal response, but in *addition to it*. It's one of those "letters-that-don't-need-to-be-written" which we discussed in an earlier chapter . . . letters that people do not expect, and are therefore especially delighted to receive.

When a luncheon is given to present a celebrity, a new bride, or an out-of-town guest to a group of friends, that fact should be clearly specified in the invitation. If it's a personal note, as it's very likely to be, it should be brief and to the point:

Dear Mrs. Pratt:

   Miss Marta Lang, the portrait painter, is visiting me
this week and I am inviting a few friends to meet her.
I am giving a luncheon on Thursday, September the
third, at one o'clock; and I do hope you can come.

   Miss Lang is a most charming and fascinating person, and I know you'll enjoy her company as much as
she will enjoy yours. So please write and say you'll be
here!

Cordially yours,
Elizabeth K. Benton

   If it's a formal invitation instead of a personal note, the
phrase "To meet Miss Marta Lang" is used as the *first* or
last line of the invitation:

To meet Miss Marta Lang

Mrs. Thomas Matthew Benton
requests the pleasure of

Mrs. Wayne L. Pratt's

company at luncheon
on Thursday, September the third
at one o'clock
250 Park Avenue

Please respond

or

Mrs. Thomas Matthew Benton
requests the pleasure of
your company at luncheon
on Thursday, September the third
at one o'clock
to meet Miss Marta Lang

250 Park Avenue

   Whether an invitation specifically calls for a response or not,
send an acceptance or regret promptly. It's difficult and inconvenient for a hostess not to know how many guests to
expect. The reply to a personal note is, of course, a personal
note.

The reply to a formal invitation can be only a formal acceptance or regret. A personal note or a telephone message may accomplish the same purpose, but does not do it properly from a social standpoint.

Sometimes a large and elaborate luncheon is given by two or more women. The invitations are usually engraved, and the names of all the women appear on it. For example:

Mrs. Carl Whitney
Mrs. Robert G. Scully
Mrs. Thomas Matthew Benton
request the pleasure of
your company at luncheon
on Wednesday, April the second
at half past one o'clock
The Savoy Plaza

Please reply to
Mrs. Thomas M. Benton
250 Park Avenue

Your reply to the above invitation should list *all* the names of the hostesses, exactly as in the invitation. But the envelope should be addressed only to the person whose name and address are indicated in the lower left corner. If no name and address are given, the envelope should be addressed to *all* the hostesses and sent to the hotel, as it can be assumed that arrangements have been made to receive them there.

INVITATIONS FOR SIMPLE
INFORMAL LUNCHEONS

Up to this point we have been discussing formal, ceremonious luncheons.

But far more familiar to most of us are the gay, informal luncheons that are planned for no other purpose than to enjoy the company of a few congenial, well-chosen friends.

The typical informal luncheon invitation is a brief note giving the time, the place and usually—but not necessarily— the reason for the luncheon.

Dear Ruth:

Will you come to luncheon on Friday, May the fifth, at one o'clock?

My niece, Doris Fernell, is visiting us, and I think

you will enjoy meeting her. She is a charming, witty
girl . . . and very good company!

Laura Winston and Susan Jennings will be here, and
perhaps we can play a little bridge after luncheon. Do
say you'll come!

> Affectionately yours,
> Betty

The response to an informal luncheon invitation should, of
course, be a friendly but definite acceptance or regret. Occasionally, however, a hostess, familiar with a friend's plans and
eager to have that friend attend her luncheon, writes as follows:

I know you are planning to be in Chicago on the
tenth; but if you can possibly get back in time, will
you come to my luncheon in honor of Kay Bolton, the
writer?

In that case, the person who receives the invitation may
answer in kind, giving neither a definite acceptance nor regret,
but promising to come if she can:

I'll try my best to be back by the tenth, as I'd like
very much to come to your luncheon and meet Kay
Bolton. But please don't count on it, as I wouldn't like
to disappoint you.

If she returns in time—even if it's the very morning of the
luncheon—she should telephone and say, in effect: "Well, I
made it! I'm home and I'm coming to lunch today!"
If she does *not* get home in time, she should telephone or
write immediately upon her return to say she was looking
forward to the luncheon and was very sorry to have missed it.

INVITING SOMEONE YOU
DO NOT KNOW

The most important thing to bear in mind when inviting a
stranger to luncheon (or to any other social affair) is that you
must *explain the reason* for the invitation. Be sure it's a real
reason, a *legitimate* reason, otherwise your invitation may
seem offensive and in poor taste. It's important also to make
your luncheon sound as though it will be interesting and enjoyable. Most people have busy social lives of their own, and
do not like to accept invitations from strangers unless they

know *why*, and can be reasonably sure they'll enjoy themselves if they accept.

Dear Mrs. Johnson:

If you have no other plans for Wednesday, April the sixth, will you come to a little informal luncheon here at my home?

My Richard and your Larry have been roommates at Andover for so long that it's about time their mothers got to know each other—don't you think so?

I have asked two friends whom I think you will like; and perhaps we can play some bridge in the afternoon.

Luncheon is at one, and I'll expect you at that time unless I hear from you to the contrary.

Cordially yours,
Elizabeth K. Benton

If you receive a luncheon invitation like the above, and plan to accept it, you may reply or not as you prefer. An acknowledgment is not actually required, as your appearance on the day of the luncheon is expected if you do not send regrets within a day or two. However, a note like the following paves the way for a more friendly and cordial relationship:

Dear Mrs. Benton:

I'll be delighted to come to your luncheon on Wednesday, April the sixth, at one o'clock.

Larry has often spoken to me of Richard, and has told me how very much he enjoys having him for a roommate. Although I have never met Richard, I feel as though I know him from hearing so much about him.

I assure you it will be a very great pleasure indeed to meet Richard's mother! Thank you so much for asking me.

Sincerely yours,
Mildred Johnson

If you receive an invitation from someone you don't know, and you cannot accept it, be sure that your reply is very carefully and very tactfully worded. For it would be most unkind to give the impression that you do not *want* to accept an invitation so graciously extended.

Dear Mrs. Benton:

I have heard so much about Richard from Larry that I almost feel as though I know him. I would certainly enjoy meeting his mother!

But unfortunately I expect guests myself on Wednesday, the sixth of April; and therefore cannot accept your invitation for luncheon on that day.

It was thoughtful of you to invite me, and I am extremely sorry I cannot accept. I do hope you will ask me again some time!

Sincerely yours,
Mildred Johnson

However disappointed the hostess may be to receive a note like the above, she cannot feel hurt or resentful. For it is a gracious and friendly note, expressing sincere regret, and it gives a real excuse for not coming. In other words, it does not slam the door shut . . . as *this* note does:

Dear Mrs. Benton:

I'm sorry I cannot accept your invitation for luncheon on Wednesday, April sixth, as I have other plans for that day.

Sincerely yours,
Mildred Johnson

Surely a cold, curt note like that leaves no further possibility of friendly overtures! It stamps the writer as rude and ill-mannered . . . and totally lacking in the social graces.

SUPPER INVITATIONS

Supper parties are the most *informal* of all types of entertaining. Guests are generally intimate friends or members of the family; and invitations are almost always telephoned.

"How about you and Ted coming to supper next Tuesday night?" is the way supper guests are most likely to be invited.

A written note of invitation should be on about the same general level. If you customarily say to a friend, "How about supper Tuesday night?"—don't suddenly become stilted in your letter and write, "May we have the pleasure of entertaining you at supper next Tuesday evening?" Formal language doesn't go with simple supper party informality. *Write it as you would say it.*

Dear Ann:

We're having a buffet supper Sunday night, June the fourth—and of course we want you and Bob!

Come at six, if you can. We'll have supper early and play some bridge afterwards. The Clarks and the Prestons will be here, and I know you always enjoy their company.

We'll be expecting you on the fourth, so don't disappoint us!

With love,
Marjorie

No response to the above is necessary unless you like to be especially courteous and considerate. In that case, you write a note telling your hostess you'll be there. But if you *cannot* attend the party, you must reply—and promptly.

Dear Marjorie:

I'm so sorry we can't come to your buffet supper Sunday night! Bob's mother is ill, and we're going to Philadelphia this week end to see her.

Thanks for asking us, Marjorie. We certainly hate to miss any of your parties . . . they're always such fun!

Affectionately,
Ann

Guests do not ordinarily expect to meet strangers at an intimate supper party. Therefore if you are inviting someone outside your usual circle of friends and acquaintances, it's a good idea to explain about the details beforehand in your note of invitation.

In other words, the invitation should "sell" the idea of accepting the invitation—should give a real reason for accepting it, and for looking forward to the occasion with pleasure and anticipation.

Dear Susan:

I know you are interested in old china and glassware, so I'm sure you'll be interested in the Bartons! They are coming here to supper next Sunday night, October the twelfth, and we'd like you and Walter to come, too.

The Bartons are that very charming couple we met in Montreal last summer. They have a wonderful collection of old china and glassware; and I understand that Mrs. Barton is quite an authority on English china. I'm sure you and Walter will thoroughly enjoy an evening in their company.

We're planning supper at six; that will give us a nice long evening to talk. If I don't hear from you before then, I'll be expecting you on the twelfth!

Affectionately yours,
Laura

It is not easy to turn down an invitation so cordially and personally extended. The hostess who invites congenial people and plans an evening for their special enjoyment—and who goes to the trouble of writing notes to "sell" the evening to her guests—*should not be turned down unless absolutely necessary*. When an evening is so obviously planned for certain people, those people should make every effort to accept—even though it may mean a change in previous plans for the evening. If such plans cannot be changed, and the invitation cannot therefore be accepted, the hostess should be notified immediately. It is then up to her either to proceed according to plan, or to postpone the supper until the people she wants can be there.

Dear Laura:

We would *love* to come to your supper on Sunday, the twelfth, and meet the Bartons. But that's the night Walter's brother is arriving from England, and he is expecting us to meet him at the airport and drive him home.

If it were anything else, Laura, we'd just change our plans and come. You know that, I'm sure. But we haven't seen Paul in nearly a year, and Walter is practically counting the hours to his arrival! We couldn't possibly disappoint him when we know he'll be expecting to see us as he steps off the plane. He is scheduled to arrive at six-fifteen; and as we are driving him out to Westchester, we couldn't get to your party until much too late.

We're *most* sorry to miss the opportunity of meeting the Bartons! Walter and I would have enjoyed so very much talking with them about old English china. But perhaps we'll have that pleasure at some future time.

You were sweet to ask us, Laura, and we appreciate it. Our very best to you and Jim!

> With love,
> Susan

Occasionally a supper of more elaborate and ceremonious proportions than the usual intimate type for friends, is given for some special purpose. For example, instead of the elaborate formality of a dinner *preceding* the theater or opera (for a group of people who are to be entertained for one reason or another)— a supper is given *following* it. This is not, as a rule, the popular buffet supper, but a more impressive "sit down" affair. Nevertheless, invitations are still in the form of friendly, informal notes.

Dear Mrs. North:

We have eight tickets for the opening of the new Moss Hart show on Wednesday, September third. We are asking a group of friends to join us at the theater, and come back with us later for a little supper party at the house. Dr. Benton and I hope that you and Mr. North have no previous engagement, and can join us for the evening.

We are meeting in the lobby of the Globe Theater at eight-fifteen. Please let us know if you *cannot* come; otherwise we will expect to see you there.

> Cordially yours,
> Elizabeth K. Benton

Even when an invitation specifically says to answer only if you cannot come, it is more gracious to send a note of acceptance.

4. Party Invitations and Acknowledgments

The invitations you send out for your simple informal parties at home may be as original and "different" as you wish. It is not necessary to conform to any special wording or style. Birthday invitations may be in the form of amusing jingles. Shower invitations may be in the form of tiny, umbrella-shaped cards, if that appeals to your fancy. Invitations for holiday parties—such as Easter, Christmas, New Year—may be whatever is cleverly in keeping with the occasion.

But there are certain generalities of good taste that apply to *all* invitations. And there are certain basic "unwritten laws" of good hospitality that everyone should know about.

In the first place, no matter how informal the party may be, invitations should be sent out—or telephoned—at least one week in advance. Obviously this doesn't apply to unplanned, impromptu parties for which no regular invitations are issued. It applies to the parties you plan ahead of time . . . and to which guests should be invited far enough in advance to make it *convenient for them to accept.*

The second "unwritten law" of hospitality is to *choose your guests carefully.* Always try to invite people who are congenial and have something in common, and can therefore be reasonably expected to enjoy one another's company. Don't, for example, invite experts and beginners to the same bridge party. Don't invite two people you know dislike each other, or who are for one reason or another uncomfortable or unhappy in each other's company.

CARD PARTY INVITATIONS

Many hostesses prefer to telephone their card party invitations, as this provides an immediate acceptance or regret from each guest, and tables can be arranged accordingly. However, notes of invitation are a shade more gracious, and somehow seem to give greater social significance to the occasion. If they are sent out well enough in advance, and answered promptly, the hostess will have time to fill in, if necessary, and arrange the right number of players for each table.

Dear Ruth:

How would you and Bill like to play bridge on Friday evening, March the fourth? The Prestons and the Clarks are coming, and as you know, they're excellent players.

I hope you and Bill have no other plans for that evening, and that you can come. We're starting at about eight-thirty. Do try and make it, Ruth—we're looking forward to seeing you!

Affectionately yours,
Betty

An invitation calls only for an acceptance or regret—not for a long, chatty letter giving the local gossip and the family news. So answer briefly and to the point.

It's always better not to accept an invitation at all, than to accept it and be unable to go at the last minute. This is especially true of bridge invitations; for if you are expected and you fail to put in an appearance, others are left out of the game. So if there's a possibility you may not be able to keep the engagement, say so frankly in a note of regret:

Dear Betty:

I wish I could accept your very tempting invitation to play bridge on Friday, March the fourth—but I hesitate to do so.

Bill has one of his usual deadlines to meet. He has been working night after night until ten or eleven o'clock; and although he says he may be through by the fourth, there's a very good chance that he *won't* be.

I wouldn't like to say "yes," Betty—and then find at the last minute that we can't come. So count us out this time; but many thanks for including us, and I hope you'll ask us soon again!

Affectionately,
Ruth

Many women like to entertain their friends at afternoon card parties; and frequently such parties are preceded by a luncheon. If it's a simple, informal party at home, the invitations are extended by telephone or personal note. But if it's a large bridge luncheon at a restaurant or hotel—perhaps to announce an engagement, or to honor a special guest—engraved invitations are usually sent out.

FOR AN INFORMAL
BRIDGE LUNCHEON

Dear Marcia:

I understand you've been taking bridge lessons recently. Well, here's your chance to show us what an expert you've become!

I'm having a group of friends here for luncheon and bridge next Tuesday, June the eighth. Can you come at one o'clock, and stay for most of the afternoon?

Betty and Susan will be here, and I know they'll be disappointed if you can't come. But I'll be even *more* disappointed—it's such a long time since I've seen you! So please try your best to make it.

Affectionately yours,
Janet

FOR A FORMAL
BRIDGE LUNCHEON

When a mother and daughter entertain at an afternoon party, the names of both appear on the invitation:

Mrs. Thomas Matthew Benton
Miss Anita Benton
request the pleasure of your company
at luncheon
Thursday, the twentieth of September
at one o'clock
The Hampshire House

Please reply to   Bridge
250 Park Avenue

FOR AN INFORMAL
COCKTAIL PARTY

Dear Ruth:

We're having some friends in for cocktails on Friday, June the eighth, from four to six. Can you and Bill come?

Tom and I are looking forward to seeing you, so don't disappoint us!

Cordially yours,
Betty

FOR A FORMAL
COCKTAIL PARTY

When invitations are issued for a cocktail party, the exact time of arrival and departure should be given—otherwise guests may stay too long and interfere with plans for the evening.

Dr. and Mrs. Thomas Matthew Benton
At Home
Friday, June the eighth
from four until six o'clock
250 Park Avenue

Cocktails

FOR AN INFORMAL
TEA PARTY

A tea or "at home" is a type of reception, and is more strictly *social* in character than other forms of afternoon entertaining. Therefore even a quite small and informal tea party calls for *written* invitations. It's not considered good form to telephone your invitations for this type of party.

Dear Mrs. North:

I have asked some friends to come for tea on Tuesday, April the eighth, at four o'clock. Will you join us?

I know you have just returned from Bermuda, but I hope you're not too busy to come. I'm looking forward to seeing you.

Cordially yours,
Elizabeth K. Benton

If some special entertaining is planned for the afternoon, that fact should be mentioned. An invitation is always more likely to be accepted if a *good reason* for accepting is given!

Dear Mrs. North:

Some of your good friends and mine are coming for tea on Tuesday, April the eighth, at four o'clock. I hope you can join us.

Rosa Cantrell is one of the guests, and she has promised to sing for us. And Mrs. Winston is planning to show her Samoan movies. So *do* come if you can—it promises to be a most interesting afternoon!

Cordially yours,
Elizabeth K. Benton

Your acceptance or regret should be sent promptly and should be of the same warm and friendly character as the invitation.

FORMAL TEA PARTIES

Teas, like luncheons and other afternoon parties, are generally given by women alone; but sometimes they are given by "Mr. and Mrs." jointly. Such teas are formal and ceremonious, as a rule, and are given for some special purpose like honoring an important guest, presenting a debutante daughter, or announcing an engagement. The invitations for such teas or receptions may be handwritten; but usually they are engraved—especially if the affair is away from home, at a club or hotel.

For a formal tea given at home by a mother and her debutante daughter, the invitations are written or engraved as follows:

Mrs. Thomas Matthew Benton
Miss Anita Benton
At Home
Friday afternoon, October fifth
from four until seven o'clock
250 Park Avenue

For a formal tea given by a mother and her debutante daughter *away* from home, in a hotel, the invitations are exactly the same as the above . . . except that the name of the hotel is given instead of the home address. If a reply is requested, that fact is indicated in the lower left corner, and the address for the reply is given.

When *both* parents receive with a debutante daughter, the invitations are issued by them jointly . . . and men as well as women are invited to the party. Instead of "Mrs. Thomas Matthew Benton" in the invitation above, the top line reads "Dr. and Mrs. Thomas Matthew Benton." The rest of the invitation remains the same.

Sometimes a large formal tea is given at a hotel by the parents of two debutantes who are friends. For an important social function of this kind, invitations are almost always engraved—and read as follows:

> Dr. and Mrs. Thomas Matthew Benton
> Mr. and Mrs. Walter Jennings
> Miss Anita Benton
> Miss Suzanne Jennings
> At Home
> Friday, November the seventeenth
> from four until seven o'clock
> The Savoy Plaza

When a tea or reception is given in honor of a distinguished guest—or "to meet" a well-known personality—that person's name should appear first on the invitation.

> To meet
> Miss Rosa Cantrell
>
> Dr. and Mrs. Thomas Matthew Benton
> request the pleasure of your company
> Tuesday, the fourth of March
> from four until seven o'clock
> The Sert Room
> Waldorf-Astoria

Please respond to
250 Park Avenue

Formal tea invitations should be sent out ten days to two weeks in advance. The customary phrase is "At Home"—which simply means a social gathering, or reception. If the purpose of the tea is to meet a celebrity, the phrase "request the pleasure of your company" is preferred.

All such invitations are answered as written—in the same third-person phraseology, and with the same formal spacing. As a rule, one accepts an "At Home" simply by attending it

. . . unless a reply is specifically requested. But if one cannot accept, a regret should be sent promptly. All the names that appear on the invitation should be repeated in the acknowledgment.

If no name and address for a reply are given on the invitation, it should be sent to the hotel where the reception is scheduled to be held. The envelope should be addressed to all the persons in whose names the invitations are issued.

GARDEN PARTY INVITATIONS

By "garden party" is generally meant a tea or reception held out-of-doors. If it's an important social function and formality is desired, the invitations may be engraved as follows:

> Mr. and Mrs. Robert G. Scully
> At Home
> in the garden
> Thursday, June the twenty-fifth
> from three to six o'clock

But nowadays most garden parties are charmingly informal, and invitations are by friendly note:

Dear Joan:

Our garden has never been as lovely as it is now! We'd like our friends to see it, so we're having tea on the lawn next Thursday, June the twenty-fifth, from three to six o'clock.

We hope you and Ralph can come. You simply *must* see what a magnificent display of June roses we have this year!

> Affectionately yours,
> Martha

The acceptance or regret must of course follow the tone of the invitation—formal replies for formal invitations and warm informal replies for informal invitations.

INVITATIONS FOR HOUSE AND
WEEK-END PARTIES

All invitations for house parties, whether for a week end or longer duration, should be by letter. There are many things the guest needs to know, and these should be included in the invitation.

For example, house guests must know the exact duration of the visit: when they are expected to arrive and when they are expected to leave. They should be given some idea of the activities planned, so that they will know what clothes and sports equipment to take with them. They should be told the best way to come, with marked road maps or timetables enclosed for their convenience.

A week-end visit is generally from Friday or Saturday until the following Monday morning. Guests should be invited at least two weeks in advance, to give them time to make all necessary arrangements. If several members of a family are invited, they should all be mentioned specifically by name. The thoughtful hostess mentions what other guests have been invited, to avoid the possibility of bringing uncongenial people together for a week end.

Dear Jane:

I hope you and Fred haven't any plans for the week end of July twenty-fourth, as we'd like you to spend it with us at Far Acres. It's simply *beautiful* here now, with everything in bloom!

I think we can promise Fred some good fishing this year. The trout are biting better than ever! So bring your fishing clothes; and be sure to bring your tennis things, too, because the Owens are coming and I'm sure you'll want to get out on the courts with them.

There's a very good train Friday night; I've marked it in red on the timetable. It gets you here about seven-thirty, which is just in time for dinner. You can get a late train back Sunday night, or there's an early express that Bob usually takes on Monday morning.

We hope nothing will prevent you from coming, as we're looking forward to your visit . . . and I know the Owens are looking forward to seeing you again, too. Be sure to let us know what train you are taking so that Bob can meet you at the station.

Affectionately yours,
Martha

Acceptance

Dear Martha:

Fred and I are counting the days to our week end
with you at Far Acres! We are delighted that you have
asked us; and we certainly won't let anything prevent
us from coming.

We plan to take the five o'clock train on Friday
night, July twenty-third, as you suggest. And we'll
take the early express back to town on Monday morning.

Thanks so much for asking us, Martha! We're looking forward to two wonderful days with you and the
Owens.

Affectionately yours,
Jane

Regret

Dear Martha:

How awful to have to turn down your very, very
tempting invitation! I can't think of *anything Fred*
and I would enjoy more right now than a week end
at Far Acres. But I expect my mother just about that
time—either on the twenty-third or twenty-fourth of
July. She is stopping over on her way to Canada, and
plans to spend a few days with us. Under the circumstances, we cannot make any plans for the week end.

But thanks so much for asking us, Martha! I know
we're missing a marvelous time! Please remember us
to the Owens, and tell them how sorry we are not to
have been able to join them for the week end.

Affectionately yours,
Jane

People who own country houses often invite friends to house
parties that may last anywhere from three days to three weeks.
The invitation must give the exact date of expected arrival and
departure, so that there can be no question about the duration
of the visit. And like the week-end invitation, it should indicate the best and most convenient way to come, the sports and

activities planned, the clothes likely to be needed, and so forth.

The acceptance or regret should be similar to those used as illllustrations for the week-end party.

INVITATIONS FOR SHOWERS

The setting for a shower may be a luncheon, an afternoon tea, or an evening party . . . and the invitations may be telephoned, or they may be in the form of any attractive shower cards that appeal to you. Written invitations are simply informal notes giving the time, place, type of shower, and so forth.

Dear Miss White:

I am giving a linen shower for Miss Mary Crawford on Saturday, April sixth, at four o'clock. I hope you can come, and stay for a buffet supper afterward.

This is a surprise for Mary, so please don't mention it to her if you see her before Saturday.

I have heard a great deal about you from Mary's friends, and I am looking forward to the pleasure of meeting you.

> Sincerely yours,
> Suzanne Jennings

The acceptance or regret should be sent as promptly as possible and should follow the friendly, informal character of the invitation.

INVITATIONS FOR CHRISTENINGS

Most christenings are very informal affairs. Invitations are usually telephoned, or friends are asked when seen. But it is also correct to write brief, friendly notes:

Dear Mrs. Whitney:

Our new baby is to be christened at the Community Church next Sunday at four o'clock. We are planning to call him "Robert." Wouldn't you and Mr. Whitney like to come to the service?

> Sincerely yours,
> Dorothy Evans

To an intimate friend, the note would naturally be less dignified and reserved:

Dear Kathleen:

That precious young son of ours is going to be christened next Sunday at four o'clock, at the Community Church. Come and see him make his first public appearance. He's simply *adorable*, Kathleen! We're planning to call him "Robert"—I hope you approve.

I'll be looking for you on Sunday—so be sure to come!

Affectionately yours,
Dorothy

Sometimes a business associate is invited to a child's christening and is unable to attend. When business interferes with the acceptance of any kind of invitation, it's gracious to imply you would have been *delighted* to accept otherwise.

Dear Mrs. Evans:

I am leaving for Los Angeles today on business. But it's with great reluctance that I do so, as I had hoped to attend your son's christening at the Community Church on Sunday.

I'm very sorry I won't be able to be there. Allow me, however, to wish you great joy in your son; and to wish the young fellow himself a long and happy life.

Sincerely yours,
John T. McElroy

There are usually two godmothers for a girl and one for a boy—two godfathers for a boy and one for a girl. They are chosen from among the relatives and intimate friends, and generally well before the baby's arrival. However, if someone living at a great distance is asked to be a godparent, a telegram is sent on the day of the child's birth—or very soon afterward.

It's a boy! Will you be godfather?

or

The baby arrived and it's a girl! We'd like you to be godmother.

A letter asking someone to be a godparent should be written with due regard for the seriousness of the occasion. It is no time to be flippant or facetious:

Dear Joan:

Our son is to be christened at the Community Church on Sunday, April the tenth, at four o'clock. We have decided to call him "Robert."

Joan, you and I were confirmed together; it would make me very happy if you would consent to be Robert's godmother. Peter Dawson and Kenneth Ayres will be the godfathers. I think you know them both.

We are planning to have a small dinner party at the house after the service, and we expect you to join us.

Affectionately yours,
Dorothy

The purpose of godparents is to provide "substitute parents" or protectors for a child, should it be left alone in the world. To be selected as a godparent is therefore somewhat of an honor—certainly an expression of trust and confidence in the person so selected. The request cannot very well be refused; on the contrary, it should be accepted with evident pleasure and pride, and with an appreciation of the responsibilities involved:

Dear Dorothy:

I'm proud and happy to be chosen as godmother for little Robert!

I warn you I shall take very seriously my share of the responsibility for your son's welfare, and shall keep a careful eye on the young man in the years ahead.

I'll be at your house about three o'clock on Sunday so that I can go to the church with you, and perhaps be of some help on the way.

Affectionately yours,
Joan

5. Dance Invitations and Acknowledgments

The days of large, colorful balls and receptions are over; but the dance as a social function remains as popular as ever.

The word "ball" is rarely used on invitations nowadays, except for a large public subscription dance or a charity affair. For ordinary social invitations, formal or informal, the word "dance" is used. The phrase "a small dance" frequently appears on formal invitations, regardless of the size of the function.

Invitations for formal dances are usually engraved, and are sent out from two to three weeks in advance. Following are the most familiar and acceptable forms:

> Dr. and Mrs. Thomas Matthew Benton
> request the pleasure of your company
> at a small dance
> Thursday, the eighth of November
> at ten o'clock
> The Savoy Plaza
>
> Please reply to
> 250 Park Avenue

The fill-in type of invitation (with the guest's name written in by hand) is somewhat more personal, and for that reason many people prefer it. Instead of "at a small dance" in the body of the invitation, the word "Dancing" may be used in the lower right corner.

The most formal and precise invitation of all is the "At Home" with "Dancing" in the lower left or right corner. It may be used whether the dance is for twenty or thirty people in a private house—or for several hundred people, with an entire floor of a large hotel engaged for the purpose:

> Mr. and Mrs. Paul Preston
> At Home
> Tuesday, the third of April
> at ten o'clock
> The Drake
>
> Kindly send reply to   Dancing
> 20 Lake Drive

When a dance is given by two couples, the names of both should appear on the invitation. If a reply is requested, the name of the person to whom it should be sent and the address are indicated in the lower left corner.

Dances are frequently given in honor of an important guest or someone who is to be especially honored. The name of that guest should always appear on the invitation. Either of the two following forms is correct and may be used:

Dr. and Mrs. Thomas Matthew Benton
request the pleasure of your company
at a dance in honor of
Miss Doris Fernell
Thursday, the eighth of November
at ten o'clock
The Savoy Plaza

or

To meet
Miss Doris Fernell

Dr. and Mrs. Thomas Matthew Benton
request the pleasure of

Mr. and Mrs. William Forster's

company on Thursday, the eighth of November
at ten o'clock
The Savoy Plaza

Dancing

Masquerade and costume dances are based on the idea that people like to throw off conventional garb once in a while, and dress up to represent an entirely different character or personality than their own. Such dances are especially suitable for young people home from school for the holidays. Invitations are exactly like any formal dance invitations, except that "costume dance," "masquerade" or "fancy dress" appears either in the body of the invitation or in the lower right hand corner.

If a special kind of costume is to be worn—representing famous personalities of the past, characters from books, the dress of colonial times, and so forth—that fact should be indicated in the lower left corner of the invitation.

DEBUTANTE DANCES AND
DINNER DANCES

The most popular form of invitation for a dance in honor of a debutante daughter is as follows:

Mr. and Mrs. Walter Jennings
request the pleasure of

Miss Anita Benton's

company at a dance in honor of their daughter
Miss Suzanne Jennings
Wednesday evening, October the seventh
at ten o'clock
One East Sixtieth Street

R.s.v.p.

The formal "At Home" is also correct for a debutante dance, with the name of the daughter at the top of the invitation with those of her parents:

Mr. and Mrs. Walter Jennings
Miss Suzanne Jennings
At Home
Wednesday, October the seventh
at ten o'clock
One East Sixtieth Street

Please respond   Dancing

If the dance is held away from home, at a club or hotel, the following invitation is correct:

Mr. and Mrs. Walter Jennings
request the pleasure of your company
at a small dance in honor of their daughter
Miss Suzanne Jennings
on Wednesday, October the seventh
at ten o'clock
The Ambassador

A dinner dance is by far the favorite type of entertainment for a debutante daughter. Often two groups of guests are invited: one group for dinner and dancing, another for dancing only. In that case two separate sets of invitations are issued: regular dance invitations for those who are to come *after* dinner, and invitations like the following for those who are invited for both dinner and dancing:

Mr. and Mrs. Walter Jennings
request the pleasure of your company
at dinner
in honor of their daughter
Miss Suzanne Jennings
Wednesday, October the seventh
at eight o'clock
The Ambassador

Please reply to   Dancing at ten
One East Sixtieth Street

or

Mr. and Mrs. Walter Jennings
request the pleasure of

Mr. and Mrs. James Winston's

company at a dinner dance for their daughter
Miss Suzanne Jennings
on Wednesday, October the seventh
at eight o'clock
The Ambassador

Please address reply to
One East Sixtieth Street

SUPPER DANCE INVITATIONS

Nowadays supper parties are frequently given to honor a special guest or a debutante daughter, or to introduce a new daughter-in-law. These dances are simple and unpretentious compared to the great "balls" of the past; but the same precise formality is maintained in the invitations. Following is the correct invitation for a debutante's formal supper dance at home:

Mr. and Mrs. Walter Jennings
Miss Suzanne Jennings
request the pleasure of your company
at a supper dance
Wednesday, October the seventh
at half past ten o'clock
One East Sixtieth Street

The favor of a reply
is requested,

If the supper dance is held at a hotel, and is for the purpose of presenting a new daughter-in-law to one's friends, either of the following two invitations may be used:

To meet
Mrs. Arthur Blanchard

Mr. and Mrs. Floyd T. Blanchard
request the pleasure of your company
at a supper dance
on Tuesday, September the fifth
at ten o'clock
The St. Regis

R.s.v.p.
One University Place

or

Mr. and Mrs. Floyd T. Blanchard
request the pleasure of

Mr and Mrs. Frederick Steele's

company at a supper dance in honor of
Mrs. Arthur Blanchard
on Tuesday, September the fifth
at ten o'clock
The St. Regis

Please send reply to
One University Place

Occasionally an afternoon tea with dancing is given for a debutante, or to introduce a son's bride. The invitation is generally a formal "At Home," with the name of the hostess and her guest of honor at the top:

Mrs. Floyd T. Blanchard
Mrs. Arthur Blanchard
At Home
on Tuesday, the fifth of September
from four until seven o'clock
The St. Regis

Dancing

HOW TO ACKNOWLEDGE
FORMAL DANCE INVITATIONS

All formal invitations should be answered in formal, third-person phraseology. The acceptance or regret should be carefully handwritten on one's best white note paper, in the same arrangement as the invitation and following the same wording. The regret should contain the reason why, as follows:

Mr. and Mrs. Frank North
regret that owing to illness
they are unable to accept
Dr. and Mrs. Thomas M. Benton's
kind invitation to a costume dance
for their daughter
Miss Anita Benton
on Thursday, the eighth of November

Frequently a formal regret is followed up by a personal note a week or so after the dance. This is not an obligation, but it's a courteous and thoughtful thing to do. If the dance was for a debutante or a special guest, it's a friendly gesture to send flowers a few days after the dance, with a brief note saying how sorry you were to miss it.

RECALL OR POSTPONEMENT
OF FORMAL DANCE INVITATIONS

If an invitation must be recalled, it is always more polite to give the reason for it. A simple announcement like the following is usually sent out. It may be either printed on cards, or carefully written by hand on plain white note paper. As a rule, there is not enough time to have such announcements engraved.

Dr. and Mrs. Thomas Matthew Benton
regret that they are obliged to recall their invitations
for Thursday, the eighth of November
owing to the illness of their daughter

The postponement of a dance may be indefinite, or another date may be specified. It is always best to repeat the hour and the place, even though they are the same as in the original invitation. If an invitation is merely postponed and not canceled, it isn't necessary to give a reason or make an explanation.

SUBSCRIPTION DANCES
AND CHARITY BALLS

When a large dance is given by a club or association, and attendance is by paid subscription, a return card and envelope are usually enclosed. The return of the card with a check for tickets is the only acknowledgment required.

Bear in mind that the word "ball" may be used only in invitations like the following—invitations to large public or semi-public affairs:

> The Entertainment Committee of the Ferndale Club
> requests the pleasure of your company
> at a Ball
> to be held at the club house
> on Friday, the fifth of October
> at ten o'clock
> for the benefit of
> The Community Hospital

> Tickets five dollars

Frequently the invitations to a dance issued by a club list the names of the patrons or patronesses. If there are just a few names, they may appear on the face of the invitation, as shown below. But if there are many names, they should be listed separately on the inside or reverse side of the invitation. Occasionally the addresses of the patrons are also given when tickets are on sale at their homes.

> The pleasure of your company is requested
> at a
> Spring Dance
> on Saturday evening, the second of May
> at ten o'clock
> The Wynnfield Club

> Patronesses

> Mrs. Robert Bruce   Mrs. Charles Cort
> Mrs. John T. Price   Mrs. Earle Higgens
> Mrs. Arthur Hervey   Mrs. Charles Gordon

> Please send reply to
> Dance Committee   Tickets five dollars
> The Wynnfield Club   for each person

Invitations to subscription dinner dances usually give the name of the person through whom reservations can be made. For example:

The Graduating Class of 1938
Hahnemann Medical College and Hospital
invites you to attend a
Dinner Dance
at
The Bellevue-Stratford
Wednesday, the fourth of October
at half past seven o'clock

Make reservations through
Miss Margaret Baker
11 Rittenhouse Square

Tickets five dollars
for each person

INVITATIONS FOR
INFORMAL DANCES

Some people still cling to the custom of using visiting cards as informal invitations to dances, teas, musicales, even luncheon and supper parties. They simply scribble the few necessary words in a corner of the card—usually the lower left corner—and let it go at that!

We cannot approve this use of visiting cards for invitations. It's a careless and "sloppy" social habit, and should not be encouraged. Originally intended as a convenient substitute for engraved third-person forms, visiting card invitations have a curt and unflattering connotation. They sound *hurried*. They have neither the dignity of formal engraved invitations, nor the warmth and charm of friendly informal notes.

However, as some people still use visiting cards for invitations, and you will no doubt continue to receive them from time to time, you should know what kind of party they represent—and what kind of acknowledgment you are expected to write.

If you receive such an invitation you can expect a not-too-formal party, somewhat more important socially than a simple little supper or dance for intimate friends would be, but not important or elaborate enough to warrant engraved invitations.

These invitations should be answered at once whether a reply is requested or not, and they should be answered by personal note. It may be more convenient to write, "Delighted! Sunday at eight" on your own visiting card and send it to your hostess. And fundamentally, of course, that's no more incorrect than the invitation is. But it's so much more courteous to write a friendly note . . . just as it would have been more courteous to write a friendly *note of invitation* instead of sending a visiting card!

If you cannot accept the invitation, explain why in your note. If there is no real reason, if you just don't want to go, the easiest way out is to say you have another engagement . . . but say it graciously and with apparent regret.

THE FRIENDLY NOTE
OF INVITATION

When you plan a simple, informal dance to celebrate a birthday or anniversary, to entertain a son or daughter home from school, or perhaps merely to repay a group of friends for their hospitality to you—you invite your guests either by telephone or by note. It's always more desirable to write notes if you have the time. They may be as short as you like, but they should be *cordial*. Following are several examples for various types of small dances:

Dear Mrs. Brown:

Will you and Mr. Brown give us the pleasure of your company on Thursday, March eighth, at ten o'clock? We are planning a small, informal dance; and Dr. Benton and I should like very much indeed to have you join us.

We do hope you have made no other arrangements for the eighth, and that we can look forward to seeing you.

						Sincerely yours,
						Elizabeth K. Benton

Dear Ruth:

Next Friday, September the fifth, is Tom's birthday —and I thought it would be pleasant to have some of his friends here to help him celebrate. Will you and Bill come? We'll have dancing from nine until midnight, and then cut the birthday cake!

Tom and I are both very eager to have you here, so don't disappoint us!

						Affectionately yours,
						Betty

Dear Suzanne:

Richard will be home for Thanksgiving next week. We are having some of his friends in for dancing on Friday evening, the twenty-third, and I hope you can come.

The dancing will be from nine-thirty to midnight, and we'll see that you get home safely. So *do* come!

> Sincerely yours,
> Elizabeth K. Benton

Dear Julie:

If you meet a witch or a ghost on the way here Saturday night, October the sixteenth, don't be alarmed! They'll just be guests on their way to our masquerade.

I'd like you and your brother Bob to come. You can dress here if you like, or you can come all dressed and masked so that nobody recognizes you. I think that's more fun!

Come at nine, Julie. There'll be dancing until eleven, and a buffet supper afterward. I hope that both you and Bob can make it.

> With love,
> Anita

It's entirely proper to write, "I'd like you and your brother to come" in an informal invitation. But do *not* address the envelope to "Miss Julie Clark and brother." That's distinctly bad form. A note written to one person should never be addressed in any way except to that one person.

The acceptance or regret to such an invitation should be written as promptly as possible and should be as warm and informal as the invitation.

Remember that even between good friends, such notes should be brief and to the point. Don't let yourself be tempted to write of other things.

ASKING AN INVITATION FOR A RELATIVE OR FRIEND

It is never permissible to ask for an invitation of any kind for yourself. Nor is it permissible to ask for a luncheon or dinner

invitation for someone else. But if you are invited to an informal dance, and you have someone staying with you at the
time—or you would like to take someone along whom you
think your hostess would enjoy meeting—it's entirely proper to
ask for an invitation.

Dear Mrs. Benton:

   I know that you and Dr. Benton are interested in
Indian folklore and legend. My nephew, Ralph Harris,
who has just written a book about the Indians of New
York State, is staying with us—and I would like to
bring him to your dance on Thursday, March the
eighth. I think you will enjoy meeting him; and I
know *he* will enjoy seeing your unusual Indian collection.

   May I bring him? I know he'll be delighted to receive your invitation. But if you feel you cannot invite
another guest, please say so frankly and I'll understand.

   Mr. Brown and I are looking forward with pleasure
to the eighth!

                                    Cordially yours,
                                    Millicent Brown

Dear Betty:

   Bill's brother has just arrived unexpectedly from
California; and as he'll only be here a few days, we
don't like to desert him even for an evening.

   So may we bring him to your dance on the fifth?
He's a most charming and congenial person, and I'm
sure you and Tom will enjoy meeting him.

   But if you'd rather not have an extra guest, Betty—
please say so! We'll get him a ticket for the theater or
something, and come help Tom celebrate his birthday
anyway!

                                    Affectionately yours,
                                    Ruth

   The hostess who receives such a note should reply at once,
either extending a courteous invitation to the stranger, or explaining frankly why she cannot do so.

6. Wedding Invitations and Announcements

In the start of their social life together, a bride and groom naturally want to be *correct*. They want their wedding to be perfect in every detail, as traditionally beautiful and dignified as they can make it.

With all the many other things to plan and decide in connection with the ceremony and reception, it's nice to know that in the matter of invitations there need be no problem, no difficulty. Here at least it's easy for the bride and groom to make their choice, and to know that their choice is the right one. For whether a wedding is of great social importance or great simplicity, the forms are fixed by custom and long usage . . . and it's necessary only to select the particular invitation or announcement that suits the circumstances.

All the approved engraved forms for church and home weddings are given in this chapter, as well as suggestions for the simple, informal notes that are written by hand when the wedding is a very small and intimate one. But first, here is a general commentary on the etiquette of wedding invitations . . . answers to the questions people ask most frequently on the subject:

1. Everything about a wedding should be in quiet dignity and good taste, including the invitations and announcements. Only white paper of finest quality should be used, and it should be entirely without decoration—except, perhaps, for a family crest or coat of arms embossed without color. Gilt edges, borders, monograms, entwined initials are all in extremely bad taste.

2. Engraved invitations are traditional for all weddings, large and small, as they reflect the great importance of the occasion. But if it's a very simple and informal wedding for just a few friends—or if it's a very quiet wedding due to a recent death in the family—invitations may be by personal note, or even by telephone. In this case, formal announcements are usually sent on the day of the wedding, or very soon afterward, to everyone on the mailing list of both families.

3. Engraved wedding invitations come in two sizes. There are the *large* double sheets which must be folded in half to fit

the envelope; and there are the *smaller* double sheets which slide right into the envelope without folding. Both are correct and in good form. But it is *not* good form to use cards or single sheets for wedding invitations.

4. The lettering used on wedding invitations depends on what is fashionable at the moment. Script and shaded roman are always in good taste, but there are several other styles of lettering that are equally desirable. It's always a good idea to look at samples of invitations at a reputable stationery or department store before making your own choice.

5. All wedding invitations and announcements are enclosed in two envelopes. The inside envelope contains the invitation, the reception card, and whatever other cards or enclosures are necessary. This envelope is not sealed, and only the *name* of the guest or guests is written on it. (The names of children invited to the wedding may be written on this inside envelope, under the names of their parents.) The outside envelope is for mailing and carries the complete address. It protects the invitation and enclosures, and assures their delivery in a clean envelope.

When you place the first envelope into the second, be sure that the name of the guest will be "face forward" when it's taken out. Just insert the inside envelope with its back, or flap, facing the raised flap of the outside envelope . . . and it will be in the proper position.

6. Be sure to order an adequate supply of invitations. It's better to have a few left over than to discover at the last moment that you forgot a distant cousin or an old school friend, and that you simply haven't another invitation to send!

Start making your guest list weeks ahead of time. This can be quite a job, if you have a lot of family and friends . . . but not if you go about it systematically. Make a *neighborhood* list, a *relative* list, a *family-friend* list, an old *school* list, a *club* list. Consult the groom and his mother and get *their* lists.

For a large church wedding, the guest list may be as long as you like, with all the relatives and friends of both families invited—including those in distant places and those in mourning even though they are not expected to attend. But for a home or hotel wedding, the guest list should include only as many relatives and friends as can be comfortably accommodated.

7. Wedding invitations are sent out earlier than other invitations. They should be mailed at least one month before the big event, so that friends will "save the day." Then too, the sooner invitations go out, the sooner wedding

presents start coming in and can be enjoyed and acknowledged more leisurely.

As engraving take time, *see your stationer early.* You will find it very helpful to have the outside envelopes delivered a week or two ahead of time so that they can be all addressed and ready to mail by the time the engraved invitations arrive.

8. Announcements should be ordered at the same time as the invitations, and should be similar to them in style and wording. Announcements are never mailed before the ceremony. They are mailed on the day of the wedding or after it, and only to those who did not receive invitations.

9. Invitations and announcements are issued by the bride's parents, even though she may not be living at home. If one parent is dead, the invitations are issued in the name of the remaining parent. If neither parent is living, the invitations are issued by the nearest relative (like a married brother and his wife)—or by a guardian. In rare cases, when there are no relatives and no guardian, the invitations may be issued by an intimate friend—or the bride and groom may send them out in their own names. In the latter case, the bride's name comes first. When invitations or announcements are issued by someone other than the bride's parents, or a relative with the same name as her own, the bride's *full name* should be used to prevent confusion.

10. Parents who are separated may unite their names on the occasion of their daughter's wedding, if they so wish. Thus the invitations may be issued by "Mr. and Mrs. Frank B. Mitchell"—even though "Mr." and "Mrs." have been living apart for many years. But if parents are legally divorced, and especially if one or the other has remarried, the invitations should be issued only in the name of the parent with whom the daughter has been living. If that parent has remarried, the invitations should be issued in the names of the parent and the new mate. It would be a glaring discourtesy to issue the invitations in the name of a parent alone, when that parent has remarried and the bride has been making her home with both.

When a bride has lived part of the time with one parent and part of the time with the other, the invitations are usually issued in the name of her mother.

11. The year is not necessary on wedding invitations, and is not ordinarily used. But if it *is* used, it should be written as spoken: "Nineteen hundred and forty-seven." The form, "One thousand, nine hundred and forty-seven" is an affectation and should be avoided.

12. The year *should* be given on wedding announcements—
    also the city or town in which the ceremony was held.
    This applies even after an elopement, and regardless of the
    time that has elapsed between the marriage and the an-
    nouncement. But the name of the church or the house
    address where the ceremony was performed is not neces-
    sary, though it is frequently given.

13. Numbers, names, street addresses, dates should all be
    spelled out in full on an engraved invitation or announce-
    ment. Numerals may be used only if an address is unusually
    long and would look clumsy and unattractive if spelled
    out on the invitation.

14. If necessary, the street address may be engraved under the
    name of the church. Also "daylight saving time" may be
    engraved after the time of the day on an invitation, to
    avoid the possibility of mistake or confusion.

15. The word "to" is used between the names of the bride and
    groom on announcements and on invitations to the cere-
    mony. But the word "and" is grammatically necessary in-
    stead of "to" on invitations to a wedding breakfast or re-
    ception—because by that time the bride and groom are
    already man *and* wife.

16. The words "honor" and "favor" are frequently spelled
    with a "u" on wedding invitations and announcements.
    But this is now looked upon as an affectation in this
    country—and the Americanized form (without the "u")
    is recommended.

17. The phrase "request the honor of your presence" is always
    used for church weddings. It may also be used for home,
    club or hotel weddings—but as such invitations include
    the reception following the ceremony, the phrase "request
    the pleasure of your company" is considered more suitable.

18. "Wedding breakfast" is the term generally used for the
    reception following the ceremony if it's before one o'clock
    in the afternoon. If it's *after* one o'clock, "reception" is the
    correct word to use.

19. At the typical wedding, family and intimate friends are
    invited to the reception and the ceremony; less intimate
    friends, neighbors, acquaintances and business associates
    are invited to the church only. Two sets of invitations may
    be ordered for the two groups of guests: one for the cere-
    mony only, the other for the ceremony and reception. Or
    the same invitation may be sent to all guests, with a
    separate card enclosed for those invited to the reception.

20. When an invitation is for the church ceremony only, a
    reply is not ordinarily required—and as a rule none is

requested. But when the invitation is to both the ceremony and the reception following it, a reply is generally requested. The letters "R.s.v.p." or the phrase "Please reply" may be engraved in the lower left corner of the invitation; or a separate card to be filled out and returned by the guest may be enclosed.

21. Occasionally, when one of the bride's parents is an invalid, the wedding ceremony is very small and private, with only the immediate families present; but a big reception follows for all the relatives and friends. In this case, *reception invitations* only are issued. Invitations to the ceremony are either given verbally to the few who are to be present; or "Ceremony at three o'clock" is written on a small card and enclosed with the invitation to the reception.

ANNOUNCING AN ENGAGEMENT

Engagements are usually announced informally at a luncheon or supper party. Or public announcement is made by telephoning the society editor of the local papers. But occasionally formal announcement of an engagement is sent to members of the family and to friends. The correct wording for an engraved formal announcement is as follows:

Mr. and Mrs. George Coleman
have the honor to announce
the engagement of their daughter
Harriet
to
Mr. John Anthony Wayne

If the engagement is subsequently broken off, an announcement to that effect must be sent to all who received the original announcement. That's one reason many people prefer to tell the news casually and informally, instead of issuing engraved announcements. But if such announcements *have* been sent out and the engagement is then broken off, an announcement like the following should be sent to the same people:

Mr. and Mrs. George Coleman
wish to announce
that the engagement of their daughter
Harriet
and
Mr. John Anthony Wayne
has been broken by mutual consent

THE CHURCH WEDDING

Here is the correct form for an invitation to a church ceremony:

Mr. and Mrs. Gerald Weylin
request the honor of your presence
at the marriage of their daughter
Margaret
to
Mr. Donald Blaine
on Thursday morning, the seventh of June
at ten o'clock
St. Thomas Episcopal Church
New York

If preferred, the fill-in type of invitation may be used, with space for the guest's name to be written by hand.

The reception card to go with the above invitation would read as follows:

Mr. and Mrs. Gerald Weylin
request the pleasure of your company
at breakfast
Thursday, the seventh of June
at half past twelve o'clock
Forty-five Park Avenue

Please respond

Or instead of the above form, a small card may be enclosed with the invitation reading simply:

Breakfast
immediately following the ceremony
Forty-five Park Avenue

Please respond

Remember that *"breakfast"* is the proper term for a reception held before one o'clock . . . *"reception"* is the proper term after one o'clock.

The invitation for an afternoon or evening church ceremony is exactly the same as the invitation for a morning ceremony—except, of course, for the difference in time.

There are several types of reception cards suitable for afternoon and evening weddings. The simplest and most familiar type is a card reading:

Reception
at ten o'clock
The St. Moritz

Please send response to
Forty-five Park Avenue

Another popular type of reception card leaves space for the guest's name to be written in:

Mr. and Mrs. Gerald Weylin
request the pleasure of

Mr. and Mrs. Alan Brewster's

company immediately following the ceremony
The St. Moritz

Please address reply to
Forty-five Park Avenue

These cards are enclosed in the envelope with the invitation to the ceremony—for those guests who are invited to both the ceremony and the reception. For guests who are invited to the reception only, an invitation like the following is more acceptable:

Mr. and Mrs. Gerald Weylin
request the pleasure of your company
at the wedding reception of their daughter
Margaret
and
Mr. Donald Blaine
on Thursday, the seventh of June
at four o'clock
The St. Moritz

Please reply to
Forty-five Park Avenue

If all guests, or most of the guests, are invited to both the ceremony at the church and the reception following it, a combined invitation like the following may be used:

Mr. and Mrs. Gerald Weylin
request the honor of your presence
at the marriage of their daughter
Margaret
to
Mr. Donald Blaine
on Thursday, the seventh of June
at twelve o'clock
St. Thomas Episcopal Church
New York
and afterwards at breakfast
at the St. Moritz

Please reply to
Forty-five Park Avenue

Occasionally a reception is given for the bride and groom at
the home of a relative or friend. The invitation should be in
the name of the bride's parents, regardless of who gives the
reception. Here is the correct wording for a card enclosed with
the invitation to the ceremony:

Mr. and Mrs. Gerald Weylin
request the pleasure of your company
at the residence of
Mr. and Mrs. John Ridgley
Nine Hundred Riverside Drive
immediately following the ceremony

The reply to such an invitation is always sent to the parents
of the bride and not to the people in whose home the reception
is held.

CHURCH ADMISSION CARD

When the wedding is large, the church small, and the
general public is not to be admitted, cards of admission are
necessary for the guests. These are usually engraved in the
same style as the invitations, and are enclosed with them. The
wording is simply:

Please present this card
at St. Thomas Episcopal Church
on Thursday, the seventh of June

For members of the family and intimate friends, the number of the pew may be written on the admission card in ink. If they are not to occupy individually reserved pews but a special area "ribboned" off at the front of the church, the phrase "Within the ribbon" may be written in the lower left corner of the admission card. If admission cards are not necessary, "Pew No. 7" or "Within the ribbon" may be written on a small white card and enclosed with the invitation.

THE HOME WEDDING

The invitation to a *church* wedding is solely for the ceremony, which is why a separate invitation to the wedding breakfast or reception must be enclosed with it. But the invitation to a *home* wedding is for both the ceremony and the reception. Obviously a second invitation to stay on at a house to which the guest is already invited is unnecessary.

Either "honor of your presence" or "pleasure of your company" may be used on the invitation for a home wedding. One is used as much as the other, and both are correct . . . but "honor of your presence" belongs more rightfully to the sacred and solemn dignity of the church.

Here is a typical invitation to a wedding held at the home of the bride:

Mr. and Mrs. Anthony Duncan
request the pleasure of your company
at the marriage of their daughter
Edith Anne
to
Mr. Eugene Griffith
on Tuesday, the tenth of October
at four o'clock
Sixty-four Lake Drive
Chicago, Illinois

The favor of a reply
is requested

If the invitations are issued by the parents of the bride, but the wedding ceremony takes place in a home other than their own, this is the form of invitation to use:

Mr. and Mrs. Anthony Duncan
request the pleasure of your company
at the marriage of their daughter
Edith Anne
to
Mr. Eugene Griffith
on Tuesday, the tenth of October
at four o'clock
at the residence of Mr. and Mrs. John Porter
Twenty-six Ivy Street
Chicago, Illinois

If the ceremony is private and guests are invited to the reception only, the following form is used. Note that the word "and" is used instead of "to"—as by the time of the reception the bride and groom are already married.

Mr. and Mrs. Anthony Duncan
request the pleasure of your company
at the wedding reception of their daughter
Edith Anne
and
Mr. Eugene Griffith
on Tuesday, the tenth of October
at eight o'clock
The Drake
Chicago, Illinois

Please send reply to
Sixty-four Lake Drive

For an outdoor wedding, the same form of invitation is used as for any other home wedding . . . except that the phrase "in the garden" appears just above the address. For example:

As a rule, a rain card is enclosed with the invitation to an outdoor wedding. This is a small card engraved to conform with the invitation, and reads simply:

In the event of rain
the ceremony will be held
at Saint Paul's Church

TRAIN AND DIRECTION CARDS

When a wedding takes place at a country home, the transportation of guests is sometimes arranged by the bride's parents. They may have a special car added to a regular train for the convenience of the guests; or if it's a very big wedding, they may charter a special train for the occasion. Train cards are generally enclosed with the invitation and guests use them in place of tickets. If it's for a special car, this is the best form to use:

A special car will be attached to the train
leaving Pennsylvania Station, New York
for Southampton at 10.40 A.M.
and to the returning train
leaving Southampton at 8.20 P.M.

Please present this card in place of ticket

If it's for a special train, this is the way the card is customarily worded:

A special train
on the Long Island Railroad
will leave the Pennsylvania Station, New York
for Southampton at 10.40 A.M.
and returning
will leave Southampton at 8.20 P.M.

Please present this card in place of a ticket

When transportation is not provided, a small card is often enclosed with the invitation to indicate the best trains to take. This is a thoughtful gesture that guests appreciate. The information may be neatly written by hand on plain white cards; or engraved cards for the purpose may be ordered at the same time as the invitations. This is the usual wording:

Train leaves Pennsylvania Station
for Southampton at 10.40 A.M.

Returning train leaves Southampton
for New York at 8.20 P.M.

Route maps and direction cards are also frequently enclosed with the invitation to a country wedding. A simplified map may be printed or engraved on a card for all guests coming from a certain point, like New York. Or a direction card like the following may be used to help guests find their way to the wedding without too much difficulty:

Automobiles from New York follow
Route 27 to Old Town
then turn right at the white arrow
and follow Hedgerow Road
to Shady Acres

Train and direction cards do not need to be enclosed in separate envelopes. They are merely slipped into the same envelope as the invitation. However, it's a good idea to use sheets of tissue between the cards and the invitation to prevent smudging. Suitable tissue for this purpose—very thin and in the proper size—can be provided by your stationer.

WEDDING ANNOUNCEMENTS

When a wedding is small and private and no general invitations are issued, it is customary to send out formal announcements on the day of the ceremony or very soon afterward. Such announcements should have all the traditional beauty and dignity of wedding invitations—being engraved on the finest white paper and, like invitations, enclosed in two envelopes.

The announcement is made by whoever would have sent out the wedding invitations. That means the parents or nearest relative, whether actually present at the ceremony or not. For example, even if the bride's mother is an invalid—even if her father is abroad at the time of the ceremony—the announcements are issued in the names of both parents.

Announcements are never sent to those who were present at the ceremony. Nor are they sent *instead* of invitations to relatives and friends living at a great distance. An *invitation* sent to someone far away means, "We would have loved to have you with us!" But an *announcement* means, "We couldn't invite you to the wedding, but we want you to know about it."

Here is the correct wording for a formal wedding announcement:

> Mr. and Mrs. Anthony Duncan
> have the honor of announcing
> the marriage of their daughter
> Edith Anne
> to
> Mr. Eugene Griffith
> on Tuesday, the tenth of October
> Nineteen hundred and forty-seven
> Saint Paul's Church
> Chicago, Illinois

Instead of "honor of announcing" it is also correct to use "honor to announce" or just "announce." For example, here is the form customarily used for announcements after an elopement. Notice that the name of the city or town in which the ceremony was held is given; but the name of the church or the house address where the ceremony was performed is not necessary (though it is frequently included):

> Mr. and Mrs. Clyde Peters
> announce the marriage of their daughter
> Marion
> to
> Mr. Nelson Crowinshield
> on Friday, the twentieth of June
> Nineteen hundred and forty-eight
> Carson City, Nevada

If the bride is a young widow or divorcée, the announcement is still made in the name of her parents or nearest kin:

> Mr. and Mrs. Clyde Peters
> announce the marriage of their daughter
> Marion Peters Armstrong
> to
> Mr. Nelson Crowinshield
> on Friday, the twentieth of June
> Nineteen hundred and forty-eight
> Carson City, Nevada

But if the widow or divorcée is a woman of mature years, the announcement may be made in her own name and that of the groom, as follows:

> Mrs. Helen Wallace Smith
> and
> Mr. William Tracy Hamilton
> announce their marriage
> on Friday, the twenty-first of May
> Nineteen hundred and forty-eight
> at Saratoga Springs, New York

Ordinarily "Mrs." is not used before the name of a widow or divorcée of an announcement of her remarriage, when the announcement is issued by her parents or other relatives. But it is *always* used on announcements issued by the bride and groom themselves.

ENCLOSING "AT HOME" CARDS
WITH THE ANNOUNCEMENT

If the bride and groom want to let their friends know where they are going to live, they send them cards of address—or as they are more familiarly called, "at home" cards. These are usually enclosed with the announcements of the marriage; or they are sent out separately after the bride and groom are settled in their own home and ready to receive visitors.

The typical at home card is about the size of a visiting card and reads:

> Mr. and Mrs. Eugene Griffith
> will be at home
> after the first of November
> at Twenty-five Little Plains Road

Or a joint visiting card of the new "Mr. and Mrs." may be used, with the address indicated in the lower right corner.

At home cards engraved with the bride's new name should not be sent out *before* the ceremony—for the reason, of course, that she has not yet acquired her new name. However, cards without any name may be enclosed with the invitations. These would read:

> At home
> after the first of November
> Twenty-five Little Plains Road

WEDDING INVITATIONS FOR
SPECIAL AND UNUSUAL CIRCUMSTANCES

Not all weddings conform to type; and those involving special or unusual circumstances—such as the bride with one parent, the bride whose parents have remarried, the double wedding for sisters, and so on—require special wording of the invitation.

The forms that follow are for these special cases; and though they are for invitations, they apply also to wedding *announcements* issued under the same circumstances.

INVITATION TO A DOUBLE WEDDING

Mr. and Mrs. Henry Hassett
request the honor of your presence
at the marriage of their daughters
Nancy Joan
to
Mr. Robert Kinnaird
and
Amy Jean
to
Mr. Harrison Colt
on Friday, the second of October
at four o'clock
Grace Church
Brookline, Massachusetts

Sometimes friends or cousins are married on the same day, at the same time, and invitations are issued jointly for both ceremonies. The wording of a double wedding invitation when the brides are *not* sisters should include the surnames of the brides to prevent any possibility of confusion:

Mr. and Mrs. Henry Hassett
and
Mr. and Mrs. John Ward Sheldon
request the honor of your presence
at the marriage of their daughters
Nancy Joan Hassett
to
Mr. Robert Kinnaird
and
Marion Sheldon
to
Mr. Frederick Bowen
on Thursday, the fourth of October
at four o'clock
Grace Church
Brookline, Massachusetts

THE BRIDE WITH ONE PARENT

If a bride's mother is dead and her father has not remarried
the invitations are issued in his name alone:

> Mr. James Norman Walsh
> requests the honor of your presence
> at the marriage of his daughter
> Edith
> to
> Mr. Curtis Phelps
> and so forth

If the bride's father is dead and her mother has not remarried the invitations are issued in the name of the mother.

But if the mother *has* remarried and the bride has a step-
father, the invitations are issued in the names of both. Following are the two forms that are most frequently used. Both
are correct; the choice is entirely a matter of personal preference. The bride's *full name* should always be used; and
in the first of the two forms given below, "her daughter" may
be used instead of "their daughter."

> Mr. and Mrs. Benjamin Crane
> request the honor of your presence
> at the marriage of their daughter
> Mary Alice Thorne
> and so forth

or

> Mr. and Mrs. Benjamin Crane
> request the honor of your presence
> at the marriage of
> Mrs. Crane's daughter
> Mary Alice Thorne
> and so forth

If the bride has a stepmother, the invitations may read "the
marriage of their daughter," "the marriage of his daughter,"
or "the marriage of Mr. Walsh's daughter"—depending on
which wording best suits the circumstances and the wishes
of those most intimately concerned. In this instance, of course,
the bride's full name does not need to be used as it's the
same as the name in which the invitations are issued.

WHEN THE PARENTS OF THE BRIDE ARE DIVORCED

Parents who are divorced and remarried do *not*, under any circumstances, combine their different names on invitations or announcements for their daughter's marriage. It's not only a question of taste and propriety. The names of divorced parents and their new mates appearing together on a wedding invitation is an affront to the sacred dignity of marriage.

Invitations should be issued in the name of the parent with whom the bride has been living. If that parent has remarried, the invitations are issued in the names of the parent *and* the new mate. If the bride has lived part of the time with one parent and part of the time with the other, the invitations are usually issued in the name of the mother.

Here is the wording to use when the bride's mother is a divorcée who is not remarried:

Mrs. Preston Hodges
requests the honor of your presence
at the marriage of her daughter
Carolyn
and so forth

Here is the wording to use when the bride's mother is a divorcée who *has* remarried:

Mr. and Mrs. Ronald Fischer
request the honor of your presence
at the marriage of her daughter
Carolyn Hodges
and so forth

or

Mr. and Mrs. Ronald Fischer
request the honor of your presence
at the marriage of
Mrs. Fischer's daughter
Carolyn Hodges
and so forth

WHEN THE BRIDE HAS NO PARENTS

As a rule, when a bride has no parents the invitations are issued by her oldest brother, whether he is married or not. Or a sister, aunt, grandparent or other close relative gives the wedding and issues the invitations. If there are no relatives and no guardian, the invitations may be issued by intimate friends.

And in those rare cases when there are neither relatives nor
friends to issue the invitations, the bride and groom invite
their own guests—using the form immediately below:

> The honor of your presence
> is requested at the marriage of
> Miss Laura Ellen Kay
> to
> Mr. Thomas Field Macfarlane
> on Thursday, the eighteenth of June
> at twelve o'clock
> Trinity Church
> Detroit, Michigan

When wedding invitations are issued by a married brother
and sister-in-law of the bride, this is the proper wording:

> Mr. and Mrs. Henry Fairchild
> request the honor of your presence
> at the marriage of their sister
> Janet Fairchild
> and so forth

Following is the correct form to use when a married sister
and brother-in-law give the wedding and issue the invitations:

> Mr. and Mrs. John Alan Wright
> request the honor of your presence
> at the marriage of their sister
> Eleanor Rogers
> and so forth

When friends give a wedding reception at their home for a
bride who has no parents, this is the way the invitation should
read:

> Mr. and Mrs. Maxwell Burton
> request the pleasure of your company
> at the wedding reception of
> Miss Martha Helstrom
> and
> Mr. Raymond Frank Peterson
> at four o'clock
> Six Beach Lane Road
> Manhasset, Long Island

Please respond

INVITATIONS FOR A SECOND MARRIAGE

If a widow or divorcée is young, the invitations to her second marriage are issued in the name of her parents or nearest relative; and the form is the same as for her first wedding except that the full name is used. For example:

Mr. and Mrs. Henry Hassett
request the honor of your presence
at the marriage of their daughter
Nancy Hassett Kinnaird
to
Mr. William Kingston
and so forth

If the bride is a mature woman, or if there are no relatives or old family friends to issue the invitations, this form is acceptable:

The honor of your presence is requested
at the marriage of
Mrs. Nancy Hassett Kinnaird
and
Mr. William Kingston
and so forth

The name of the bride always comes first on invitations and announcements issued by the bride and groom.

A divorcée uses whatever name she has taken after the divorce. If she has legally resumed her maiden name, it it entirely permissible for her to use it on the invitations and announcements of her second marriage.

WHEN THE GROOM IS IN THE MILITARY SERVICES

The generally accepted rule at present is that for the rank of Captain or above in the Army—Lieutenant, senior grade, or above in the Navy—the title is used in front of the name. For example:

Captain Arthur Cunningham
United States Army

For officers under these ranks, the title goes on a line directly below the name. For example:

Harold Creighton
Lieutenant, junior grade, United States Navy

If the groom is in the regular Army or Navy, the wording "United States Army" (or Navy) appears in the line below his name. But if he has been called into the Army or given a temporary commission, the positioning is the same but the wording is "Army of the United States"—or for the Navy, "United States Naval Reserve." In the case of a private or non-commissioned officer, the name is on one line and the branch of service is designated below it. For example:

Frank Pearson
Signal Corps, United States Naval Reserve

or

John Hamilton
Coast Artillery, Army of the United States

The title of "Mr." is not used in military invitations or announcements.

Army Officer's Wedding Invitation

Colonel and Mrs. Charles Higgins
request the honor of your presence
at the marriage of their daughter
Marilyn
to
Captain Richard Anderson
United States Army
on Tuesday, the tenth of October
at four o'clock
Christ Church
Santa Barbara, California

Army Officer's Wedding Announcement

Mr. and Mrs. John Curtis
announce the marriage of their daughter
Catherine Alice
to
David Alan Sewall
Second Lieutenant, United States Army
on Thursday, the seventh of September
Nineteen hundred and forty-seven
Boston, Massachusetts

Naval Officer's Wedding Invitation

Mr. and Mrs. Winston Evans
request the honor of your presence
at the marriage of their daughter
Marion Elaine
to
Theodore Spencer
Ensign, United States Navy
on Friday, the first of August
at twelve o'clock
Saint Paul's Church
New York

Naval Officer's Wedding Announcement

Mr. and Mrs. Thomas Rourke
announce the marriage of their daughter
Adelaide
to
Commander Ralph Cummings
United States Navy
on Thursday, the seventh of June
Nineteen hundred and forty-seven
Trinity Church
Washington, District of Columbia

RECALLING A WEDDING INVITATION

A sudden death in the family, serious illness or an accident
may make it necessary to recall the invitations issued for a
wedding. If it's very close to the date set for the wedding,
someone in the family should notify immediately all who received invitations. But if there's time, small cards should be
printed or engraved and sent to the list of expected guests.
The announcement should be formal in wording, but is not
necessarily arranged with indented lines. The reason for re-
calling the invitation is always given:

Mr. and Mrs. Gerald Weylin regret
that owing to their daughter's
illness they are obliged to recall the invitations to her
marriage on Thursday, the seventh
of June.

When a wedding is canceled after the invitations have
been issued, announcements should be sent out as quickly as
possible. If comparatively few guests are expected—or if time

is short—someone close to the bride (preferably her mother) should telephone the people who must be notified. No explanation need be given on the telephone or in the announcement; just a matter-of-fact statement that the wedding will not take place is all that's necessary:

> Mr. and Mrs. Gerald Weylin announce
> that the marriage of their daughter
> Margaret and Mr. Donald Blaine will
> not take place.

HOW TO ACKNOWLEDGE WEDDING INVITATIONS

An invitation to a church wedding does not require written acknowledgment—unless a reply is specifically requested, or unless an invitation to the reception is included. But a prompt acceptance or regret *is* definitely required for a home, club or hotel wedding, or for an invitation to a wedding reception. Always write your reply and mail it *promptly*, within a few days after receiving the invitation. Write it by hand, on the first page of a double sheet of your best white note paper.

The answer to a formal wedding invitation should not be written like a friendly note, but should be in formal third-person phraseology. It may be written in straight box form, without indented margins, if that is preferred; but the wording should follow the exact wording of the invitation—even to the repetition of date, place and time. That helps prevent the possibility of a misunderstanding. A *regret*, of course, does not require repetition of the time, as that is unimportant if one does not plan to attend. But whenever possible, the regret should include a reason for not being able to accept.

A combined invitation to the ceremony and reception would be acknowledged as follows:

Acceptance

> Mr. and Mrs. Edward Willis
> accept with pleasure
> Mr. and Mrs. Anthony Duncan's
> kind invitation to be present
> at the marriage of their daughter
> Edith Anne
> to
> Mr. Eugene Griffith
> on Tuesday, the tenth of October
> at four o'clock
> and afterward at the wedding reception
> at the Drake

Regret

Mr. and Mrs. Edward Willis
regret exceedingly that
owing to the illness of their son
they are unable to accept
Mr. and Mrs. Anthony Duncan's
kind invitation to be present
at the marriage of their daughter
Edith Anne
to
Mr. Eugene Griffith
on Tuesday, the tenth of October
and afterward at the wedding reception

The *announcement* of a wedding does not call for formal acknowledgment, like an invitation. You may write a note of congratulation, if you like (see page 151). Or you may send a wedding gift if that is your generous impulse. But these are entirely of your own pleasure and volition; no response is required.

THE INFORMAL WEDDING INVITATION
WRITTEN BY HAND

Personal notes are written when the wedding is very small and informal, and only a few relatives and intimate friends are invited. They should be written *by hand*, on plain white paper —preferably double sheets like those used for engraved invitations. Colored, decorated or odd-shaped stationery, or correspondence cards, are not good taste even for the most informal wedding invitations.

These little notes of invitation to a small and intimate wedding should always be written by the bride herself. Even if she is extremely busy (as most brides are before their wedding!) she should not ask a sister or a friend to write the notes for her. No one is ever too busy to write a few short notes to those they really care about and whose presence they desire at their wedding.

There is one exception to the rule that the bride always writes her own notes of invitation. If the bride's mother has an old and cherished friend, she may want to write her about the plans and invite her personally to her daughter's wedding. For example:

Dear Martha:

At last my Helen has set the day! She and David are
to be married very quietly at the Community Church

on Thursday, June the twelfth, at noon. They have invited just a very few relatives and intimate friends; and they are all coming here after the ceremony for a simple little wedding breakfast I'm planning for them.

Helen had your name at the very top of her guest list, but I said I'd write to you myself. We'll see you at the church at twelve, Martha—and of course we expect you to come back here with us afterward for the wedding breakfast.

I am very happy, as you can imagine. I am already as devoted to David as though he were my own son!

Affectionately yours,
Sarah

Bride's Note of Invitation to a Close Friend

Dear Betty:

David and I have set the date—and we want you to be the first to know it! We're going to be married *very quietly* at the Community Church on Thursday, June the twelfth, at noon. We're asking only a few people— just our nearest relatives and our very special friends.

Can you be at the house about eleven, Betty, and go to the church with us? Then we'll all come back here after the ceremony; mother's giving a little wedding breakfast for us.

Let's hope it's a bright sunny day on the twelfth! With much love,

Helen

To a Relative

Dear Aunt Kate:

David and I are to be married at the Community Church on Thursday, June the twelfth, at noon.

We want you to come to the ceremony, and also to the wedding breakfast afterward at home.

We'll be looking for you, Aunt Kate, on the twelfth!

With love,
Helen

If There Has Been a
Recent Bereavement

Dear Julia:

We have changed our plans for an elaborate church wedding because of the death of my uncle.

Instead, Bill and I are going to be married very simply and quietly at my home on Sunday, June the sixth, at four o'clock. We have invited only those we love best, and of course we want you!

There will be a small supper party at six, so plan to stay on for the evening.

Affectionately,
Grace

To an Old Friend of the Groom
—a Stranger to the Bride

Dear Mr. Knox:

Paul Lawrence and I are to be married on Sunday, May the eighth, at the Presbyterian Church on Main Street in Lenox. The ceremony will be at three o'clock.

I know Lenox is a long way from Philadelphia, but we would both love to have you come if you can possibly make it. Paul has spoken so often and so fondly of his old roommate at Exeter that I feel as though I know you! I am looking forward with very great pleasure to meeting you at last.

So *do* come if you can, and stay on for the small reception at my home in the evening. There is a train that leaves here at 9:20 and would get you back to Philadelphia before midnight.

It will make us both very happy to have you come to our wedding!

Sincerely yours,
Marjorie Willis

TO A BUSINESS ASSOCIATE
OF THE GROOM

The bride writes all the notes of invitation, including those to business associates of the groom. If a business associate is married, the note should be addressed to his wife. For example:

Dear Mrs. Harris:

Frank Peters and I are to be married at my home on Tuesday, October the fourth, at eight o'clock in the evening.

Frank has been so long and so happily associated with Mr. Harris, that the wedding just wouldn't be complete without him! We hope you can both come, and that you will stay on for the small reception following the ceremony.

Sincerely yours
Catherine Miller

INVITING A FRIEND TO
THE RECEPTION ONLY

Dear Harriet:

Jim and I are going to be married on Friday morning, June the twentieth.

In view of circumstances with which you are familiar, the ceremony will be *very private* . . . with only my sister and one of Bill's friends as witnesses.

But we are having a small reception at the Terrace Club on the evening of the twentieth, at eight o'clock, and we want you to come. We are asking only a few of our best friends. Bill wants me to say he's as anxious to have you come as I am.

So we'll see you, won't we, Harriet—Friday at eight at the Terrace Club!

Affectionately yours,
Madeline

Informal notes of invitation like the above should be answered promptly, briefly and with a definite acceptance or regret. Sometimes relatives or friends telephone to say whether or not they are coming . . . and while that's not incorrect, it may be *inconvenient* for a busy bride and her mother to receive many calls. It is always more gracious to answer a note of invitation with a note.

INVITATION TO WEDDING ANNIVERSARIES

If the celebration of a wedding anniversary is simple and informal, the invitations are written by hand or are telephoned.

Frequently, however, a formal reception is given to celebrate a twenty-fifth or fiftieth wedding anniversary. The invitations are engraved, and usually the year of the wedding and the year of the anniversary are given at the top. These significant dates—or even the entire invitation, if so desired—may be engraved in silver lettering for a twenty-fifth anniversary, in gold lettering for a fiftieth anniversary. Following are the two forms generally used for an afternoon reception. The wording is the same for an evening reception, except for the time; and if it's a dinner or a supper dance, that fact is of course specified.

1900—1950

Mr. and Mrs. Edward Paul Sullivan
request the pleasure of your company
on the Fiftieth Anniversary of their marriage
on Thursday, the seventh of October
from four until seven o'clock
The Inn
Andover, Massachusetts

1900—1950

Mr. and Mrs. Edward Paul Sullivan
At Home
on Thursday, the seventh of October
from four until seven o'clock

The Inn
Andover, Massachusetts

These invitations are answered like all other formal invitations: a definite acceptance or regret in the same precise, third-person phraseology—handwritten on plain white note paper of good quality.

7. Letters of Thanks

One kind of letter most people enjoy writing is the letter of thanks or appreciation. It's pleasant to say "thank you" to someone who has been generous or thoughtful.

Every gift, however trifling, should be acknowledged with a note of thanks. Every favor or courtesy—every kindness or attention on the part of a neighbor or friend—every expression of hospitality—certainly every letter of condolence or congratulation—deserves sincere and gracious acknowledgment.

And it doesn't matter if you have already expressed your appreciation in person; a letter of thanks must still be written! It can be as brief and simple as you like; but it should express your appreciation with sincerity and warmth. Remember that half the joy of giving is the anticipation of receiving pleased acknowledgment; and surely the person who has been thoughtful or generous toward you deserves that satisfaction!

Sincerity is by far the most important quality of all in a note of thanks. If it's just a run-of-the-mill "duty" note—a brief but uninspired thank-you written because such a note is expected and must be written—it defeats its own purpose. It does not give the pleasure and satisfaction a note of thanks should give.

So be sure your letter has the unmistakable ring of sincerity to it. That's much easier to accomplish when you feel grateful and appreciative than it is later on when the emotion has cooled and the enthusiasm worn off. The whole secret is this: *don't wait too long to write your note of thanks!* Don't procrastinate and keep putting it off. Write your letter quickly . . . while the glow is still with you! Then you won't need to grope for words, trying to sound sincere. The words will come of their own accord, will spring naturally and sincerely from the warmth of your own enthusiasm.

We cannot tell you the exact words to put in your personal letters of thanks. After all, the very essence of sincerity is the expression of your own true feelings and sentiments. But we *can* make suggestions. And that, precisely, is what you will find in this chapter: suggestions we hope will prove helpful and stimulating when you "just don't know what to write!"

WHEN AND HOW TO ACKNOWLEDGE
WEDDING GIFTS

As soon as the wedding invitations go out, the gifts start coming in. And the smart bride starts writing her notes of thanks right away, as each gift arrives. She doesn't wait until the thank-you's pile up and get ahead of her, becoming a problem instead of a pleasure.

The bride who is systematic as well as smart, keeps a little gift book. It may be one of the handsome little books that are published for this purpose and kept as a souvenir . . . or it may be just a blank notebook such as children use at school. In it she records each gift as it arrives: what it is, from whom it came, the sender's address, where the gift was purchased, when the note of thanks was written and mailed. Then she never needs to wonder, "Did I ever thank Aunt Mary for the picture?" Or, "Did I ever write and acknowledge Uncle Pete's check?"

Then, too, if the bride is swamped with gifts a few days before the wedding, and it just isn't humanly possible to write all the necessary thank-you's in time, she can take the gift book along on the honeymoon and write the notes while she's away. Of course, if she's only going to be gone a week or two, the notes can wait. But if she's going to be away for a month or more, she should take the list with her and write the notes of thanks as soon as she can. This is a task that cannot be evaded . . . nor should any gracious bride want to evade writing cordial notes to those who showered her so generously with gifts!

The bride acknowledges all gifts, for her husband and herself—including gifts from friends or business associates of her husband whom she has never seen and doesn't know. All notes must be personally written by the bride herself; she cannot relegate someone else to do it for her. If gifts arrive while she is away, her mother may acknowledge them—but only to say: "Helen had already gone when your beautiful gift arrived. She will, of course, write and thank you as soon as she gets back." Or better still, the mother may write to the bride and describe the gift so that she can acknowledge it herself. This isn't necessary, of course, if the bride will be back in a reasonable time.

Printed or engraved cards of thanks won't do for wedding gifts—or any gifts! They are not sincere, and they are not in good taste. A letter and *only* a *letter* in the bride's own handwriting is correct for thanking relatives and friends for their wedding gifts. These thank-you's should be written on formal paper—not on cards or so-called "informals." There is no objection to the use of "informals" for brief notes to friends, acknowledgments of kindness or hospitality, even for invitations to card parties and other simple home functions; but they should not be used for acknowledging wedding gifts.

The bride's notes should be an expression of her own personality; but the following provide a variety of acceptable patterns from which she can easily design her own.

To Relatives

When a present is sent by a married couple, the note of thanks may be written to both—or it may be written to the wife alone, with thanks to both in the letter. For example, here is a typical note of thanks to a married cousin:

Dear Margaret:

Thank you so much for the perfectly *beautiful* little boudoir clock you and Bill sent us! It's one of the very nicest wedding gifts we have received.

David sends thanks too; we hope you'll come soon and see how lovely the clock looks on our dresser. You just couldn't have made a better choice!

With love from both of us,

Helen

Bachelor uncles are usually very generous. This letter is to a favorite uncle who sent an expensive silver tea service:

Uncle Joe, darling!

I'll be the proudest hostess in all New York when I use my handsome tea service! What a simply *magnificent* gift—and how generous of you to select it for David and me! We were quite overwhelmed when we unpacked it this morning. It's standing on the table

right near me as I write this note, and I keep looking at
it and *gloating* because it's really and truly mine!

Thank you, darling—for David and me. We're expecting you to be a *very frequent visitor* at our house,
and don't think for a minute we'll let you disappoint
us!

Love from both of us, and a special hug and kiss
from me.

Helen

To Intimate Friends

Dearest Carolyn:

I just can't get over the English hunting prints you
sent us! They're exactly what David and I want for
our dining room; but we didn't think we'd be lucky
enough to get them as a gift!

David and I are delighted, Carolyn. Thank you very,
very much!

We're looking forward to seeing you at the wedding.

Affectionately yours,
Helen

It's always more gracious to mention the specific gift. For
example, don't write, "Thanks for the beautiful gift" but
"Thanks for the beautiful lamp." And it's nice to mention
something special about the gift if possible—how it just goes
with something else, or just fits into a certain decorative
scheme, or is in some other way the perfect choice. People like
to be told they selected the ideal gift; it's part of the pleasure
of giving we mentioned earlier in the chapter.

A gift received from an intimate friend of the groom should
be acknowledged by the bride, of course. And although she
does not know him well, her letter should be very friendly
and cordial . . . as she is writing for the groom and herself.
A well-written note of thanks is enthusiastic but not profuse.

Dear Bob:

How very sweet of you to send David and me such a beautiful pair of candlesticks! We're delighted with them, and we just can't thank you enough.

David and I are looking forward to seeing you Tuesday at the wedding.

Thanks again for your *wonderful* gift!

Affectionately,
Helen

To Less Intimate Friends

Dear Miss Walsh:

Thanks for the lovely, lovely salad bowl! I'm sure it will be one of our most useful gifts. David said to be sure and send *his* thanks, too!

With best wishes from both of us,

Cordially yours,
Helen Curtis

Neighbors who were not invited to the wedding but who sent a gift should receive an especially cordial note of thanks:

Dear Mrs. Howland:

It was most kind of you and Mr. Howland to send us a gift—and such a handsome one! We are simply *thrilled* with the book ends; they are just what we needed for our library desk.

We hope that you and Mr. Howland will come real soon, and see for yourselves how beautiful the book ends look.

Cordially yours,
Helen Curtis

To a Business Associate of the Groom

Dear Mr. Kingston:

Thank you for the beautiful carving set you sent David and me. It's a lovely gift, and a useful one—and we appreciate it very much.

Sincerely yours,
Helen Curtis

If the card accompanying the gift is from "Mr. and Mrs. Kingston," the note of thanks should be addressed to Mrs. Kingston—even though neither the bride nor groom know her personally. If Mr. Kingston does not customarily address the groom by his first name, it's advisable to use his surname in the note of thanks. The use of first name or surname in any note of thanks depends upon the degree of intimacy between the persons involved.

To an Old Classmate of the Groom —a Stranger to the Bride

Dear Mr. Foster:

David and I think it was most generous of you to send us such a beautiful gift! We love the little carved Chinese figures, and they'll be just *perfect* on our mantel!

I'm delighted to know you are coming to New York for the wedding. David has talked of you so often, and with such great affection, that I'm looking forward to meeting you.

Many thanks for the gift, from David and me!

Sincerely yours,
Helen Curtis

SHOWER GIFTS SHOULD BE INDIVIDUALLY ACKNOWLEDGED

When an engaged girl is given a shower of gifts by her friends, it's not enough to express verbal thanks at the party.

An individual note of thanks should be written to each person who contributed a gift.

Dear Anne:

   I was so thrilled and excited on Saturday that I'm sure I didn't thank you adequately for the beautiful guest towels. They are lovely—and exactly the color I would have selected myself!

   Thanks so much, Anne. I'm looking forward to seeing you on the twelfth.

Affectionately,
Janet

A special note of thanks goes to the hostess who planned the party and provided the refreshments.

Susan, dear:

   You were sweet to give a shower for me, and I appreciate it more than I can say. I don't know how you managed to keep it such a secret! It was a complete surprise to me . . . and a thrill I'll never forget.

   Bill and I are overwhelmed by the wealth of lovely linens we have suddenly received. Your tea cloth is especially lovely, Susan. I am *doubly* indebted to you— for the party and for your generous gift!

   Thanks from both of us—to a swell gal and a wonderful friend!

With love,
Janet

NOTES OF THANKS FOR
CHRISTMAS GIFTS

   Instead of a run-of-the-mill note that merely acknowledges the gift you received and says a casual "thank you"—try to show real appreciation. You can do that by pointing out certain features of the gift that especially appeal to you. Of you can tactfully point out that it's just what you've been wanting—just what you've been hoping for. The point is to make the person who sent the gift feel that it was a very good selection, that you are delighted and pleased with it.

Dear Aunt Mary:

What a simply *gorgeous* Christmas gift! A fitted bag is something I've wanted for a long time, but could never get for myself.

Thanks you so much, Aunt Mary. I'll have the bag for years and years, and I'll think of you with gratitude and affection every time I use it.

> Lovingly yours,
> Carolyn

Dear Mrs. Carter:

John and I have been displaying your Christmas gift with great pleasure and pride.

The cups and saucers are *exquisite*—and we think it was wonderful of you to remember that collecting Spode is our hobby.

Many thanks to you and Mr. Carter for your thoughtful and generous gift, and our best wishes to you for the new year!

> Sincerely yours,
> Carolyn Brewster

FOR BIRTHDAY GIFT

Dear Alice:

If you had asked me what I wanted for my birthday, I'd have said, "A charm for my bracelet." You just couldn't have selected anything I'd like more!

The little stagecoach is adorable—I can't wait to have it put on the bracelet. Isn't it cute the way the tiny wheels turn?

Thank you, Alice. You have a positive *genius* for selecting the right gift!

> With love,
> Dorothy

FOR WEDDING ANNIVERSARY GIFTS

The wedding anniversaries that are most frequently cele-
brated, and for which friends and relatives customarily send
gifts, are:

> 1 year, Paper
> 5 years, Wood
> 10 years, Tin
> 15 years, Crystal
> 20 years, China
> 25 years, Silver
> 50 years, Gold
> 75 years, Diamond

Such gifts should, of course, be graciously acknowledged
by a written note of thanks. The note is written by the wife,
for her husband and herself.

Dear Carl:

Your flowers came this morning and turned our living room into a garden. Fifty yellow roses for our fifty
golden years! How wonderful of you to remember, Carl
. . . and so generously!

Steve and I are humble and grateful for our many
years of happiness together. And we are grateful, too,
for the many good friends we have accumulated along
the way. You rank high among them, Carl . . . our
dear and loyal friend through all the years.

So we send you our love on our golden anniversary!
And we send you our thanks, Carl, for the beautiful
roses.

> Affectionately,
> Lucy

FOR A GIFT FOR A
NEWBORN BABY OR YOUNG CHILD

Dear Mrs. Langston:

Thank you ever so much for the beautiful little dress
you sent the baby. She wore it home from the hospital,

and I just wish you could have seen how sweet she looked in it!

You were very kind to send a gift, and Mr. Cummings and I appreciate it very much. We hope you will come and see the baby now that we are home.

Sincerely yours,
Mary Cummings

Dear Marj:

I just wish you could see how Patsy adores the cute little panda with the big black eyes! I'm sure that if she could write, she'd say, "Thank you, Aunt Marj, for sending me this beautiful panda to love! You are the very best aunt in all the world!"

But little Patsy can't write as yet . . . so let me thank you for her. You are always so thoughtful and generous.

Come and see us soon, Marj. It's a long time since you have been here.

With love,
Kate

FOR A BON VOYAGE GIFT

Often when people leave for foreign shores, their relatives and friends send *bon voyage* gifts to the ship or plane. These may be books, flowers, baskets of fruit . . . but whatever they are, each gift should be promptly and cordially acknowledged.

Dear Laura:

It was certainly grand of you and Ted to come and see me off! I know it wasn't easy for you to get to the airport at such an early hour, so I appreciate it all the more.

Flying over water can get dreadfully boring after the first few hours, and your book of detective stories came in very handy. It was sweet and thoughtful of you to think of it.

The flight was uneventful and we arrived in Paris on schedule time. Jeanne and Paul met me at the airport, and we went straight to their charming little house. I know I am going to love it here; I'm looking forward to two *marvelous* weeks with my sister and her husband!

I'll write to you again, Laura. In the meantime, my thanks to you and Ted for your many kindnesses to me —and my love to you both, always!

                                                    Blanche

Dear Mr. Peterson:

Your basket of fruit was waiting in my cabin when I got on board this morning. And a more magnificent basket I have never seen!

It was kind and generous of you to do this for me, Mr. Peterson, and I appreciate it more than I can say.

                                            Sincerely yours,
                                            Martha Ellsworth

THE BREAD-AND-BUTTER LETTER

If you have received hospitality at the home of a friend, for a week end or longer, courtesy requires that you write a cordial note of thanks within two or three days after your return home. The fact that you personally and enthusiastically thanked your hostess before leaving doesn't count. You must still express your appreciation *in writing*. This is a so-called "duty" note which is expected of you and which you *must* write. It has become known as a bread-and-butter letter, because it thanks the hostess for the "bread and butter"—or hospitality—she provided.

Kate, dear:

This is to tell you again how very much I enjoyed the week end at Pine Ridge. Everything was just about perfect: the weather, the company, the beautiful surroundings—no wonder I'm finding it difficult to get down to business this morning! The office seems so dull and prosaic after Pine Ridge.

I hope you and Fred know how much I appreciate your hospitality, and your many kindnesses to me. I count myself fortunate indeed to have two such generous and charming friends!

> Affectionately yours,
> Maureen

Dear Mrs. Franklin:

I'd like you to know how much the week at your lovely house in Southampton has meant to me. I not only enjoyed myself immensely, but I feel relaxed and refreshed as I haven't felt in months!

Please give my love to Betsy. It was so nice being with her again—just like our old days together at school!

Many thanks to you and Mr. Franklin for asking me.

> Sincerely yours,
> Evelyn McCormack

Dear Mrs. Benton:

Thank you very much for those four wonderful days at Shady Acres! Every moment was a delight; I can't remember ever having enjoyed myself so thoroughly *anywhere!*

It was good of you and Dr. Benton to invite me, and I deeply appreciate your hospitality.

> Sincerely yours,
> Walter Hanley

THANKS FOR GIFTS TO A
PATIENT OR INVALID

If friends send you books, flowers or fruit while you are in the hospital—or ill at home—it is not necessary that you write immediately. But you should write a brief note of thanks as soon as you can, or have someone very close do it for you.

Dear Mr. Martin:

I want to thank you for the beautiful roses you sent Mrs. Granby. She was very happy and pleased when she saw they were from you.

I'm glad to say she is improving rapidly, and I hope she will soon be able to leave the hospital.

We both send you our warmest thanks for the flowers and for your very kind wishes.

Sincerely,
John Granby

Dear Mary and John:

Now that I can finally sit up and write letters, I want to thank you both for the flowers and books you sent me while I was ill—and most of all, for your many cheerful notes. You have no idea how much they meant to me!

You've been more than kind, you two, and I won't ever forget it. My love and deepest gratitude, now and always!

Jane

THANKS FOR A FAVOR RECEIVED

The gracious person does not accept favors without an expression of thanks and appreciation. Not every favor requires a written note, of course. If you borrow the lawn mower from your neighbor, or ask a friend to send her piano tuner next time he comes—verbal thanks are sufficient. But if a neighbor or friend goes out of the way to do something special for you or a member of your family, nothing but a cordial note of thanks will do to show how grateful you are.

For example, if a member of your family is visiting in a distant city, and an acquaintance to whom you gave her a letter of introduction is kind and attentive, you naturally write a note of thanks.

Dear Mrs. Hackett:

My niece, Jane Barlow, has written to tell me how very kind you have been to her during her stay in Washington.

Mr. Crawford and I deeply appreciate your courtesy, and we hope to have the opportunity of reciprocating when you are in New York.

With many thanks to you for entertaining Jane so generously,

> Sincerely yours,
> Margaret F. Crawford

THANKS FOR A LETTER OF CONDOLENCE

Every letter of condolence should be acknowledged by personal note. Commercial "thank you" cards are in bad taste and should be avoided, except in the case of a public official or person of prominence who receives an overwhelming number of letters from strangers. In private life, sending an engraved form of thanks to a friend or acquaintance who has expressed sympathy is looked upon as rude and ungracious.

The reply to a note of sympathy or condolence need not be written as promptly as other notes of thanks. It can be mailed any time within six weeks after receipt of the flowers or note of sympathy. It can be brief to the point of saying nothing more than a simple "Thank you for your kind expression of sympathy." Or it can be as wordy as one's feelings and impulses at the time prompt. To an intimate friend, for example, one might write:

Dear Anne:

I shall always remember with gratitude the letter you wrote me when you learned of Claire's death. No one but you, who knew my sister and loved her as her own family did, could have written that letter. It brought me comfort, Anne, at a time when I needed it badly.

Thank you from the bottom of my heart, for your letter and for your many kindnesses to Claire during her long illness.

> Affectionately,
> Carol

To a friend who has asked in her note of sympathy if she can help in any way, one might reply:

Dear Ida:

Thank you for your kind note of sympathy, and for your offer to help.

I'm afraid there's nothing anyone can do to help us right now. Only time can help us get over the terrible shock of Philip's death.

But it was good of you to make the offer, and I appreciate it more than I can say.

Always affectionately,
Gail

A woman who has lost her husband may find it difficult to write notes of thanks even to her most intimate friends. She may ask a son or daughter, or some other close relative, to acknowledge the flowers and the letters of condolence she received.

Dear Mrs. Hartley:

Mother has asked me to write to you, as she cannot do so herself just now.

She would like you and Mr. Hartley to know how much she appreciates the flowers and the letter of sympathy you sent. You have both been very kind.

Sincerely yours,
Virginia Baxter

This is the type of letter one generally writes to a neighbor who has sent flowers and made a call of condolence:

Dear Mrs. Davis:

You were very kind at the time of my mother's death.

I want you to know how much your sympathy and

thoughtfulness have meant to me, and how grateful I am for all you did.

With heartfelt thanks,

Sincerely yours,
Thelma Conners

A girl called home from college by the death of her father, might receive flowers and a note from her classmates. She would write a note to the girl closest to her at school, asking her to thank the others for their expression of sympathy.

Dear Grace:

The letter and the flowers came on Tuesday. Will you please give my thanks to all the girls, and tell them how much mother and I appreciate their thoughtfulness?

I shall try to return to school on Tuesday if mother is feeling well enough by that time.

With affection,
Annette

A difficult note of thanks is the one a man writes at the time of his wife's death to friends they have known intimately for many years, and with whom they have shared many happy experiences.

Dear Kate:

I don't need to tell you and Paul how greatly I appreciate all you have done for me in these trying weeks —and how grateful I am for the comfort and understanding you gave me when I needed them so desperately.

No one knows better than you two what Christine meant to me, and what an aching void my life has become without her. But I am trying to take your advice, Kate—and I hope that returning to my work next week will help fill some of the emptiness.

You and Paul have been splendid. I really don't know what I would have done without you. Thank you for everything.

> Affectionately,
> Todd

THANKS FOR A LETTER OF CONGRATULATION

When friends take the trouble to write and congratulate you on your birthday or anniversary, on your engagement or marriage, on a talk you gave, or a distinction you earned . . . you owe them a gracious note of thanks in acknowledgment. Whether it's a brief and formal note, or a long and newsy letter, depends upon the circumstances and upon the degree of intimacy with your correspondent.

On a Birthday

Dear Mrs. Martin:

I just can't tell you how flattered I am that you should have remembered my birthday. It was a real pleasure to receive your charming note this morning.

Thank you so much for your good wishes!

> Sincerely yours,
> Hilda Rankin

On an Engagement

Dear Louise:

What a wonderful letter! Thanks so much for your good wishes, and for all the nice things you wrote about Alan and me.

I guess I'm just about the happiest girl in the world, Louise. I know now what you meant when you said you and Phil were made for each other. I feel the same way about Alan!

Thanks again for your letter. If the future holds only half the fine things you hope for us, we'll be lucky indeed!

> Affectionately,
> Judy

Dear Tom:

You're right! Judy's the cream of the crop and I'm the luckiest fellow in the world!

Thanks so much for your letter. Judy and I appreciate your congratulations and good wishes.

Sincerely,
Alan

On a Marriage

Dear Mrs. Snowden:

Thank you ever so much for your charming note of congratulation. My nice new husband and I appreciate your letter, and your good wishes for the future.

We will be at home after November first, and we hope you will come and see how cozy we are in our little apartment.

Cordially yours,
Judith T. Powell

Dearest Elaine:

Of all the letters Alan and I have received since our marriage, we enjoyed yours the most! Thank you, darling, for all those good wishes. If our life together proves half as rosy as you predict, we'll be well content!

You say Alan is to be congratulated, but I think *I'm* to be congratulated, too. He's a wonderful, wonderful, wonderful husband, Elaine, and I just can't tell you how happy I am!

Thanks again for your good wishes. Alan joins me in hoping you'll come often to see us in Garden City.

With affectionate greetings from us both,
Judy

On a Wedding Anniversary

Dear Cynthia:

Your letter took us back twenty years, and brought so many happy memories to mind! Thank you, dear, for remembering our anniversary and for your kind thoughts of us. Paul joins me in sending our love and appreciation.

Affectionately,
Janice

On the Birth of a Child

Dear Mrs. Hanson:

What a lot of fine big wishes you made for our very tiny new daughter! Thank you ever so much—for Mr. Bradley and myself. We deeply appreciate your good wishes and congratulations.

Sincerely yours,
Vera Bradley

On Graduating from College

Dear Mr. Kimball:

That was a wonderful letter you wrote me! I certainly appreciate your congratulations, and your invitation to come and see you about a job.

But as Dad must have told you by now, I am interested in industrial design and hope to find an opening in that field.

It's quite an exciting adventure, starting out in the business world—and I guess I'll need all the good wishes my friends have been sending me!

Thanks ever so much for your interest, Mr. Kimball, and for your very kind offer.

Sincerely yours,
Edwin Halleck

On Winning an Honor or Distinction

Dear Dr. Benton:

Thank you very much for your note of congratulation on my election as president of the state medical association.

It was good of you to take the time and trouble to write, and I sincerely appreciate your kindness.

Cordially yours,
Frederick P. Harmon, M.D.

8. Letters of Congratulation

If you hear of a friend's engagement or marriage, if you hear of the birth of a child, or of an honor or distinction that has come to someone you know—sit down right away, while you are elated and excited by the news, and write a letter of congratulation. Sincerity comes more easily and naturally to your written words at such a time, and your note has a truer ring to it.

Letters of congratulation should be especially easy and pleasant to write, for we all like to share in the joy of some happy event. These are cheerful messages, in which you can spread yourself to your heart's content. The note may be brief and formal, or it may be chatty and informal—depending on the circumstances.

CONGRATULATIONS ON AN ENGAGEMENT

Always be sure that the *occasion* for congratulation is mentioned specifically in your letter. Don't write "I've heard the news and hasten to congratulate you" but "I've heard the news of your engagement and hasten to congratulate you."

A young lady is not customarily congratulated either on her engagement or her wedding. It's the *man* who is congratulated; the lady is sent good wishes for her happiness.

Dear Lenore:

I have just learned of your engagement to Shelley Travers. Let me be among the first to wish you both every happiness.

I've known Shelley for years, and I'm very fond of the lad. But I think he's lucky to have won a grand girl like you; and tell him for me, my dear, that I congratulate him!

> Affectionately,
> Hilda K. Brandon

Dearest Lenore:

Your mother has told us of your engagement to Shelley Travers. I can't tell you, my dear, how pleased your Uncle Fred and I are by this news. We have been very close to Shelley's family for years, as you know —and we have always thought of him as an unusually fine and dependable young man. In fact, we don't know anyone we would rather have you marry than him!

So we send you our love, Lenore—and our wishes for a lifetime of happiness. Give Shelley our love too, and tell him how delighted we are to welcome him into the family.

> Always affectionately,
> Aunt May

Dear Shelley:

That's great news about you and Lenore! She's a wonderful girl in every way, and we congratulate you on your good fortune.

Best wishes from us both on your engagement. We hope you will have nothing but joy and happiness in your life together.

> Affectionately,
> Ethel and George

Dear Shelley:

I know how crazy you've always been about that precious Lenore of yours; and from what you've told me about her, she's something to be crazy about! So I guess you're a pretty lucky fellow, and I congratulate you.

Some day I hope to meet Lenore. In the meantime tell her your old pal sends his best wishes for her happiness. And that goes for you, too!

As ever,
Bob

CONGRATULATIONS ON MARRIAGE

When an announcement of a marriage is received, congratulations are usually sent to the bride and groom. The note is customarily written and addressed to both; but it may also be written to the bride individually, or to the groom individually—as indicated in the various examples below.

Dear Anne and Jerry:

We were thrilled and delighted to receive the announcement of your marriage in Springtown last Tuesday.

Tom and I send you both our love, and best wishes for every happiness that life can bring.

We hope you'll let us know when you return to New York, so that we can give you our congratulations in person.

Affectionately,
Barbara

Dear Anne:

You will always be little Anne to me . . . even though you're now a staid and dignified married woman! It's hard for me to believe you are old enough to be married. Why, it seems only yesterday I dangled you on my knee!

Give my congratulations to that nice new husband of yours, and tell him I think he's a mighty lucky fellow.

My very best wishes to you, for a lifetime of happiness.

Affectionately,
Wilbur T. Ross

My dear Carter:

Congratulations on your recent marriage.

I wish you and your bride the best of luck, and ever-increasing happiness as the years go by.

Sincerely yours,
Robert F. Wheeler

CONGRATULATIONS ON A WEDDING ANNIVERSARY

Dear Harriet:

It doesn't seem possible that it's five years since you and Bob were married! Somehow I still think of you as a bride and groom. Maybe it's because you're just about the most devoted couple I know!

Congratulations to you both, and may the years ahead bring you continued joy and contentment.

Affectionately,
Janice

Dear Mrs. Dearing:

We have heard that you and Mr. Dearing are celebrating your fiftieth wedding anniversary this week.

It must be a great source of pleasure and pride to have reached this milestone in your long and happy life together, and to be able to look back upon a rich and full life and know you have accumulated so many devoted friends.

Mr. Phillips and I send you warm congratulations, and we hope that there are many more years of happiness ahead for both of you.

Cordially yours,
Myra L. Phillips

CONGRATULATIONS ON A BIRTHDAY

Birthday cards are universally used, and there is no real objection to them. At least they show you have not forgotten the day. But a written message, no matter how short, always means twice as much. So if you have real affection for your relatives and friends, write them personal notes of congratulation instead of sending ready-made congratulations printed on a card.

Jane, dear:

You may not like to be reminded that you are a year older today—but that's not going to keep me from saying "Happy Birthday!"

Let's see. . . . Is it twenty-seven, or twenty-eight—? Or perhaps I'd better not ask!

Anyway, my love to you on your birthday, Jane —and many, many happy returns of the day! Next time you come into town to do some shopping, call me and I'll meet you for lunch. It's been too long since we had one of our good old-fashioned chats!

Affectionately,
Sonya

Dear Uncle John:

To everybody else in the world, this may be Columbus Day. But to *me* it's a far more special day than that! It's the birthday of my favorite uncle—the uncle who never *ever* forgot my birthday when I was a child and who always made me so happy!

I wish you weren't way out there in Highbridge, Uncle John. I'd love to see you on your birthday and help you celebrate. But I can't—so I'm sending you a little gift I hope you'll like. With it go my congratulations, and all my love. I hope you'll have many, many happy birthdays, and that you'll never lose the cheerful outlook and gay spirits that have made you so well-loved by all the family.

Bill and the children join me in sending congratulations. Love from all of us.

Cornelia

Dear Babs:

So you're a year older today—or don't you want to be reminded? Anyway, congratulations and best wishes and all that sort of thing.

If you feel in the mood for celebrating, will you let me take you to dinner and the movies, as a sort of birthday treat? You name the day. And in the meantime, many happy returns!

Cordially,
Harold

CONGRATULATIONS ON THE BIRTH OF A CHILD

Everybody's happy when a baby is born. To express your pleasure and share in the joy, you write the proud new mother a note of congratulation.

Marjorie, dear:

What wonderful news! I know you wanted a baby girl—and I can just imagine how thrilled and happy you must be.

Dan must be just about bursting with pride. Tell him that Carl and I send congratulations and best wishes—and that goes *double* for you, Marj!

We wish you both all possible joy and happiness in your new little daughter.

Fondly,
Claire

Dear Marjorie:

Congratulations on the new baby! I hear she is simply beautiful, even at five days old. But she'll have to go a long way to be even half as lovely as her mother!

Bill tells me you are calling her Marianne. It's a charming name. . . .

Hurry and get well so that I can come and see you, and judge for myself whether little Marianne is as beautiful as they say.

Affectionately,
Edgar

Dear Mrs. Harper:

Your husband just told me the good news. I'm so glad to hear it's a boy, for now little Barbara will have that baby brother she's been wanting!

Congratulations from Mr. Martin and myself. We wish you joy and happiness with your son.

Sincerely yours,
Nellie Martin

CONGRATULATIONS ON GRADUATION

Dear John:

Congratulations upon having received your doctorate in philosophy from Princeton University. I know this has meant years of study and hard work on your part, and it's an achievement you can well be proud of.

Your Aunt Emma and I have followed your progress with pleasure and interest; and we are sure, from the fine record you have made, that you will be a success in whatever you undertake.

No doubt you are tired after the strain of the past few months; and if you would like to come to Lake Talbot for a few weeks this summer, we'd be very happy to have you. We remember that you always used to like it here as a boy; and although it may be too quiet for you now, the rest and relaxation might do you a lot of good. And we'd certainly enjoy hearing about your plans, now that you have completed your college course.

Think it over, John, and let us know.

> Affectionately,
> Uncle Clint

Dear Mrs. Malcolm:

We hear that John has graduated from Princeton and that he made a very fine record for himself there. You must be proud of his splendid accomplishment, and we are very happy for you.

Please give John our congratulations, and our best wishes for success and happiness in his chosen work.

> Sincerely yours,
> Myra T. Clark

CONGRATULATIONS ON WINNING AN
HONOR OR DISTINCTION

Dear Dr. Harmon:

My warm congratulations to you on your election as president of the state medical association. It's a fine tribute from your colleagues, and a reward you richly deserve for your many years of splendid service to the profession and to the people of the state.

I can't think of any man who would have been a better choice. My very best wishes to you!

> Sincerely yours,
> Thomas M. Benton, M.D.

CONGRATULATIONS ON A PROMOTION
OR A NEW VENTURE

Dear Mr. Forthright:

I read in this morning's paper that after twenty-five years with Courtway and Pratt, you are branching out for yourself and opening your own advertising agency.

I would like to add my congratulations to the many you must be receiving. With your brilliant background and long record of fine achievements, I'm sure the new agency will be a great success. I sincerely hope you will find in this new venture the happiness and satisfaction you so richly deserve.

Cordially yours,
Lillian E. Watson

Dear Al:

I ran into Carl the other day, and he tells me you were recently appointed managing editor of the Middletown *Star*.

It's great news, Al—and I'm delighted to hear it! I knew it would be only a matter of time before your unusual abilities were recognized.

It's fine to know you have achieved the goal you've been working toward all these years, and I wish you the greatest possible success. In my opinion, the *Star* at last has an editor who can make it the dominant, outstanding daily of the Middle West!

My heartiest congratulations!

Sincerely yours,
Bert Fellows

CONGRATULATIONS ON A SPEECH OR A PERFORMANCE

Dear Miss Vuillimet:

Congratulations on your triumph last night! Everybody in Middletown is talking about your brilliant piano recital.

Mother and I are especially fond of the Tchaikovsky Concerto, and your rendition of it was simply *superb*. I just can't tell you how much we enjoyed it!

Sincerely yours,
Fredericka Hollings

9. Letters of Condolence

Among the most difficult letters of all to write are letters of condolence. Many people find them so difficult that they send telegrams, printed cards, flowers—anything to avoid writing a personal note of sympathy!

And yet, there is probably no time when a letter can mean so much and be so deeply appreciated. It always helps to know that friends are sympathetic and understanding. A few sincere, well-chosen words can give comfort even to the most grief-stricken . . . can renew the faith and courage of those cruelly hurt and embittered by their loss.

So even though you send flowers or make a condolence call, always write a letter as well to any relative or friend who has suffered a bereavement. Put your sympathy and understanding on paper—*write down* the way you feel—for the greater comfort such written words can give.

A good letter of condolence is like a handclasp, warm and friendly. It is written with dignity and restraint, not filled with gushy sentiment. It's brief, for this is no time to be wordy. It says only what you truly feel: that and nothing more. It doesn't dwell on details of the illness or death, nor quote "comforting" passages from poetry or the Bible. It doesn't touch on memories that reopen the floodgates of pain and sorrow.

Often, in a note of condolence, it's not so much what you say as what you don't say that counts. Surely there can be neither comfort nor compassion in a letter that says, "She was too young to die!" or "Your life will be desolate without him!" It's better not to write at all than to write so tactlessly.

It shouldn't be difficult to write a good letter of condolence if you are genuinely moved to sympathy by a friend's misfortune. It shouldn't be difficult to write with kindness and understanding if you feel that friend's grief and share in the tragic impact of it. The important thing is to write promptly, as soon as you hear the news—and before the shock of it has worn off. For if you write while your heart is filled with sadness, your letter will have the ring of sincerity to it. Your letter will be a warm and convincing expression of the sympathy you really feel.

When you sit down to write a note of condolence, don't think about the right words and phrases to use. Don't strive for eloquence and effect. Remember, it's the feeling behind the words that counts, not the words themselves. Think of the person who is gone. Think of the heartache and sorrow of the person to whom you are writing. Put down simply and truthfully what you think and feel at that moment. Just remember that the three most essential qualities of a good condolence letter are *tact*, *sincerity* and *brevity*.

Following are examples of condolence letters representing a wide range of circumstances. These are not intended as set forms, to be used word for word; but as models or patterns to help you write comforting and understanding messages of your own.

ON THE DEATH OF A PARENT

Margaret, dear:

If only I knew what to say to comfort you! But words cannot say what is in my heart, nor tell you how deeply I feel for you in your sorrow.

I loved your mother, too, Margaret, and I'll never get over missing her. You know I share your grief, but how I wish that sharing it could lighten the burden for you!

I send you all my love, darling, and all my sympathy.

Devotedly,
Jane

Dear Margaret:

I know words aren't much comfort at a time like this. But I'd like you to know I'm thinking of you; and that my family and I send our heartfelt sympathy.

Sincerely,
Jim

Dear Margaret:

Today I heard you had lost your mother. I know the suddenness of it must have been a dreadful shock; and I just can't tell you how sorry I am. Having been so recently through the same sad experience, I know only too well what it means. . . .

I wish there were something I could do or say to soften your grief. But only time can do that, Margaret —and it *will*, as surely as it did for me.

With deepest sympathy to you and all your family,

> Affectionately,
> Vera T. Hubbard

Dear Miss Conners:

Please accept my very deepest sympathy on the death of your mother.

I can well appreciate what a great loss this must be to you.

> Sincerely yours,
> Frederick T. Warner

Dear Paul:

I've just heard the sad news, and I hasten to offer my sympathy.

Please call on me if there is anything I can do to help.

> Sincerely,
> Bob

Dear Paul:

I feel it's almost an intrusion to write at a time like this. But I must tell you how saddened we are by the news, and how deeply we feel for you in your sorrow. It was a privilege to have known your mother; and her loss will be felt by many, for a long time to come.

Fred and I hope that time will quickly soften the blow, and leave you only cherished memories.

> Affectionately,
> Mary Haskins

Dear Mr. Owen:

We have just learned with profound sorrow of the death of your mother.

She was well-loved in this community for her charities and good work, and she will be long remembered by many.

We send you our heartfelt sympathy.

Sincerely yours,
Jan and Tom Stevens

My dear Owen:

I cannot tell you how sorry I am to hear of your great loss. Please accept my sympathy and best wishes.

Sincerely,
Jonathan P. Stevens

Dear Alice:

We just learned of the sudden death of your father. The shock was a great one. But he went as he would have wished—quickly and without suffering. That should be some consolation to you.

We send our deepest sympathy to you and your family. We hope that time will soon heal your sorrow.

Affectionately,
Leslie Blair

Dear Mrs. Taylor:

It was a great shock to hear of your father's death. He was a wonderful neighbor and friend, and he'll be missed by many.

Mr. Henderson and I send kind thoughts and sympathy to you and your family.

Sincerely yours,
Agnes Henderson

Dear Jim:

I sympathize with you on the loss of your father, to whom I know you were deeply devoted.

I hope you will find what comfort you can in the fact that he was with you to a fine old age . . . and that you made his life such a happy one. He was so proud of you, Jim—so proud of your splendid accomplishments. That should help soften your sorrow a little.

Lillian joins me in sending affection and sympathy. You know that if there's anything we can do, you have only to tell us.

Sincerely,
Walter

Dear Mr. Hartwell:

We were saddened to read of your father's death in this morning's paper. He was a fine old gentleman, well-loved and admired by all who knew him.

We can well appreciate your great sense of loss. But we hope you'll find some small measure of comfort in the good wishes and heartfelt sympathy of your great host of friends—among whom I hope you include Mr. Travers and myself.

With affectionate regards from both of us,

Sincerely,
Marian Travers

ON THE DEATH OF A HUSBAND
OR WIFE

A message of sympathy to someone who has just lost a beloved husband or wife is especially difficult to write. The following examples may prove helpful when you are at a loss for words.

Dear Mary:

We are shocked by the sad news. Is there anything Fred or I can do?

Our hearts are filled with sympathy for you in this

hour of trial. We send you our love, and our assurance of devoted friendship—now and always.

Lillian

Dearest Mary:

No one knows better than I what you are thinking and feeling, for I have so recently gone through the same bitter experience.

I know well how meaningless words are to you now; and how little even your best friends can do to comfort you. But time is a great healer, Mary—and it will soon soften the pain and bring you peace of mind, just as it did for me.

You have your children, Mary—and you can be very grateful for that. I am all alone. But I have my memories of my beloved husband, and they grow more precious to me with every passing day. You will have that too, my dear. You will have beautiful memories that no one can take away from you, *ever*.

So try and be brave these first difficult weeks. I send you a heart full of sympathy and understanding; and you know you have my love always.

Janet

Dear Mrs. Bishop:

I am profoundly sorry to learn of the death of your husband, for whom I had the greatest admiration and regard.

Please accept my deepest sympathy.

Sincerely yours,
Gerald P. Searle

Dear Tom:

There's not much we can say at a time like this. But Marge and I want you to know how deeply we feel for you in your sorrow—and how much we would like to help. Will you call on us if there's anything we can do?

With profound sympathy,

Sincerely,
Jerry

Dear Mr. Bailey:

It is with great sorrow that I have just learned of the death of your wife.

I know there is little I can say to lessen your grief; but I'd like you to know you have my deepest sympathy in your bereavement.

Sincerely yours,
Horace Mitchell

ON THE DEATH OF A CHILD

How heartbreaking the death of a child can be! And how cruel a long, wordy message is at such a time, especially if it probes into the details of the child's illness or manner of death. It's far better not to write at all than to write carelessly or thoughtlessly to grief-stricken parents. Remember that a note to bereaved parents should be short, very short—and should scrupulously avoid mention of any subject that could possibly give pain.

Dear Julia:

I'm thinking of you, darling . . . and hoping you'll be as brave as you've always been.

My love and deepest sympathy to you and David.

Affectionately,
Joan

Julia, my dear:

We know only too well the shock and grief you and David are suffering today, for it's only a little more than a year since our own son was taken.

Our hearts are filled with sympathy for you both. We hope that time will soon ease the pain. In the meantime, Julia, you must be strong and brave—for the sake of David and the other children. They look to you for guidance and comfort.

With all our love,

Martha and Henry

Dear Julia:

There are no words to express our grief at the sad news. Our hearts are filled with sorrow for you and David.

Is there anything we can do? You know how grateful we'd be if you let us help in some way.

Joel and I send our love, and our deepest sympathy to you both.

Affectionately,
Charlotte

Dear Mr. and Mrs. Andrews:

I hope you will forgive me for intruding on your grief. Although I'm a new neighbor and almost a stranger to you, I must tell you how deeply I feel for you in this great sorrow.

Mr. Mulhall and I extend to you our warmest sympathy. Please count us among those who share your grief and whose hearts are heavy for you today.

Sincerely yours,
Dorothy K. Mulhall

Dear Mr. Andrews:

I have just learned with deepest sorrow and regret of the death of your little boy.

I realize the inadequacy of words to comfort you in your great grief. But I'd like you and Mrs. Andrews to know my thoughts are with you in your bereavement; and I stand ready and eager to help in any way I can.

With sympathy and warmest personal regards,

Sincerely yours,
Edwin Corbett

ON THE DEATH OF A RELATIVE

When someone loses a relative, it's kind and thoughtful to write a brief note of sympathy. If you knew the person who died, you may want to include a word of praise in your message. Otherwise a simple expression of sympathy, a word or two of comfort, are all that are necessary.

Dear Mr. Forrest:

Word of the recent death of your brother has just come to me, and I hasten to offer condolences.

I had the privilege of knowing your brother in years past, and I realize your great loss. He was a fine and brilliant man, and he will not soon be forgotten by the many who admired and respected him.

Please convey my sympathy and my warm personal regards to all your family.

Cordially yours,
Gerald M. Larkin

Dear Paula:

I have just this moment learned of the sudden death of your brother, Eric. I can't tell you how shocked I am by this sad news. I know what he meant to you and your sister, and I send you both my deepest sympathy.

I'm sure that many hearts must be heavy with sorrow today; for I never knew anyone with such a host of friends as Eric. He'll be keenly missed by everyone who knew him.

Is there any way I can help, Paula? You know I would gladly do anything I can.

With love,
Emily

Dear Miss Travers:

I have just been told of your aunt's death; and knowing your devotion to each other, I realize what a great loss this is to you.

I'd like you to know how sorry Mr. Patton and I are; and how deeply we sympathize with you in your bereavement.

With kindest thoughts from us both,

Sincerely,
Jennifer R. Patton

Dear Mrs. Drummond:

We read in this morning's paper of the death of your talented young nephew. We share with many the shock and sorrow of this tragic news; and our hearts go out in sympathy to you and your family.

Mr. Rankin and I send our heartfelt condolences; and we hope you will find some consolation in the record of brilliant achievements he leaves behind him.

Sincerely yours,
Bessie G. Rankin

WHEN DEATH IS A RELEASE

There are times when death is clearly "for the best," and may be looked upon almost as a blessing rather than a great sorrow. Under these circumstances, the expression of sympathy or condolence should be for the long illness or suffering of the deceased, rather than the immediate death.

Here are typical examples of such letters, written when death was a release from long and hopeless suffering.

Carol, dear:

All my thoughts are with you and your mother today. My heart is filled with sympathy for you both— for the long year of suffering, and for your sorrow now that Jean is gone.

I loved your sister, Carol; I'm sure you know that. I shall miss her more than I can say. But I know how she suffered this past year, and I'm grateful that her suffering is over at last. I try to find comfort in that thought, and I hope you will, too.

Affectionately,
Lucy

Dear Mrs. Carleton:

Yours has been a long and tragic sorrow, and now that it is over at last, I am sure that time will soon bring comfort and peace.

Mr. Jamison and I want you to know how deeply we sympathize with you for all you have endured through the years, and now. We assure you of our affectionate regard, and hope you will let us know if there is anything either of us can do—as neighbors and friends.

Sincerely yours,
Laura Jamison

Dear Dick:

You have been through a great deal these past few months, and all my thoughts and sympathies are with you now.

I hope you will look on Barbara's death as a release from cruel and hopeless suffering. John and I feel deeply for you in your present sorrow, but we are grateful that the long ordeal is over.

Try not to look back, Dick. You have your two fine sons to think about. So keep your eyes on the future and the life that lies ahead.

Always affectionately,
Carolyn

WHEN SOMEONE IS KILLED
OR COMMITS SUICIDE

When death strikes cruelly and without warning, it leaves shock and anguish to those left behind. Only relatives and close friends should write; others should not intrude upon the horror and heartache of sudden death.

Dear Christine:

We are stunned, as all your friends are, by the tragic news. Jerry and I send you our heartfelt sympathy, and we beg you to let us help you in any way we can.

Will you have someone call us if there's anything we can do? In deepest sorrow and affection,

Yours devotedly,
Sue

Mary, darling:

Ed and I are too grieved and shocked even to try and express our sympathy.

Our hearts are filled with sorrow for you and Pete. We hope and pray that time will quickly soften this terrible blow.

We send you our love, and we're standing by to help in any way we can. Have someone call us, darling, if you want us.

Devotedly,
Jane

Dear Claudia:

I just can't believe the terrible news. I wish with all my heart I could help or comfort you in some way.

It may be some slight consolation to you to know that your grief is shared by everyone in Middletown.

With deepest sympathy to you in your great loss,

Affectionately,
Kathryn

SOME FAMOUS LETTERS OF CONDOLENCE

Often it helps, in writing your own letters, to know what others have written to family and friends in time of tragedy or bereavement.

Princess Alice of England, the devoted daughter of Queen Victoria, wrote the following letter to her mother on the anniversary of her father's death:

Darmstadt, December 11, 1866

Beloved, precious Mama:

On awakening this morning, my first thoughts were of you and of dear darling Papa! Oh, how it reopens the wounds scarcely healed, when this day of pain and anguish returns! This season of the year, the leafless trees, the cold light, everything reminds me of that time!

Happily married as I am, and with such a good, excellent and loving husband, how far more can I under-

stand now the depth of that grief which tore your lives
asunder!

                                                          Alice

When Charles Dickens' infant daughter died, his wife was
ill . . . and he broke the tragic news to her gently, tenderly, in
a letter that has become a classic of its kind. He didn't actually
tell her the child was dead; he prepared her slowly for the
shock, let her realize for herself that there was no hope.

> You would suppose her quietly asleep, but I am
> sure she is very ill, and I cannot encourage myself with
> much hope of her recovery. I do not (and why should
> I say I do to you, my dear?) I do not think her re-
> covery at all likely. . . . Remember what I have often
> told you, that we never can expect to be exempt . . .
> from the afflictions of other parents. . . .

By far the most famous condolence letter ever written—and,
in fact, one of the most famous letters in American history—
is the one Abraham Lincoln wrote to Mrs. Lydia Bixby, con-
soling her on the loss of five sons in the Civil War.

                                      Executive Mansion
                                      Washington, Nov. 21, 1864

To Mrs. Bixby, Boston, Mass.

Dear Madam,

> I have been shown in the files of the War Depart-
> ment a statement of the Adjutant General of Massa-
> chusetts that you are the mother of five sons who have
> died gloriously on the field of battle. I feel how weak
> and fruitless must be any word of mine which shall
> attempt to beguile you from the grief of a loss so over-
> whelming. But I cannot refrain from tendering you
> the consolation that may be found in the thanks of the
> republic they died to save. I pray that our Heavenly
> Father may assuage the anguish of your bereavement,
> and leave you only the cherished memory of the loved
> and lost, and the solemn pride that must be yours to
> have laid so costly a sacrifice upon the altar of freedom.

                          Yours very sincerely and respectfully,
                                      A. Lincoln

10. Notes of Sympathy on Illness, Injury, and Material Loss

Not all letters of sympathy are written on the sad occasion of death. They are written also to cheer friends who are ill, or who have been injured in an accident. They are also frequently written to relatives or friends who have suffered material loss by fire, flood, theft or other unfortunate circumstances.

A note of sympathy, like a note of condolence, should be tactful and *sincere*. If the illness or loss is a relatively minor one, the letter may be written in a light and bantering vein. But when a person is gravely ill or has suffered a really serious loss, any attempt to be facetious is in very bad taste and should be avoided. Even though your bright and witty letter may be written with the best intentions in the world, to cheer the invalid or unhappy victim of misfortune, you can be sure it will be resented. For people take their troubles seriously, and expect you to do likewise.

That doesn't mean your note of sympathy should be gloomy or pessimistic. Quite on the contrary! It should bring courage and comfort to the person who receives it.

TO THOSE WHO ARE ILL

Always try to write to a sick person as though complete recovery were just around the corner—and he, or she, will soon be up again, sound and well as ever. Minimize the illness, if you can; don't dramatize its seriousness. Unless a note of sympathy makes the person who receives it *feel better*—unless it gives that person a mental lift and a more cheerful outlook—it should be dropped into the wastebasket and not the mailbox! For a gloomy or thoughtless letter can do more harm than good to someone already depressed by illness or suffering.

A note of sympathy may be quite brief, just a paragraph or two. Or it may be long and chatty, like the letters you write to friends who are *not* ill. The length of the letter is not important. But what you say in your letter is very important indeed to the person confined to a lonely room, ill . . . and perhaps in pain. Your letter should be like a warm and friendly visit with that person, bringing brightness and cheer into the sickroom, bringing at least momentary escape from the loneliness or pain.

When writing to an invalid or convalescent you know well, try to bring the outside world to him by writing of the things in which he is interested and with which he is familiar. For example, if he's a golf enthusiast, tell him about the 90 your neighbor shot the other day. If his hobby is tropical fish, tell him about the exhibit you saw recently . . . or the article you read in a magazine . . . or the new kind of tank just developed for Siamese fighting fish. If necessary, go out of your way to get some interesting tidbit of information to include in your letter. Remember that you are able to get around and the sick person is not. He'll appreciate news of the outside world, especially in his own field or hobby.

To a woman whose great love is gardening, you might write about the flower show . . . or tell her how lovely her garden looked as you went by it that morning . . . or confide plans for your own garden next Spring. Or you might mention that you saw her children recently, and how lovely they looked— or how surprised you were to see how big they were getting. You can always find something to write about that's of interest to the patient, if you really want to. If you are writing to someone who has no special interests or hobbies, you can always write about people. Everyone is interested in people: what they are doing, where they are going, what they have accomplished.

The following examples cover a variety of circumstances, and are written with different degrees of intimacy. Some are formal and reserved in tone, but cordial—the type of notes you might write to neighbors or acquaintances with whom you are friendly but not intimate. Others are chatty and informal in tone, and are the type of notes you would send to relatives or close friends.

Bear in mind that the most important thing is to write *optimistically*, with the cheerful assumption that the sick person is well on the road to recovery.

Dear Mrs. Corbin:

I was so sorry to learn of your illness. You must hurry and get well! Everybody in the neighborhood misses you, and we're all hoping you'll be back soon.

Mr. Burke joins me in sending best wishes for your speedy recovery.

Sincerely yours,
Mary T. Burke

Dear Dr. Howell:

Mrs. Dunne and I are extremely sorry to hear of your illness. We often wondered how you could keep going as you did, day and night. It was bound to catch up with you sooner or later!

We *do* hope you won't rush your recovery—that you'll think of yourself, for a change, and get a good rest before you return to your practice. We're sending you some books we think you'll enjoy.

With best wishes for your quick and complete return to health,

> Sincerely yours,
> Gilbert Dunne

Dear Joe:

I've just this minute heard that you are in the hospital. I think you are very wise to find out once and for all what's causing your trouble, and get it over with.

I hope that by the time this note reaches you, you'll be feeling a great deal better. I'm sure that now it won't be long before you are entirely and completely yourself again.

By the way, Joe, the boys are postponing that fishing trip until you can join us. We've decided it wouldn't be nearly as much fun without you. So hurry and get well!

> Affectionately,
> Harry

Dear Mary:

I hear you are making such a rapid recovery that you'll soon be out of the hospital and back with your family and friends. That's wonderful news, Mary! I've missed you so much. You've been on my mind constantly, ever since you went to the hospital. I just can't tell you how sorry I was that you had such a difficult time of it.

But all that's over now, and you'll soon be as good as
new! I met Dr. Carleson at my sister's house yesterday
(her little boy has the mumps) . . . and he tells me
you are his prize patient. He says you rallied beautifully, and that from this point on you'll show steady
improvement—until you have all your old health and
strength back again.

I saw John yesterday, too. The poor man is like a
lost sheep without you! He says he's counting the very
hours until you come home. Janet was with him; my,
how she has grown in the past year! You have a lovely
daughter, Mary . . . as gracious and charming as she
is sweet to look at. You must be very proud of her.

This morning I walked by your house on the way to
the post office, and I stopped for a moment to look at
your garden. I still say it's the most beautiful garden
in town! Your roses are magnificent this year. And I
do hope you'll get home before the lilacs are gone—
they're simply *gorgeous!*

Frank sends his best wishes, and he says to be sure
and tell you how delighted he is to hear about your
fine progress. Keep it up, Mary—and come home real
soon to those who love and miss you.

Affectionately,
Lillian

TO THOSE WHO HAVE BEEN INJURED

A note written to someone who has been injured in an
accident should be as brief as possible, and genuinely sympathetic. It is better not to write at all than to write out of
curiosity. The spirit behind your message should not be, "How
did it happen? Whose fault was it? Were there any witnesses?"
—but "I'm so sorry to hear about it! I hope you weren't badly
injured and that you'll soon be all right again." In other words,
your concern should not be for the details of the accident but
for the condition and well-being of the person who has been
injured.

Dear Tom:

I just can't tell you how sorry I was to learn of your
accident. Your family tells me that you are progressing
nicely, and that you'll be out of the hospital in about
ten days. I'm certainly relieved to know that!

In the next day or so you'll receive a little package from Margaret and me. I hope you like it, and that it will help to pass the time more pleasantly.

With every good wish for your swift recovery,

> Sincerely,
> Bob

Dear Mrs. Gilbert:

I feel I simply *must* write this note and tell you how much you are in the hearts and minds of everyone in Middletown.

We were shocked and saddened beyond words by news of the crash. But we were grateful, too, that your injuries were not worse.

The affection and best wishes of the entire town are with you, and everyone's hoping for your quick and complete recovery.

> Sincerely yours,
> Cora Stanley

Dear Marjory:

I've just learned that young Pete was hurt in a football game. I'm ever so sorry to hear it, and I hope his injuries are not serious.

I know just how you feel because I had the same experience with George a few years ago—remember? I guess it's just something all mothers of growing boys must expect!

Please let me know if there's anything I can do to help. Perhaps you'd like to send Patsy here for a week or so, until Pete is better. We'd love to have her, and I'd see that she got to and from school safely. Just phone me, Marj—and I'll come and get her.

Tell Pete I'm sorry he was hurt, and that I hope he'll soon be fit as a fiddle again.

> Affectionately,
> Harriet

TO THOSE WHO HAVE SUFFERED
MATERIAL LOSS OR DAMAGE

People who have suffered material loss or damage generally appreciate a brief message of sympathy from their friends. But it should not be a probing letter, filled with questions—a letter prompted more by curiosity than kindness. It should merely express sympathy, and perhaps offer help. Here as a few examples:

Dear Mr. Thompson:

I was extremely sorry to hear of the fire which destroyed your beautiful house in Far Acres. I know well how much that house meant to you and Mrs. Thompson, and I hasten to offer my sympathy.

With best wishes to you both,

Sincerely yours,
Roger Whitney

Dear Sally:

Your sister phoned this morning and told us about the fire which damaged your house last night. Jim and I know how distressing this experience can be, as we went through it ourselves. If there's any way we can help, will you call on us? You are more than welcome to use our basement for storing things until the damage to your house is repaired.

We hope the damage is less than you think, and that your lovely house will soon be good as new again.

Sincerely,
Betsy Wall

11. Letters of Introduction

The purpose of a social note of introduction is to bring together people you feel reasonably sure will find pleasure and enjoyment in each other's company.

For example, if you have a friend going to a distant city where you have other friends—and if you believe it would be mutually pleasant and agreeable for these people to meet—you offer to write a note of introduction. Or if someone you know and like is going to Nassau for a vacation, and you happen to have very good friends who live in Nassau, you might say: "Be sure to stop in and see the Ridgways! I know you'll enjoy meeting them. Here—I'll give you a letter of introduction."

Notice that the letter is offered, not requested. No one should ever *ask* for a letter of introduction—nor should anyone write such letters carelessly or indiscriminately. It's an unkindness to your distant friend to give a letter of introduction to someone you do not know well . . . someone who may turn out to be a nuisance or a bore. It's equally inadvisable to send a letter of introduction to a casual acquaintance . . . someone who may not be at all interested in meeting your friend and who may look upon your letter as a presumption.

So make it a point never to write a letter of introduction unless you know both persons intimately and well. Even then, write it only if you feel sure that the meeting will be of interest or benefit to both of them. Ask yourself if the persons concerned have anything in common. Ask yourself if they would really enjoy meeting each other—if they are likely to get along easily and well together. If there is any doubt in your mind, don't write a letter of introduction.

For bear in mind that an introduction by letter imposes obligations and responsibilities far more binding than any spoken introduction. It's a demand upon a distant friend's courtesy, hospitality and time—a demand that cannot be denied without repudiating the friendship of the person who wrote the letter, and bluntly ignoring the person who presented it.

Before you write any letter of introduction, therefore, be sure that your friend wants it—and be sure that the person to whom it is written will want to receive it. Then write it briefly and to the point. It should give the name of the person being introduced—the reason or purpose for the introduction—and any other information that is relevant or important. As it is actually a letter of request, asking that kindness and hospitality be shown to a complete stranger, it should include an expression of thanks for any courtesies extended.

A letter of introduction may either be handed to the friend for whom it is written, to be presented personally—or it may be sent through the mail like any other letter. If it is to be delivered personally, the envelope should be left unsealed. Obviously nothing of an intimate nature should be included in a letter given to one friend for presentation to another. However a second and private letter may be written and sent by mail, giving more information about the person who is on the way with a letter of introduction. Examples of these various types of letters follow.

TO BE PRESENTED IN PERSON

Dear Jim:

The bearer of this note, Mr. Robert Mitchell, of Chicago, plans to be in Asheville for about a month. Besides being a personal friend of mine, he is radio director of a number of top-ranking shows; and knowing how interested you are in radio advertising, I'm sure you'll enjoy meeting him.

I have long wanted you and Bob to know each other, and I'm glad of this opportunity to bring you together. I'll appreciate anything you can do to make Bob's stay in Asheville more enjoyable—and I know he will, too.

With kindest regards to you and Ellen,

Cordially yours,
Kenneth Dawson

Dear Elsie:

This will introduce Janet Blair who is going to spend the winter in Washington gathering material and doing research for a new book. She plans to spend her days at the Congressional Library, and her evenings with congenial people. I told her I know of no one more congenial than you!

I'm sure you'll like Janet, and that you two will enjoy each other's company immensely. I don't need to tell you how much I'll personally appreciate any courtesies you show her.

Sincerely yours,
Edith Preston

Dear Catherine:

I'm giving this letter to Gerald Breen, a very good friend of ours. He is going to be in Chicago for a few days, and I'd like you two to meet as you happen to be interested in the same thing: child welfare.

Mr. Breen is making a study of juvenile delinquency, and I told him about the wonderful work you are doing among the underprivileged children of Chicago. He is very eager to talk with you about it.

I'm sure you'll enjoy meeting Mr. Breen, and I'm equally sure he'll be delighted and charmed to meet you.

Affectionately,
Alice

Dear Mrs. Hathaway:

The young lady who hands you this note is Miss Virginia Andrews—the daughter of one of my oldest and dearest friends. She will be in New York for the next year or so to study fashion design.

Virginia is a charming and talented girl, and I feel so certain you will enjoy her company that I have insisted that she call and present this note. She has never been in New York before; and I'll be very grateful for any help or advice you can give her. I know she, too, will deeply appreciate any courtesy.

Very sincerely yours,
Martha B. Emmons

TO BE SENT BY MAIL

When a letter of introduction is sent by mail, it imposes less of an obligation on the person who receives it. For example, if you write to a distant friend and say, "My former neighbors, the Boltons, are going to live in your city and I think you'd enjoy knowing them"—it's up to the distant friend to decide whether or not she wants to know them. She takes the initiative, saving the newcomer this embarrassment. And inasmuch as the letter was not presented personally, she is free to make advances or not, as she feels inclined.

Dear Peggy:

I've just learned that old friends of mine, Jane and Ira Hall, are now living in Chicago, at 70 Lake Shore Drive. That's practically next door to you, isn't it?

The Halls are very charming people, and I think you would enjoy knowing them. I told them all about you; so if you call them, they'll recognize the name right away and know who you are.

I hope you *will* call them, Peggy. They're really wonderful people to know, and lots of fun to be with. Bob and I have certainly missed them since they moved away!

When are you and Fred coming to New York again? It seems ages since we saw you!

Affectionately,
Lorraine

Dear Joe:

My brother-in-law, Roy Fowler, will be in Boston all next week—at the Copley-Plaza. I've often wanted you two to meet, and this seems like the ideal opportunity.

Roy is research director of an advertising agency. I told him about the book you are writing on the history of buying trends in America, and he was completely fascinated—as I knew he would be! He said he'd like to know more about it; and I think you might find it interesting and helpful to discuss it with him.

So call him if you can, Joe—but not if it's an inconvenience. If he doesn't hear from you, he'll understand that it's because you are tied up. I suggest this meeting only because I know you two are bound to enjoy each other's company.

Cordially,
Homer

"FOLLOW UP" LETTERS OF INTRODUCTION
GIVING ADDITIONAL INFORMATION

Frequently when a letter of introduction is given to a friend to be delivered in person, another letter is written at the same time and sent by mail. The purpose is to say that the letter of introduction is on the way . . . and to give any additional information that may seem necessary or desirable. Here are some examples of such "follow up" letters:

Dear Jim:

In the next day or so you will receive a telephone call from Robert Mitchell of Chicago. He is a very good friend of mine; and as he is planning to be in Asheville for a month or more, I gave him a letter of introduction to you.

I know how busy you are, Jim, and I don't want you to regard this as an obligation. But I feel certain you'll enjoy meeting Bob Mitchell; and I'll wager that once you meet him, you'll want to keep on seeing him! For Bob's good company anywhere—at bridge, golf, tennis, or just talking. I should say *especially* talking! Bob's just about the most brilliant and entertaining conversationalist I know.

I'm writing this note so that you'll know who Bob is when he calls. I'll appreciate any kindness you and Ellen may show him as a stranger in Asheville; but please don't put yourselves out or feel that you are committed in any way at all. If I didn't feel you'd be as delighted to meet Bob as he will be to meet you, I wouldn't have given him a letter.

I hope you and Ellen are well, and I look forward to seeing you on your next visit to Chicago.

Sincerely yours,
Kenneth Dawson

A FAMOUS LETTER OF INTRODUCTION

The following letter of introduction was written by the gifted composer, Felix Mendelssohn, to a friend in London. Although it was written more than a hundred years ago, it has none of the pompous phraseology of that period . . . and remains the classic letter of its kind: simple, charming and very much to the point.

Berlin, March 10, 1844

My dear friend,

The bearer of these lines, although a boy of thirteen, is one of my best and dearest friends and one of the most interesting people I have met for a long time. His name is Joseph Joachim. He was born in Hungary at Pesth, and he is going to London.

Of all the young talents that are now going about the world, I know none that is to be compared with this violinist. It is not only the excellence of his performances, but the absolute certainty of his becoming a leading artist—if God grants him health and leaves him as he is—which makes me feel such an interest in him. . . .

He is not yet very far advanced in composition, but his performances of the Vieuxtemps, Bruch and Spohr concertos, his playing at sight (even the second violin parts of difficult quartets I have heard him play in the most masterly manner), his accompanying of sonatas, etc., is in my opinion as perfect and remarkable as may well be.

I think he will become a yeoman in time, as both of us are. So pray, be kind to him, tell him where he can hear good music, play to him, give him good advice, and for everything you may do for him, be sure that I shall be as much indebted to you as possible. Farewell.

Very truly yours,
F.M.B.

Book III

*

Your Personal Correspondence

* * *

1. The General Rules of Personal Correspondence

Your personal correspondence is made up of the letters you write to family and friends. These are the letters you *want* to write and *enjoy* writing, as compared with your social correspondence which is made up for the most part of "duty" notes and letters of obligation.

The purpose of personal correspondence is to bring news and share experiences with those who are near and dear to you—to "visit" with those you like, and miss, and with whom you want to keep in contact. They are the letters you write to distant friends, to husband or wife away from home, to children at school or camp . . . the letters that reach out across space and bring you close to those you love and from whom you are separated.

In a recent national drive to promote letter writing, the post office department used the slogan: *Someone feels better when you send a letter!* Your personal correspondence is made up, or should be made up, of letters that make people feel better. A good personal letter is written with joy and received with delight. It's intimate and informal, with all the natural ease of good conversation. It's *you* on paper—what you are doing, reading, thinking, feeling—your very personality tucked into an envelope and mailed with love of affection to someone far away!

Lord Chesterfield, undisputed social arbiter of the eighteenth century, considered the ability to write good personal letters so important that he never stopped urging his son to develop to the utmost his skill and facility in this direction. Always, over and over again—through more than twenty years of correspondence between father and son—his advice remained the same: *Write as you speak! Write as though you were seated in a room with me, talking in plain, simple language about the things you have seen and done and thought and experienced since you wrote me last.*

The next time you sit down to write a personal letter, remember Chesterfield's advice to his son. Put as much of yourself as you can into your letter. Write as you speak, of things you know are interesting to your correspondent. Use words that come readily and easily to your mind, for your letter should be natural and unstudied—like the flow of conversation. Your letter should be good plain talk on paper, bringing your image, your voice, your gestures to the mind of the reader.

Unlike social correspondence, there are no fixed or standard forms for letters to family and friends. The most *natural* letters are the best in personal correspondence. You can even take liberties with the long-established customs and traditions, if you like . . . being as different and original as you please. For example, you don't need to start your letter in the usual familiar way, with a salutation:

> Dear Helen:
>
>   We've been having very bad weather here. It's been raining very hard for a week, without letup. I hope you are having better weather in New York.

You can start your letter *without any salutation at all,* if that appeals to you—making it as informal and conversational as the following:

>   What awful weather we've been having, Helen! It's been raining cats and dogs for the past week. How's the weather in New York?

That doesn't mean just being yourself is all there is to successful personal letter writing. It isn't quite as simple as that! After all, very few of us are "born" letter writers who can put ourselves on paper with the greatest of ease and charm. For most of us, good letter writing is neither easy nor natural. But by following a few well-tested ideas and suggestions, *anyone* can write more interesting letters—*anyone* can write the kind of letters that family and friends love to receive.

ANSWER EVERY LETTER PROMPTLY—
IT'S EASIER FOR YOU

Answer all your correspondence promptly, so that your letters reflect the mood and impulse in which you resolved to write. The impulse may come from within yourself, perhaps from thoughts of your distant friend—or it may be in response to a letter you have received and that needs to be answered. In either case, your letter is bound to be more interesting and readable if you write it before the impulse fades . . . before the warmth of friendly intention cools and evaporates.

Postmaster Albert Goldman of New York, in a radio address during National Letter-Writing Week, said: "We've all heard the timeworn apologies for failure to write, but how often do we really have a good excuse? It's a common trait to be careless in keeping up with one's correspondence. . . ."

Don't be careless! *Keep up with your correspondence!* Remember what we said earlier in this book, and now repeat for emphasis: *Don't wait too long to answer your letters. Write while the glow is still with you! Then you won't need to grope for words, trying to sound sincere. The words will come of their own accord, will spring naturally and sincerely from the warmth of your enthusiasm.* Any letter is easier and more pleasant to write if it's written on time and you don't need to make apologies or explanations for its delay.

YOU DON'T NEED LITERARY STYLE
TO WRITE INTERESTING LETTERS

It isn't necessary to have a distinguished or "literary" style to write the kind of letters people love to receive. A simple, kindly letter, written from the heart, is as welcome as the most brilliant epistle . . . perhaps even more so! It's the *feeling* behind your letter that counts, the warmth and understanding. So don't hesitate to write letters—lots of them!—because you feel you don't write well. Lincoln was often unsure of his spelling; he was sometimes careless with grammar and punctuation. Yet Lincoln's warm heart and generous love of mankind are reflected unmistakably in all his letters, making even the least of them shine with greatness.

Bear in mind that your style improves with practice, in letter writing as in all kinds of writing. The more you write, the more easily you will write—and the more interesting and readable your letters will be. Balzac always advised young writers to correspond freely with family and friends, for "letter writing forms one's style." Every good letter you write increases your skill and facility for writing the next one.

HOW LONG SHOULD A LETTER BE?

People frequently ask how long a personal letter should be. That depends entirely on what you have to say. It isn't necessary to write long letters. If you were talking face to face with your correspondent, you wouldn't deliver a prolonged monologue. You would say what you have to say . . . and stop. And that's exactly what you should do in letter writing. You should begin and stop writing with the same ease of transition as you begin and stop talking in conversation.

The length of your letter is not at all important. It can be as brief as the warm but hurried "hello" when busy friends meet, greet and part. Or it can ramble on and on for pages in the easy intimacy of friends who have stopped for a heart-to-heart chat. It's the *tone*, or *spirit*, of your letter that counts, not the number of pages you fill with writing.

In general, letters to family and friends should be neither so brief as to give the impression of haste—nor so long and rambling as to cause confusion and boredom. Just be sure your letter carries the feeling of friendly, informal conversation . . . and let the length of it take care of itself. The really important thing is to have something to say, something interesting and pleasant to communicate—even if it's nothing more than "I miss you—I'm thinking of you—and I'm writing to let you know you are on my mind!"

2. Friendly Letters

Friendly letters are simply the exchange of thoughts between friends—written communications between persons who, for the moment, happen to be separated. The best are those that pick up the threads of friendship and carry them forward as though no separation had occurred—letters that are like personal visits, intimate and chatty, and rich with the warmth of your personality.

It requires no special knack or ability to write such letters. Just try to imagine yourself meeting that person in the street . . . your face lighting up with pleasure . . . your hand going out in cordial greeting. Imagine yourself saying, "Well, *hello!* I'm glad to see you!"

That's the feeling a good personal letter should have. It should clearly be written because you *want* to write and *enjoy* writing, not because a letter is due and it's your "turn" to write.

HOW TO BEGIN A FRIENDLY LETTER

The old saying that "all beginnings are difficult" is certainly true as applied to letter writing. The beginning of a letter is usually the most difficult part of it. But once the first sentence is written—and especially if it's an *interesting* first sentence that gets the reader off to a good start—the rest of the letter tends to run on smoothly, one point leading to another as in conversation.

It's wise to organize your thoughts before you start to write. Decide what you want to say in your letter, then plunge right in and say it without a lot of unnecessary preliminary remarks. For example, don't start off with: "I received your letter and am sorry not to have answered it sooner." If you knew how many people start their letters with just that exact sentence, you would never use it again! Equally overworked are such opening sentences as: "I've been meaning to write for a long time" . . . "I know I should have written long before this" . . . "I would have written sooner, but there just wasn't anything to write about."

Try to avoid opening your letter with an apology or excuse for delay in writing. Such beginnings are not only commonplace and trite, but rude. When you say in a letter, "This is the first opportunity I've had to write" or "I meant to write sooner but I've been so busy"—what you are actually saying is, "I haven't written before because there were so many other more interesting and important things to do." You wouldn't dream of saying anything so discourteous to a friend; why imply it in the very first sentence of your letter? How much more gracious and flattering it is to write, "I've thought of you so many, many times during these busy months!" . . . or "If you only knew how often you are in my thoughts!"

As undesirable as an apology in your opening sentence is an announcement, right at the start, that this is a hurry-up letter written while waiting for the cake to bake or the children to come home from school. It's certainly no compliment to your correspondent to say, "I just have time to scribble a few words before John comes home for dinner" . . . or "I'll have to rush this letter, as the office is just about ready to close." A letter that is obviously dashed off in a hurry is not very likely to be received with joy or read with pleasure.

The opening sentence of a letter is very important, and should receive careful thought. For the tone of the first sentence can determine the effect of the entire letter on the person who receives it. No one can possibly be thrilled by a letter that starts out with the blunt and uninspired statement: "There's no news; everything's just about the same." Nor is there any promise of enjoyment in a letter that begins, "I said I'd write, so I will." Such remarks are dull and pointless, and should be avoided. They only bore the reader . . . and what's even worse, may annoy or offend him.

So watch that opening sentence! Always try to start off with something interesting, some important news, some information your reader will be glad to receive. If possible, start off with a compliment—a word of appreciation or praise. You might say, "What a treat to receive your letter . . . you always write such interesting news!" Or, "It's always a thrill to see your handwriting; I enjoy your letters so!" Such compliments compel attention much better than the old familiar rubber-stamp phrases that are used over and over again as the start of friendly letters—phrases that have lost all life and sparkle.

Avoid particularly starting your letter with any word that ends in "ing" . . . like "Having heard that you are in New York, I am writing to say . . ." or "Learning of your illness, I hasten to send my sympathy." Such participial openings always tend to make a letter sound stilted and formal.

Here are some interesting first sentences taken from letters written by famous people, most of them to intimate relatives or friends. They show how lively and colorful the opening sentences of letters can be.

> Things have happened quickly since I last wrote you.
> *Edward M. House*

> Truth is such a rare thing, it is so delightful to tell it.
> *Emily Dickinson*

> Nothing could have given me greater pleasure than to get news of you!   *Pierre Curie*

> My heart is singing for joy this morning!
> *Anne Sullivan Macy*

> I shall not forget how good you were to take time to write to me!   *Walter H. Page*

I am going to be married!   *Lord Byron*

You'll be thunderstruck to hear what I've been asked
to do.   *Helen Keller*

My heart is so full that I must tell you about it!
                                          Felix Mendelssohn

Thank you, thank you without end, for the photograph . . . it made me very happy, made my world
glow and my heart light and warm. *Nadejda von Meck*

There are moments in life when high position is a
heavy burden.   *Napoleon Bonaparte*

Whatever you do will always affect me . . . one
way or another.   *Lord Chesterfield*

WHAT TO WRITE IN A FRIENDLY LETTER

There is only one real reason for writing a friendly letter
. . . and that is the mutual pleasure to be derived from it.

Therefore letters to friends should be written on a gay and
cheerful note, whenever possible. They should tell of pleasant
and amusing things, not of sickness, heartache, family problems
or other disturbing or distressing things.

That doesn't mean every letter you write must be filled with
joy and cheer. Some of the best letters ever written tell of great
tragedy or sorrow. In fact, many letters are written expressly
for the purpose of sharing an unfortunate or unhappy experience with a friend.

But we are not here discussing such special letters, based on
tragic or unhappy circumstances. In the general run of friendly
correspondence, it's always best to write of pleasant and agreeable things. No one can be said to enjoy a letter that's filled
with "peeves" and complaints. No one can derive real pleasure
from a letter that's one long recital of worries, troubles and
grievances.

So don't write when you are discouraged or depressed;
wait for a happier frame of mind. Don't write when you are
angry or annoyed; or if you do write, wait until the next day
to mail your letter. You may not want to mail it when you
read what you have written.

The letters you write to friends should be warm and cordial
—should be newsy and alive. They should be filled with the
kind of information that is of interest to your correspondent,

the kind of news he or she will enjoy hearing. Write of actual people and places . . . of amusing, exciting or unusual things you have seen, heard or done. Don't scorn even the weather, for it's an interesting subject despite all the jokes we hear about it. People like to know what kind of spring New York has had . . . how much rain there's been in California . . . whether it's been a pleasant winter in Florida.

Don't waste a friend's time with a long letter about unimportant trivialities, of no possible significance to anyone but yourself. But if you have heard a good story or a lively joke, remember to tell it in your letter. Or if someone you both know has won a prize, or had a baby, or built a house . . . pass on the news. If you are in Shanghai and you are writing to someone back home, *write about Shanghai* (not about how homesick you are or how your husband's hair is falling out!). If you are writing to someone from your home town who is living in Shanghai, don't just ask how he likes it there and when he expects to return; *give him news of the town and the people in it*. Any news about familiar persons or places is important news to someone far from home.

The letters you write to friends should be narrative in style, not just a series of questions like: "How are you? How do you feel? How are the children?" But on the other hand, if you receive a letter containing a number of questions, be sure to answer them. For even the most intimate friends may be offended if the questions or comments contained in their letters are ignored. It's a good idea to keep all letters from friends until you have answered them. Reread each letter just before answering it, and try to give whatever news or information is requested.

WHAT NOT TO WRITE IN A FRIENDLY LETTER

Try not to discuss illness in your letters to friends—though, of course, if you or a member of your family has been seriously ill, you should certainly not try to conceal that fact. It's just as important to be truthful and straightforward in your letters as in your conversation. But don't go into a long and tedious discourse on the nature and treatment of the illness. Don't give all the unimportant and uninteresting details. That can be as boring as backing someone into a corner and telling him all about your operation!

Don't write at length about your children . . . except, perhaps, to a doting grandparent or to an intimate friend who has children of her own. Remember that the bright sayings of children never sound quite so bright outside the boundaries of their own indulgent homes. Nor does the average person care to read a long letter about Junior's first unintelligible word or his first amazing tooth. Save that kind of letter for grandma! She adores hearing about every detail of the baby's progress, but nobody else does.

It is not advisable to write of domestic difficulties or business reverses in the letters you write to friends. There may be occasions, of course, when you feel you must confide in someone—must write about your troubles to someone you know will sympathize and understand. But don't make it a practice to broadcast your personal affairs in your letters.

Don't discuss your servant problems in letters to friends, for such problems are of no interest to anyone but yourself. It may relieve your injured feelings to write a long tirade on your maid's insolence or incompetence; but it won't make an interesting or enjoyable letter. Furthermore, it's quite as bad taste to complain about servants in your letters as in your conversation . . . and as boring.

Always try to avoid bad news in your letters, if you can. But if you must give such news, tell it all. Don't hold back part of it, with the idea of sparing your friend as much as you can. That defeats its own purpose; for it can be very upsetting to receive bad news that is only half-told, that leaves a lot of disturbing questions unanswered.

Try also to avoid the impact of shock in the first sentence. If you have had an accident, for example, don't start off with a blunt statement of that fact, such as: "We had a bad accident in the car on the way back from Maine." It's much more thoughtful and considerate to write, "Well, we're back home again, after three wonderful weeks in Maine! It was the best vacation ever. We had a little more excitement than we bargained for, as we had an accident on the way home. But don't be alarmed as we are all fine! Nothing more than a few bruises and scratches to show for it. The car was badly damaged though . . ." and so on. Even in the case of a serious accident with major injuries to members of the party, the news can be eased into the letter without too much shock to the reader.

"We have just had the most terrible excitement; but thank God, everyone is safe and well. So don't be worried by the news in this letter," wrote blind Helen Keller to her friend, Mrs. Macy—telling of the fire that nearly destroyed her home and could easily have taken her life. "Everyone is safe and well . . . don't be worried . . ." she wrote, before even mentioning the fire.

CONSIDER THE PERSON
TO WHOM YOU ARE WRITING

No letter is a good letter if it fails to interest the reader. Therefore don't write exclusively about yourself, but *keep your correspondent in mind*. What are his interests, his hobbies? What exciting news can you give him? What would he most enjoy hearing about?

Naturally you wouldn't write the same kind of letter to a neighbor's teen-age boy away at school as you would to a dignified, elderly friend of the family. You must consider the person to whom you are writing. For people are different; their tastes and interests are different; and obviously the best letters are those written from the reader's point of view, with the reader's interests and problems in mind.

A boy likes an exciting letter, full of news. He enjoys hearing who won the local sports events—what his former friends are doing—little anecdotes about dogs, horses, pets—descriptions of unusual or interesting places and people.

A girl likes the same kind of letter, newsy and full of information . . . keyed, of course, to her own interests or hobbies. She especially likes to know what other girls of her age are doing, and what they have accomplished. She enjoys letters that tell her about hobbies or collections—about movies or movie stars—about parties or pretty clothes.

Women like to know about fashions, people, plays, books. Men are interested in sports, politics, business, world affairs. Older people love letters that tell them about the very young . . . letters that describe birthday parties, picnics, school plays, graduations, all the gay, exciting highlights of childhood. But the *really* old live a great deal in the past, and enjoy most the letters that tell about people and places they once knew . . . letters that bring back happy memories.

All people, young and old, like to feel important! Remember that, whenever you write a letter. People not only like to feel important, but they resent very much any implication that you consider yourself superior. So make it a point never to boast about yourself or your accomplishments in letters to friends. You'll write a much more successful letter if you *make your reader feel important*.

"What kind, beautiful souls live on this earth!" wrote the great composer, Tchaikovsky, to his beloved friend, Nadejda von Meck. "Meeting such people as you on the thorny road of life, one grows to feel that humanity is not as selfish and wicked as the pessimists say. . . . Among a million others, if such a one as you appears, it is enough to save a man from despair."

Surely that letter must have made Madame von Meck feel happy and proud! It must have made her feel very important.

HOW TO CLOSE YOUR LETTER

When you have said everything you want to say in a letter, take your leave promptly—but graciously. Don't tag on a lot of pointless remarks, like an uncertain visitor standing in the doorway ready to go but not quite knowing how to say "good-by." Remember what we said in an earlier chapter (page 28). It's a wonderful quality in letter writing to know what you want to say—to say it—*and to stop*.

Your closing sentence is important. As your last thought, it's likely to make a strong impact on your reader's mind, and remain long in his memory. So watch that closing sentence, and write it carefully! Try to avoid such offensive phrases as: "I must close now as I have something important to do" . . . "That's all for now, I'm in a big rush" . . . "I guess I'll close as there's nothing else to write." Such expressions are rude and abrupt, and are certainly no way to take leave of a friend. Avoid also any use of the phrase "In haste" as that clearly says you are busy, or bored, or impatient . . . that you want to get the letter over and done with.

Try to give your letter a gracious, a friendly, closing—like a handclasp and a smile. Let your last thought be, not of yourself, but of the person to whom you are writing. For example, "I'll write again very soon, Claire, and keep you informed of Bob's progress." Or, "I'll look up that recipe you want, Anne, and send it to you next time I write." Or, "I loved your letter, Bess, and I hope you'll write soon again!"

Here are some examples of interesting closing sentences, from the actual letters of famous people:

God bless you, dear Barbara—you are very precious to us.
                                                    George Eliot

Be happy, my dearest ones—I will write, be sure!
                                                    Elizabeth Browning

Heaven bless my love and take care of him!
                                                    Mary W. Godwin

Au revoir. I don't want to say 'Good-bye' because I don't want this letter to end. Devotedly yours.
                                                    Nadejda von Meck

You are everything to me.   *Sarah Bernhardt*

There never was a more generous, nor a kinder heart than yours. . . . Good night, my dear old friend.

Robert Southey

So come along; I will show you every nook and corner of my Paradise. *Anne Sullivan Macy*

EXAMPLES OF LETTERS
TO PERSONAL FRIENDS

When you sit down to write a letter to a friend, remember that the best letters are newsy, informal and easy to read. If possible they should take up where you left off in conversation with the person to whom you are writing.

Friendly Letter from One Man to Another

Dear Fred:

Remember that television set we were talking about, last time you were here? Well, Anne and I decided to give it to each other for our anniversary. It's being delivered next Monday. Now you can come and watch the basketball and hockey games with us . . . and maybe we'll see a little more of you than in the past!

By the way, I ran into Jim Ellis the other day. He's living right near you in Pelham, so I gave him your address and he said he'd get in touch with you. He's with the Bell Laboratories—some sort of research engineer, I think. He seems to know quite a lot about television, and he says I made a very good choice in my set.

Jim tells me his brother Pete just came back from Mexico City; he went there to open a branch office' for his company. Didn't you say that Chalmer-Holt was thinking of opening a branch office in Mexico? It might be a good idea to look up Pete Ellis and talk with him about it. You remember Pete, don't you? He was a junior the year we graduated, and he lived in the Delta Sigma Pi house right next to ours. I think he played end the year Bill Hickey was captain of the team. Anyway, he's a swell fellow—and I'm sure he'll be glad to tell you whatever you want to know about Mexico.

Have you read any good books lately? I just finished *The Cat's Claw*—a really creepy mystery, the kind you like. Perhaps you'd like to borrow it. That reminds me—you promised to lend me your copy of *The Lincoln Reader*. Will you bring it along next time you come? And make that real soon, Fred!

I'll phone you next week after the television set is installed. If it's working properly, I'd like you to come and watch the basketball game between City College and UCLA next Sunday night. It ought to be good!

How's your hay fever this year, Fred? Are you still taking the injections, or don't you need them any more? Anne doesn't seem to be bothered nearly as much this year as last. . . . Maybe it's because they cleared away a lot of the ragweed around here.

We're looking forward to seeing you next week, Fred. So don't get yourself all dated up! Best wishes from Anne,

Cordially,
Jack

Letters to Friends in Distant Places

Friends far from home are interested in everything that has happened in their absence. They want all the news, down to the last detail. Information about familiar people and places make any letter thrilling and exciting to receive.

Dear Paul:

Just wait till you hear all the news I have to tell you! So much has happened these past few weeks that I could fill a book telling you all about it.

In the first place, remember that big old red brick house at the top of Cornish Hill, where the Redfields used to live? Well, before the Redfields, the Pettys lived there—and it seems that *five generations* of Pettys lived right in that same house without changing the interior or the furnishings very much. Now the trustees of the estate are turning the house into a museum. I understand it's full of antiques that people will pay good money to see. They are going to call it the Petty Mansion; and with the money they charge for admission, they're planning to build a beautiful park around the house and grounds. Everyone in Cornish is delighted, of course.

And as though that weren't enough excitement for this sleepy little town, Fred Waters has just won ten thousand dollars in a prize-novel competition. You remember Fred, don't you? He used to be a reporter on the Cornish *Times*. Nobody ever dreamed he had any real talent . . . yet his book was judged the best of over a thousand manuscripts submitted! It's called *Late April* and it's about a girl who hated men until she was middle-aged, then suddenly went to the other extreme and became man-crazy. I haven't read it yet; but my brother Alex read it and liked it very much. I'm enclosing some clippings about it from the *Times*.

We had quite a little excitement here last week. On Tuesday evening, two men in a black sedan stopped at the Crystal Gas Station on Main Street and held up the attendant. They got away with over two hundred dollars. The very next day we had a mysterious fire. The Jenkins' house burned down—you know that beautiful old white Colonial house on Magpie Road. Nobody knows how the fire started; the Jenkinses were at the movies at the time and there was no one at home. Anyway, it burned right down to the ground and nothing was saved—not even one piece of furniture. The fire made too much headway before the alarm was turned in. I'm certainly sorry for the Jenkinses; they lost all their possessions, including the letters and pictures of their son who was killed in the war. Maybe they can replace the other things, but they can never replace those precious letters and pictures of their son.

Well, I guess I've given you all the news, Paul. . . . Oh, there's one thing more! The Stassons are selling their store and moving to Arizona. Their little boy (the one who has asthma) was very sick this winter and the doctor recommended a change of climate. They're leaving about the first of April.

When are you coming back to Cornish, Paul? Or are you getting to like Montreal so much that you don't want to come back? We all miss you very much; Alex says he hasn't had a decent game of tennis since you went away. I hope you took a lot of pictures this time, so that you can show us where you've been and all the interesting things you've done.

Write soon and let us know when we can expect you. So many people are always stopping Alex and me and asking, "When is Paul coming back?" Well, *when is he?*

Affectionate greetings from all the family,

> Cordially,
> Annette

Letters from Distant Places
to Friends Back Home

There is no better opportunity to demonstrate your ability as a letter writer than when you are far from home, viewing new sights and scenes, and writing to friends of your impressions and experiences. Don't fill your letter with a lot of nostalgic questions about home: "What's new at the office? Have you been busy? How's everyone?" That kind of letter is dull and uninspiring, whether it's written from romantic Bermuda or the Bronx! Try to make your reader see what *you* are seeing, through *your* eyes. Try to picture as clearly as you can whatever is new, exciting, different—so that the friend to whom you are writing can share in your experiences and in your enjoyment.

Dear Bess:

This is one time I wish I had the skill of a writer, so that I could really do justice to the exotic, almost incredible beauty of Hawaii! It's the most *heavenly* place I have ever been! I just don't know how to begin to describe it to you.

We are staying at the Royal Hawaiian Hotel in Honolulu until we can find a suitable house or apartment. Frank says it will take six months or more to establish a branch office, so we'll probably be here that long at least—maybe more. I don't mind (except that I'll miss my family and friends, of course!). I really love it here, Bess; and I know I'm going to have a marvelous time while Frank is busy organizing his office.

The Royal Hawaiian is a beautiful hotel. It's made of pink coral, and when you look at it from a distance —with the sun shining on it and the colorful gardens all around—it looks fabulous and unreal. It's right on the beach at Waikiki, and from our windows we can look out and see the long rolling breakers, the surf riders, Diamond Head in the distance.

Last week end Frank wasn't busy so he took me sightseeing. I was surprised to discover that Hawaii is just one of the islands, and that there's a whole chain of them. Honolulu, which is the capital, isn't even on the island of Hawaii, but on Oahu. Then there's Molokai, where the famous leper settlement is, Maui, Kauai, and some other smaller islands that I haven't learned to pronounce or spell as yet! An interesting thing about Maui is that when you look down on it from a plane, it looks exactly like the head and shoulders of a beautiful woman.

Frank took me to see the pineapple fields and the banana plantations; but I told him I was more interested in native life so he took me to a village on one of the smaller islands. It was very interesting. I saw how the natives spear fish, and weave baskets and eat poi with their fingers (though I have an idea most of it is an "act" put on for the benefit of tourists!). I understand there aren't many pure Hawaiians left; most of them have intermarried with Japanese and Americans, and few of the picturesque old customs and habits of the people are still observed.

But they still do the *real* hula here—a graceful and charming dance—not at all like the coarse and suggestive version of it you see on Broadway! We took movies of a group of Hawaiian girls doing the hula, and we'll show them to you when we get back. You'll see how lovely it is, and how utterly different from the popular idea of a hula dance.

I could go on and on, Bess, telling you of all the fascinating things we've done and seen in the short time we've been here. But I guess I'll just have to save some of it for my next letter. I *must* tell you one thing more, though: On Sunday we took what is called "the weirdest walk in the world"—right across the top of a volcano! It was weird, all right! We walked over what were once fiery, bubbling cauldrons of lava; but all the craters are now extinct, except one. That one is called Kilauea, and it's still very much alive! We walked right to the edge of it and looked down, and we could see the lava churning and boiling way down below. It gave me a sort of queer feeling, like standing at the edge of eternity. . . .

I won't even *try* to describe my feelings the day we visited Pearl Harbor! I thought of all those Jap planes sneaking in, blowing up our ships and killing so many people. It made me mad all over again to stand on the spot where it all happened and to picture how terrible it must have been.

But I really must end my letter now, Bess, or I'll go on forever! I'll write again soon, and be sure *you* write and tell me all the news. I'm enclosing some pictures of Honolulu; they'll tell you much better than I can how beautiful it is here.

Please remember me to your mother and sister. Frank sends best wishes to all of you.

> With love,
> Edith

Christmas Letter to a Friend

Any time is a good time to write a cheerful, friendly letter to someone far away. But remembering days and occasions important to others—not by means of printed sentiments, but by personal notes—touches the heartstrings and wins affection as nothing else can. Christmas and New Year are especially appropriate times to write to distant friends . . . to let them know that, however far away they may be, they are still very close to your heart.

Dear Ruth:

Here it is Christmas again . . . and you are still in California, and I am still in New York . . . with a whole continent between us! But you are as much in my thoughts today as though you were just around the corner. It would take far more than a continent between us to make me forget the many happy Christmases we had together, and the many pleasant memories we share.

Do you remember the Christmas party you had that first year you and Ed were married? Do you remember you had a big tree in the living room, and a tiny one right beside it—and everybody wondered why? Then you and Ed began opening the packages around the little tree and taking out booties, and mittens, and Teddy bears—and everybody knew you were going to have a baby! I always thought it was such a sweet way to announce it.

That was eleven years ago, Ruth. Your Judy must be quite a young lady now. And Jimmy was born the year you moved, so he must be seven. I wish I could see them; but I guess it will be a long time before Joe and I get to California.

Joe is just doing obstetrics now. He gave up general practice about a year ago, and I thought he'd be able to take it a little easier. But he is busier than ever, Ruth, and so conscientious that he won't go away even for a week end for fear a patient may need him and he won't be there!

Is Ed still with Technicolor? Did he ever get started on that history of the movies he was going to write? It seems such a long time since I've heard from you, Ruth—I *do* wish you'd let us know how you all are, and what interesting things you are doing.

But anyway, my dear—I just want you to know that we're thinking of you on Christmas day, and remembering all the good times we used to have, and wishing you weren't so very far away! Joe and I send our love to all the family—and the hope that you'll have a gay and merry Christmas, and a very happy New Year!

> Always affectionately yours,
> Leila

3. Family Letters

The same general rules that apply to *friendly* letters apply to *family* letters—except that in correspondence with members of the family, people are usually more intimate and informal, and more concerned with personal affairs.

Just be sure that you are never careless or thoughtless when writing to a member of your family. Try not to say anything in your letter that is ungracious or unkind. Make it a point never to write anything to a member of your family that you wouldn't or couldn't say directly to that person in conversation.

A good general rule to bear in mind is that you should never sit down and force yourself to write to a member of your family, merely because a letter is "due" and expected. But on the other hand, never ignore a letter from someone in your family who is worried about your health, or concerned about your welfare or progress. Such letters should be answered promptly and fully. It isn't kind to keep someone who cares about you waiting for information important to his or her peace of mind.

THE EVER-WELCOME LETTER FROM HOME

To children away at school or camp—to someone away on vacation, or living and working in a distant city—there are few things so eagerly welcomed and thoroughly enjoyed as a *letter from home*. A long, cheerful, news-filled letter makes any day a better day, gives a real lift to the spirits. Often a letter from home goes a long way to help dispel loneliness and banish the "blues."

When John Quincy Adams took office as Secretary of State, he wrote to his mother: "My spirits will often want the cordial refreshment of a letter from you. . . . Let me not thirst for them in vain!"

When Goethe was in Rome, he begged his mother: "Write to me soon and at length how you are, and whatever news there may be." For when one is far from home, "everything is interesting that concerns friends and dear ones!"

More than any other letter, perhaps, the letter from home should be in a blithe and happy mood. It should be full of simple, homey, familiar things. It should tell about the little incidents of daily life . . . and especially about anything unusual or interesting that may have happened. Whenever possible, clippings, cartoons, news items or snapshots should be enclosed—for they add greatly to the enjoyment of a letter from home.

Don't nag, scold, complain or find fault! Don't burden your distant relative with unnecessary tales of woe! Give all the news you can . . . and your affection . . . and the warmth of your familiar, well-loved personality. *But don't give the disappointment of a letter from home that is dull, boring, unpleasant or discouraging to read.*

One thing more: Although your letter to a relative away from home should be filled with news of family and friends, it should not concern itself *exclusively* with home affairs. Your letter should show unmistakable interest in the things your son, cousin, brother or aunt is doing . . . in his or her progress and well-being . . . the job, school, sports, hobbies, friends and other highlights of his life away from you.

Here are examples of letters from home—not intended as exact models, but to stimulate your imagination and give you ideas and suggestions to help you write interesting letters of your own:

To a Daughter Living and Working in Another City

Dearest Gail:

I was so very, very happy to get your nice long letter this morning! Thank you, darling, for not making me wait too long. I was so worried about that cold of yours; but now that I know you are completely better, I won't worry any more! Just don't go back to the office too soon . . . promise, darling? After all, you can write your scripts just as easily and well at home.

You'd be surprised to know how interested everybody is in your job. Folks keep stopping me all the time to ask about you. They want to know what shows you write, and whether thay can hear them on the air. I can't help feeling proud when I tell them about "Comets of Crime" and "Little Emmy." Their expressions are so funny when they say, *"Really? Does Gail write those famous shows?"* I guess it's hard for them to realize that the little tomboy they used to know is now a very serious-minded and successful radio writer!

That reminds me, dear: I met Mrs. Murray when I was out shopping yesterday, and she told me that Agnes is graduating this June and would like to get a job in an advertising agency. You know she had some experience writing radio commercials for the local stores. Mrs. Murray wondered if you could help her get a job, or at least tell her how to go about getting started. I said I didn't know, that Agnes would have to write to you herself. So you may get a letter from her one of these days. . . .

I'm sending you a blouse for your new suit, Gail. I know you can get anything you want in New York; but I happened to see this one in Grayson's window and it's just the kind you like—with a Peter Pan collar and long sleeves. It's a lovely, delicate shade of turquoise, with tiny pearl buttons, and I think it will go beautifully with your suit. But if you don't like it, return it and I'll take it back to Grayson's.

You asked about Martha. She doesn't expect her baby until the end of July. I just heard that the girls are planning a baby shower for her at Emily's house sometime next week—I don't know the exact date. But I thought you might like to send her something from New York. It would be a nice surprise for Martha, and I know it would please her very much. You could send it right to Emily, or send it to me and I'll have Bobby take it over the day of the shower.

Bobby is doing very much better in school now. He got 90 in his last Latin test—which only goes to prove he can get good marks when he tries. But I *do* think his eyes may have had something to do with it, Gail. He seems to be able to concentrate much better since he started wearing glasses. You know, that boy must have grown *two inches* since you saw him last. Why, he can actually wear dad's clothes now! He'll be taller than dad, I think. But I wish he would fill out—he's still as thin as a rail!

Dad is fine. The only thing that seems to be bothering him these days is that he's losing his hair. (And they say men aren't vain!) By the way, dad may have to fly to New York soon to see about that Borden property; if he does, I'll go with him and see for myself how you are.

Now take real good care of yourself, darling—and don't overdo it. You know how I worry when you aren't well! Your idea for a Television Theater is wonderful, and I'm sure it will be a great success; but must you do *everything* in such a hurry? Can't you take another week or two to work out your plans? There I go delivering a long-distance lecture! But I know how you *drive* yourself, dear—and I wish you would take things a little easier and try to get more rest.

Dad and Bobby send you their love. We all miss you, darling . . . I guess we'll *never* get used to seeing so little of our Gail! Your letters help, so write soon again.

> Devotedly,
> Mother

To a Husband Away on Business

Frank, dear:

You've been gone exactly two weeks today, but it seem more like two years to me! I've been so lonely without you.

But I'm glad to hear you had such a successful trip this time. That order you got in Detroit is simply *marvelous!* I don't blame you for being so elated about it.

Are you coming directly home, dear, or do you plan to make some stops on the way? I hope you'll be home in time for Patsy's birthday party next Sunday. She's counting on you to show movies to her little friends. But if you can't make it, I'll get my brother to come in for an hour or so—he knows how to work the projector.

Patsy keeps asking every day when you'll be back. She says you never finished that story you were telling her about the train that lost its "toot." You better hurry and think up a good ending for it—you know how Patsy is! She won't be happy until she knows exactly what happened to the "toot" and how the little train got it back again!

Everything at home is fine (except that we miss you so much!). I've been busy with the spring cleaning. Yesterday I had Cora come in to wash the kitchen walls, and she did a very good job of it. The kitchen looks as though it's been repainted. I made some new yellow curtains, and they look real pretty—if I do say so myself!

The weather here has been lovely, Frank. It's almost like summer today, balmy and warm. I let Patsy go to school with just a little sweater on instead of her coat. Everything's beginning to get green, and before you know it your favorite magnolia tree will burst into bloom. I can see it beginning to stir and waken already. . . .

I went to see your mother yesterday. Her cold is all gone, and she looks very well. Your sister Jean looks wonderful! She took off about fifteen pounds since she began dieting, and it's very becoming. But now she's complaining that none of her clothes fit!

Let me know exactly what day you'll be home, dear. I want to have your favorite dinner . . . including pineapple upside-down cake! And make it *soon*, because Patsy and I are very lonely for daddy.

Love and kisses to you, darling—

Lynn

To a Married Sister
Living at a Distance

Dear Beth:

Tomorrow is your birthday, and here you are a thousand miles away! I certainly wish you lived a little closer, so we could see each other more often. It's not much fun when a favorite sister marries and goes off to another part of the country!

But anyway, "Happy Birthday, darling!" . . . even though I can't give you twenty-six whacks and an extra one for good luck. I send twenty-six kisses instead, and an extra kiss to wish you luck, happiness

and everything good—not just for next year, but for
always!

Mother and dad have sent you something special for
your birthday. I'm not going to tell you what it is, but
I know you'll be thrilled. I sent *my* gift last week, and
no doubt you have received it by now. I hope you like
it. Janey is embroidering a bridge cloth for you . . .
but you know Janey! She'll probably finish it by
Christmas. It's very pretty, though; it's yellow, and it
has hearts, clubs, spades and diamonds embroidered in
the corners in red. Janey's proud as punch of her
handiwork, and she shows it to everyone who comes
into the house. "It's for my married sister in Boston,"
she tells everybody.

She's a brat, Beth—but an awfully cute one! Do you
know what she did the other day? She sneaked an
atomizer and a bottle of "Blue Heaven" out of my
room and sprayed her cat! She said Tansy didn't smell
nice, the way a ladycat should. Poor Tansy! Mother
wouldn't let her in the house for two days. And now
I can't use "Blue Heaven" because it reminds me of the
way Tansy smelled and I get sick to my stomach!

I'm still with Colton-Fisher; but one of these days
I'm going to tell J.C. just what I think of him . . .
and walk out. I don't know why I put up with his
tempers and tantrums. Dad wants me to leave and take
that job Uncle Ed offered me, but I don't like the idea
of working for a relative. Just between you and me, I
wish I could meet someone like Henry and get married. Or is it unladylike to admit anything like that,
even to a sister?

Do you think you'll be coming for a visit soon,
Beth? I wish you would! I know it's difficult for Henry
to get away, but couldn't you leave him just for a little
while? Your old room is a handsome guest room now,
with new lamps and draperies and even a chaise longue
by the window! But the only guest we ever want in it
is *you*.

Write soon and tell us all the news. Is Henry just as
busy as ever? I'm enclosing an editorial about the
United Nations which dad clipped out of the paper
this morning. He thought Henry might enjoy reading

it. I'm also enclosing the recipe for Baked Alaska that you wanted mother to send. She says to be sure and let her know how it turns out.

Many happy returns, darling—from all of us!

With love,
Kay

LETTERS TO CHILDREN AWAY AT SCHOOL AND CAMP

Boys and girls away from home *don't* like "preachy" letters —letters that warn, scold, find fault and endlessly criticize.

A letter that makes a child feel unhappy or discouraged fails in its purpose, whatever that purpose may be. It isn't necessary to preach or scold; a point can be made tactfully—and often a great deal more effectively—by relating an incident or telling a story. After all, children are personalities in their own right. They resent being talked down to as inferiors . . . and are often made moody and dispirited by the wrong kind of letter from home.

Bear these facts in mind when writing to your boy or girl at school. Remember that your letters are tremendously important, and can have lifelong influence on your child's character and personality. Try to write on a *basis of equality*, not as a parent alone but as a friend and confidant. Avoid writing in anger or impatience—whatever your child may have done or however he may have failed you. It may relieve your feelings to threaten and scold, but surely that is not the important thing! The important thing is the effect of your words upon the child, his spiritual and emotional response to them. *No letter is a good letter that makes a child feel resentful or unhappy*.

So be sure any letter you write to a son or daughter away at school is a friendly letter, warm with affection and understanding. Be sure it's an *encouraging* letter, showing utmost faith in the child . . . even when stern correction or reproof is necessary.

Dearest Joel:

I went to Brentano's this morning to get the books you wanted, and when I got back I found your letter waiting for me. Thank you, dear, for writing so promptly! I was anxious to know how you came out in your exams, and I'm delighted to hear that you did so well. But I knew you would, Joel. . . . I have every confidence in you, and I know you will always apply yourself to your studies and try to be near the top of your class.

If you only knew how happy your letters make me! This last one is especially interesting—just the kind of letter I love to get from you—all about your work at school, and your friends. It's a wonderful letter, Joel— almost like having *you* here in the room with me for a little while!

I can just imagine how thrilled you are to be on the football team. Dad will be very pleased when he hears about it. No doubt he'll write and tell you so himself tonight, after he reads your letter. Yes, you may get whatever equipment you need, Joel. I agree with you that it's better to buy things like that in Exeter rather than send them from New York. You really have to try them on to get the proper size. So just get what you need, dear, and have the store send the bill home.

Don't worry about your fish—I'm taking very good care of them. I feed them regularly every morning, and I always put the food in the little glass ring, just the way you showed me. Yesterday when I went to feed them—guess what? There were about a dozen tiny new babies scooting around. I got them right out and put them into another tank before the big fish could eat them. They're awfully cute, Joel; but I can't yet tell just what they are. They look like guppies, but dad says they might be platties or swordtails. When they're a little bigger we'll be able to tell what they are, and I'll write and let you know.

Did you know that Dennis Thompson is a tropical-fish fan now? I guess you got him started with that pair of gold guppies you gave him last time you were home. He was here the other day to look up something in your Innes book, and he didn't stop talking about the pair of Siamese fighting fish his father gave him for his birthday. I remember how excited *you* were the first time you got a pair of them!

Clare is going riding again on Saturday in Central Park. You wouldn't know your sister, Joel—she's grown so much in the past two months! In fact, she has outgrown her riding breeches, so she's using your old jodhpurs now—the ones you had at camp, remember? I had them cleaned and they fit her perfectly. I bought her a new green jacket to go with the jodhpurs, and she looks *adorable* in the outfit! Clare misses you very much, dear. . . . I wish you would write to her once in a while. I tell her that your letters are for *all* of us, but she's always disappointed when the mail comes and there's nothing for her. If you could hear how wistfully she asks, "Didn't Joel write to me?"—I'm sure you would send her a letter every now and then, even if it's only a few words.

I do hope you won't let football practice interfere with your school work, now that you're on the team. But I'm sure you are too sensible for that! Dad and I want you to do the best you can in whatever you undertake, and we'll be proud and happy if you distinguish yourself in football or any other sport. But not at the expense of your studies! We hope you will continue the fine progress you have been making and not let your enthusiasm for football take too much of your time and effort.

I am sending you a box of those peanut cookies you like so much. In your next letter be sure to let me know if there is anything you need, like socks or underwear.

My love to you, dear . . . and many thanks for your nice long letter. I'll be eagerly waiting for the next one!

Devotedly,
Mother

Dear Paul:

Your marks have just come, and by George—I'm delighted! You really have worked hard, haven't you? I must say I'm very pleased with the steady improvement you have shown, especially in Latin and Math.

Now I'm not saying that a 70 in Latin is *good*— don't misunderstand me! But it's certainly a lot better than the failing mark you got last time; and it shows that you are really trying. That's the important thing to me. As long as you keep trying and improving, I'll be satisfied.

That was a fine mark you got in history, Paul. And 90 in English is better than your last rating in that subject. But I'm especially pleased with your showing in Latin, because you've been failing in it right along. I think the trouble has been that you dislike and *resent* Latin, and therefore have trouble concentrating on it. Naturally it's easier to concentrate on subjects you enjoy and find interesting.

You know, Paul, I'd feel much worse if you had difficulty with a subject like science or math. After all, such subjects require *intelligence*. But a fellow doesn't need much intelligence to master Latin! It's just a matter of memorizing, as I've told you in the past. All that's necessary is to buckle down to the job and lick it. That's what you are apparently doing now . . . and that's why I'm so pleased with you.

Everything at home is fine. Your mother is well, and very happy about the good report from school. She says to tell you she sent your hockey stick yesterday; you should receive it in plenty of time for the practice game on Saturday.

The girls are trying to teach Sinbad some tricks, but without much success. I must say he's a most uncooperative pup! All he wants to do is chase cats and chew bedroom slippers. But the girls are determined to keep at it until they teach him how to beg and "play dead." They read about a dog in England that can talk, and they say Sinbad ought to be able to do *something*.

Take good care of yourself, Paul. Your mother and I may drive up to see you soon. In the meantime, we all send you our love—and we hope you keep up the good work!

Affectionately,
Dad

Dear Tommy:

How are you getting along at camp? I hope you are having fun, and enjoying your friends and all the activities.

So you passed the "crib" test! That's fine, son. Now you'll be able to swim out in the lake. Your mother and I are very proud of you for learning to swim so quickly—and so well.

We miss you very much at home. But it is a good thing you are away, as it is stifling here and very unpleasant. We will come to see you next week end, and mother would like to know if there is anything you want us to bring along.

We are all fine. Your baby sister is getting fat and chubby, and very pretty. She keeps mother busy, which is a good thing—otherwise she'd miss you too much!

Next time you write, Tommy, tell us more about what you do at camp. Have you been on any hikes with your group? Are you learning how to play tennis? We enjoy hearing about all the interesting and exciting things that go to make up your day at camp.

So write again soon, son, and make it a real long letter next time!

Affectionately,
Dad

EXCERPTS FROM LETTERS TO CHILDREN
WRITTEN BY FAMOUS PEOPLE

Often it is interesting and helpful to read what others have written. We have included, therefore, the following excerpts from letters to children, written by famous men and women:

The object most interesting to me for the residue of my life will be to see you developing daily those principles of virtue and goodness which will make you valuable to others and happy in yourself, and acquiring those talents and that degree of science which will guard you at all times against ennui, the most dangerous poison of life. A mind always employed is always happy. This is the true secret, the grand recipe, for felicity. . . . Be good and be industrious, and you will be what I shall most love in the world. Adieu, my dear child.

Thomas Jefferson to his motherless 14-year-old daughter, Martha, in a convent near Paris.

Finish every day and be done with it. . . . You have done what you could; some blunders and absurdities no doubt crept in; forget them as soon as you can. Tomorrow is a new day.

> *Ralph Waldo Emerson to his young daughter at school.*

Your letter, my dearest niece, with the one before it, came quite safely, for which I return many thanks and kisses. I rejoice too, dear Dolly, to see how well you write and express yourself, and am as proud of all your acquirements as if you were my own daughter.

> *Dolly Madison, to her beloved niece and namesake, age 16.*

Great learning and superior abilities, should you ever possess them, will be of little value and small estimation . . . unless virtue, honor, truth and integrity are added to them.

> *Abigail Adams to her 10-year-old son, John Quincy Adams, later the sixth President of the United States.*

If anybody would make me the greatest king that ever lived, with palaces, and gardens, and fine dinners, and wine, and coaches, and beautiful clothes, and hundreds of servants, on condition that I would not read books —I would not be a king. I would rather be a poor man in a garret with plenty of books than a king who did not love reading.

> *Thomas Macaulay to his niece, Margaret Trevelyan, age 7.*

My own little darling! I found a nice letter of yours waiting for me here, and hope to have another by the next mail. You cannot think what pleasure they give me. They are just as I love to have you write, telling me what you have seen that amused you, and where you have been.

> *James Russell Lowell to his daughter, Mabel, age 7*

I am delighted to have you play football. I believe in rough, manly sports. But I do not believe in them if they degenerate into the sole end of any one's existence. I don't want you to sacrifice standing well in your studies . . . and I need not tell you that character counts for a great deal more than either intellect or body in winning success in life.

> *Theodore Roosevelt to his*
> *son, Ted, away at school.*

FROM A BRIDE TO HER PARENTS
ON HER HONEYMOON

Dear Mother and Dad:

I wish you could see Boca Raton! It is fabulously beautiful. Tom and I just couldn't have picked a more perfect place for our honeymoon! We know now why it is called a "Secret Paradise."

I'm so happy, darlings! Tom is a wonderful, *wonderful* husband. I know that the magic and beauty of this past week, our first week together, will always remain with me. It can never fade, not if I live to be a hundred!

Does that sound sentimental? Well, I *am* sentimental today. It's our anniversary, you know. Tom and I have been married exactly one whole week!

Wasn't the wedding beautiful? Thank you, mother and dad. . . . I'll never forget it! It's the kind of wedding I always dreamed about, ever since I was a little girl. You looked *lovely,* mother! I do hope the pictures turn out well.

I know you both like guava jelly, so we sent you a big jar of it yesterday—right from the hotel. I hope it arrives safely and that you enjoy it.

There's a linen shop here and we bought ourselves a lovely dinner cloth. . . . It's such fun buying things together for our own home! Tom and I are thrilled with all the marvelous wedding gifts we got. I've been trying to write notes of thanks for some of the things that came just before we left; but it's no use. Boca

Raton is so enchanting, and there's so much to see and do and enjoy, that I can't concentrate on *anything* but having fun and being happy!

I'm not going to try to describe Boca Raton because I know I can't do justice to it. I'm enclosing some cards instead. They show the magnificent fountain and gardens in front of the hotel—the famous Cloister Lounge —the swimming pool and the patio—the golf course and Cabana Club. Tom is taking a lot of pictures to show you when we get back. There was a professional tennis match yesterday between Vincent Richards and William Tilden, and Tom took movies of it. He also took movies of Arthur Murray and one of his instructors doing the rumba.

I'll write again in a few days. My husband—your nice new son-in-law—sends his love. Write to us soon!

> Devotedly,
> Lenore

LETTER TO A RELATIVE WHO
HAS ASKED FOR ADVICE

When a relative writes and asks for advice, give it honestly and sincerely—and to the best of your ability. Make it the subject of your entire letter. Don't cloud the issue by writing about a number of other matters.

Dear Joe:

You asked for my advice and I am going to give it to you: *This is not the time to start a new business.* I think you should wait until conditions are better, until the downward spiral is stopped and the prospect for small new businesses is more promising.

I'd like to quote to you from an editorial in this morning's *Wall Street Journal*. It says: "The death rate among businesses this year will climb like a kite in a spanking spring breeze! . . . Only a miracle can pull a number of new small businesses, particularly retail establishments, through the new year without a collapse."

So there's the answer to your question, Joe. You'd be taking a big chance; and I don't think you have the right to take that chance with Martha seriously ill and young Joe about ready for college.

Now I'm not saying you should stay in the groove indefinitely. I don't think any man should let himself get into a rut of living or thinking. I believe in change, and I understand fully the impulse that makes you want to strike out against regimentation and find new interest and adventure in a business of your own.

But this just isn't the time for it, Joe! So I say *wait* . . . perhaps six months, or a year, or maybe even longer. Be patient, and make your plans; then when the time comes you'll be ready. And *I'll* be ready then, too, Joe—to help you financially and in any other way I can.

If you want to talk this over more fully, I'll be glad to meet you for lunch some day next week. But I strongly advise against trying to buck the trend.

Agnes and I send affectionate greetings to all the family. We hope Martha will soon be well and strong again.

Sincerely
Don

4. Love Letters

There are few letters more eagerly awaited, more joyously received, than love letters. They banish lonely hours, reassure lonely hearts. They keep the precious glow alive, and sustain devotion when loved ones are apart.

"What cannot letters inspire?" asks Heloise of Abelard in one of the most passionate and enduring of all the love letters of history. "They have souls; they can speak; they have in them all that force which expresses the transports of the heart; they have all the fire of our passions, they can raise them as much as if the persons themselves were present; they have all the tenderness and the delicacy of speech, and sometimes even a boldness of expression beyond it."

The most essential quality of a love letter is *sincerity*. And to be sincere, it must come from the heart, spontaneously. It must be a simple and unaffected expression of your feelings. It may be impulsive, restrained, romantic, gay, sad, impassioned, boastful, pleading, jubilant or despairing. It may be any or all of these. But whatever else it is or is not, *it must be sincere*. It must ring true.

Therefore love letters should follow no set rules. They should be unstudied and unstilted. They should be fresh and alive. So write what you truly think and feel; write what you want to say . . . what you want your loved one to know . . . not in flowery or poetic language, but in simple words that come from the heart.

Don't be ashamed of your sentiments when you write a love letter. Don't be embarrassed or constrained by your feelings. *Write as the heart dictates*.

Just be careful not to write anything that can be misunderstood or misconstrued. And never be guilty of saying anything in a love letter that you would be mortified to have others see . . . anything that's shocking or offensive. There need be no sacrifice of good taste to achieve sincerity and an honest expression of your deepest feelings and emotions.

EXAMPLES OF LOVE LETTERS
FROM WOMEN TO MEN

Dearest Tom:

It's wonderful to get a nice long letter from you, first thing every morning. It starts my day right! Thank you, darling. . . . Did anyone ever tell you that you're a pretty grand person?

Your letter this morning is sweet. But don't be jealous, dear! You have no reason to be. I love only you— and shall never love anyone else, *ever!*

My sister is having an anniversary party next Saturday and she wants us to come. I told her you had tickets for the ice show, but she was so disappointed that I promised I'd at least *ask* if you wanted to return them and go to her party instead. Do you, dear? Now don't say "yes" unless you really want to! It doesn't matter to me—I'll be happy and content either way, as long as I'm with you.

There I go talking in song titles again! *"As long as I'm with you. . . ."* Remember? It was on the air the other night, and we listened to it together. I think it's a lovely song, and the words sound almost as though they were written for us. I feel as though *I* could write the lyrics for a love song, Tom—I'm so thrilled and happy, and so "filled with dreams for two!"

But now you'll think I'm being sentimental and silly. . . . Well, maybe I am, darling! That's what being in love with you does to me.

Are you still so busy, dear? You didn't say in your letter whether you are still working late, like last week. You must be glad that Keenan case is settled at last. It certainly dragged on and on and *on!*

I have a new dress for Saturday night. It's red, and I bought it especially for you! Let me know about the party soon, Tom, so I can tell my sister whether or not we'll be there.

Good-by now, darling. . . . Don't ever stop loving me!

> Devotedly,
> Lou

Dear Fred:

It's easy to say I forgive you. The fault was as much mine as yours. Sometimes I'm too quick to take offense where none was intended. Dad's always telling me I'm too sensitive, only *he* calls it "thin-skinned!" He says it's a trait I must learn to control or I'll never be happy. I guess he's right. . . .

Of course I love you, Fred! And not "just a little." I love you *deeply,* and with all my heart. I'm sure you must know that, dear. I was miserable after our quarrel, and I've been longing all week to see you and straighten things out.

Wouldn't you like to come here for dinner on Sunday instead of going out somewhere? The folks are going to a church bazaar, and we'd have a nice long afternoon to talk and listen to records. I'd enjoy that,

Fred. . . . We could go out somewhere in the evening if you want to.

I'll be waiting for your call on Friday at the usual time. I'm so glad you wrote, darling. Don't ever stop loving me!

Kate

EXAMPLES OF LETTERS
FROM MEN TO WOMEN

Dearest Sally:

It's June first. That means our wedding is only three weeks away! I'm so happy, I just can't think of anything else.

Isn't it marvelous, my sweet, that with all the millions and millions of people in the world, you and I should have met . . . and fallen in love . . . and now we'll soon be married! Or do you think it was all planned that way, long ago—perhaps even before we were born?

Anyway, precious, I think I'm the luckiest man in the world! I'm going to devote my life to making you happy. *I promise.*

Darling, we really should decide between Lake George and Lake Placid right away—otherwise we're likely to spend our honeymoon in little old New York! I'm enclosing the booklets you asked me to send. Will you look them over right away, and decide which it will be? Then let me know and I'll wire for reservations. Phone me as soon as you can, pet—we should have attended to this long ago! But there's always my brother's hunting lodge in Canada, if we can't get reservations elsewhere. Bob's been asking me for weeks if we wouldn't like to use it for our honeymoon.

I'll help you address the announcements this week end. Don't try and do them all by yourself. As for the notes of thanks—just write as many as you can, Sally. The rest can wait until we get back and are in our own home.

"Our own home. . . ." Doesn't that sound wonderful, sweetheart! I wonder if you are as happy as I am. I know we're going to have a marvelous life together, Sally. . . . I love you more than I ever dreamed it would be possible to love anyone!

Love me too, precious! Don't ever *stop* loving me! You are the most important thing in life to me now—you know that, don't you?

All my love and a million kisses!

Don

Dearest:

Only a few more days, and I'll be home! I'm counting the hours, my sweet, and I hope they *fly*. Every hour is an eternity when I'm away from you. I think there ought to be a law against sending a man away from his wife for weeks at a time!

This has been a very successful trip, darling. I signed up more than fifty new dealers in the Chicago area alone. Peterson is going to be very pleased when he sees my report.

But *I'll* be very pleased when I'm *home!* That's all I can think of right now. It seems like months since I saw you, sweetheart. Does it seem like that to you, too? Or have you been so busy with your music that you haven't even missed me? See—I love you so much I'm even jealous of your music!

I bought you something very nice in Chicago, but I'm not going to tell you what it is. I'll give you a hint, though. It's something to wear, and it's something you have wanted for a long time. . . .

I'll probably leave here on Thursday—or Friday at the very latest. I'll wire when I know what plane I'm taking. Don't have any guests, precious. I want to have dinner with you alone the first night I'm home.

Do you love me? More than anyone?

Devotedly,
Chris

EXCERPTS FROM THE LOVE LETTERS
OF FAMOUS MEN AND WOMEN

I am very uneasy, my love, at receiving no news of you; write me quickly four pages—pages full of agreeable things which shall fill my heart with the pleasantest feelings. I hope before long to crush you in my arms and cover you with a million kisses.

Bonaparte to Josephine

I am a prisoner here in the name of the King; they can take my life, but not the love that I feel for you. . . . No, nothing has the power to part me from you! Our love will last as long as our lives.

Voltaire to Olympe Dunoyer

Adèle, my adorable and adored Adèle! I have been asking myself every moment if such happiness is not a dream. . . . At last you are mine! Soon—in a few months, perhaps, my angel will sleep in my arms, will awaken in my arms. . . . My Adèle!

Victor Hugo to Adèle Foucher

I always think of you and I have a thousand things to say to you. The most important . . . is that *I love you to distraction, my dear wife!*

Heinrich Heine to his wife

How I love you! Rising in the morning, my first thought is of you, and all day I am conscious that you are near; your presence seems to inhabit all the air about me . . . your nearness is a never-ending delight!

Nadejda von Meck to Tchaikovsky

Paris is a morgue without you. Before I knew you, it was Paris, and I thought it heaven; but now it is a vast desert of desolation and loneliness.

Sarah Bernhardt to Victorien Sardou

POSTSCRIPT ON
PERSONAL LETTER WRITING

During the last war, millions of letters were sent overseas—to husbands, brothers, sweethearts, sons. These letters went to men facing danger and death, to men who were lonely, homesick, often hungry and cold . . . and sometimes in agony. To many these letters brought hope and cheer and gladness. To many these letters brought joy and peace.

But not to all.

For some letters from home were *thoughtless* letters, filled with bitterness and complaint. Some letters from home were *selfish* letters . . . some were careless, impulsive, even unkind . . . letters filled with anguish and longing, with heartbreak and tears.

The world, for the moment, is at peace. But there are today, and always will be, men and women far from home, lonely and homesick as any soldier . . . and as eagerly waiting for news of loved ones. A letter that increases such loneliness, or that thoughtlessly adds worry to it, *is a letter that betrays love and trust.*

So when you write to a husband, sweetheart or son far from home—*write with courage and cheer.* Never mind your own feelings. Think of the person who is to receive your letter. Think of *his* reactions, of *his* feelings. Don't tell him how lonely you are . . . what a difficult time you are having . . . how bad conditions are at home. Write of *pleasant* things, of gay and intimate and "homey" things. Write to make him feel happier and more content.

Book IV

*

Your Business
and
Club Correspondence

* * *

1. The General Rules of Business Correspondence

A very large part of the business of the world is conducted by means of correspondence. Therefore it is extremely important to be able to write good business letters—letters that represent one's self and one's firm to best advantage.

No intelligent, forward-thinking business man would long tolerate a rude, careless or untidy salesman or representative. Yet thousands of letters go out every day that reflect discredit upon the firm they represent, letters that antagonize as surely as an offensive or bad-mannered individual. Such letters can do more harm than good, for often they destroy the very confidence and good will they seek to establish and maintain.

Before all else, therefore, consider the physical aspects of your business correspondence. Take pride in the letters you send out, just as you take pride in your own appearance. Sign and send out only letters that are well typed, well spaced, faultlessly neat and inviting to the eye . . . *letters that make a good first impression.* Here are the essential qualities that go to make up an attractive, well-groomed business letter:

1. *Good Quality Stationery*

It is advisable to use the best quality of paper you can for business correspondence. Single sheets of plain white bond paper are the best, unruled, with the letterhead printed or engraved in black. The most convenient size, and the size most generally used, is 8½ x 11 inches—though some firms now use 7¼ x 10½ inch paper for general correspondence.

The letterhead should contain the name of the firm, the address, and the nature of the business (unless the name itself gives that information). Telephone numbers, cable addresses, branch addresses and other such data may be included in the letterhead; but there should be no ornate advertising material on letterheads used for general correspondence.

Envelopes, of course, should match the letterhead in quality and weight; and any printing or engraving that appears on the envelope should conform with that on the letter sheet. Standard size envelopes are 6½ or 6¾ x 3½ inches. The large official or legal size envelopes is 10 x 4½ inches.

Quality and dignity should be the distinguishing characteristics of your business stationery. Never use loud, effeminate, highly tinted, bizarre, odd-shaped or in any way unconventional stationery for the general run of routine business letters. Such stationery is an affectation and in bad taste . . . more likely to antagonize the reader than to win his confidence and respect.

2. *Neat Typing*

All business correspondence should be typed, and at least one carbon copy made and kept on file. Whether you type the letters yourself or have them typed for you, be sure they are faultlessly neat and clean—without smudges, finger marks or erasures—otherwise they will not represent you to best advantage. Never be guilty of sending out over your signature a letter that is soiled, creased or torn, or that is in any way marred or unsightly. Avoid worn typewriter ribbons, as they produce an uneven effect that is certainly not appealing to the eye. And always keep the type of your machine shining bright and clean; for blurred type is not only difficult to read, but is very likely to smudge and spoil the appearance of your letter.

3. *Even Spacing*

No letter can look attractive if it is carelessly spaced and arranged. Whether long or short, your business letter should present an even, well-balanced appearance—neither crowded at the top of the page nor sitting lopsidedly on one side of it. Try to estimate the length of your letter and visualize its position on the page *before you begin to type it.* Then plan your margins accordingly, so that they provide an even frame or setting for your letter . . . making it look well placed and properly balanced on the page.

Bear in mind that wide margins make your letter more readable and inviting; so if your letter is a very long one, plan on using *two* sheets instead of crowding it all on one. The second sheet should be of the same size and quality as the first, but without the letterhead. When such additional sheets are used for a letter, they should be numbered at the top, either in the center of the page or in the right-hand corner. But don't use an additional sheet for only one or two concluding lines of a letter; in that case it's better to try and get it all on the preceding page. Never continue a business letter on the *back* of the sheet, using both sides of the letterhead.

Most business letters are single-spaced, with double spaces between the paragraphs. However very short letters look better when they are double-spaced, with either double or triple spaces between the paragraphs. The paragraphs may be indented or not, as preferred. But if they are indented, they should all line up exactly the same distance from the margin. Don't start one paragraph a half-inch from the margin, another an inch or more from the margin—as that gives your letter a careless and untidy appearance.

4. *Short Paragraphs*

All letters—but especially business letters—should look easy to read and inviting to the eye. As long wordy blocks of type are anything but inviting, make an effort to keep your sentences and paragraphs *short*. Use a new paragraph for each new thought or idea, and express that thought as simply and briefly as you can.

Whatever the purpose of your letter, it has a much better chance of achieving that purpose if short, swift-moving sentences and short, swift-moving paragraphs make it easier to look at and more inviting to read.

5. *Correct Grammar, Spelling and Punctuation*

Last but not least of our five essentials for an attractive, well-groomed business letter is *accuracy*. No letter should ever be permitted to go out with a misspelled word, a typographical error, or an incorrectly or poorly constructed sentence. This may seem comparatively unimportant to you at the moment, if you happen to be more concerned with the tone and spirit of your letter and what you want it to accomplish for you. But make no mistake about it! Poor grammar, misspelled words, lack of punctuation or the improper use of it, prejudice the reader against you and help to destroy the effectiveness of your letter.

So don't take chances! These, at least, are faults you can easily avoid. If you are uncertain about the spelling of a word, or the grammatical use of a word, *look it up.* It pays to check each letter carefully before it goes out and correct any errors that may cost you the confidence and respect of your correspondent.

The proper use of punctuation is especially important, for it helps to clarify and emphasize your thoughts, and makes your letter easier and more pleasant to read.

THE PARTS OF A BUSINESS LETTER

Every well-constructed business letter is made up of six parts. These are:

1. THE HEADING
     which in a business letter is the *date only,* as the address is in the letterhead
2. THE INSIDE ADDRESS
     which is the name and address of the person to whom the letter is written
3. THE SALUTATION
     which is the complimentary greeting
4. THE BODY OF THE LETTER
     which is the subject matter or message
5. THE CLOSE
     which is the complimentary conclusion or "good-by"
6. THE SIGNATURE
     which may include the official capacity in which the letter is written

This is the same general structure or form as the social letter, discussed in an earlier chapter.* The only difference is in the use of an *Inside Address,* which always appears on business letters but is not ordinarily used in social correspondence. The position of the *Inside Address* may be either, as indicated above, immediately preceding the salutation; or it may be written at the end of the letter, below the signature, in the lower left-hand corner.

The following outline shows the six parts of a business letter:

* For a detailed analysis of the parts of a letter, see pages 25 to 41.

1. HEADING   November 10, 19—

2. INSIDE   Mr. Martin L. Schiff
       ADDRESS   45 Broadway
                       New York, N.Y.

3. SALUTATION   Dear Mr. Schiff:

4. BODY   Thank you very much for your offer to co-
                       operate with us on the Wendell case.

                             We shall keep you informed as to the prog-
                       ress of the case, and call upon you when your
                       testimony is needed.

                             Mr. Davis will be in New York on Decem-
                       ber first, and he will telephone you for an ap-
                       pointment.

5. CLOSE   Very truly yours,

6. SIGNATURE

                                                John B. Brandt

                                                John B. Brandt

   Business letters are almost always written on business letterheads giving the name and address of the firm, and as a rule the
nature of the business. The heading of the letter therefore consists only of the date, as shown in the outline above. But if
paper without a letterhead is used, the heading should include
the address—as follows:

                       20 Wall Street
                       New York, N.Y.
                       December 5, 19—

The heading may be either in *block* form, as above—or in *step*
form, with each line indented:

                       20 Wall Street
                         New York, N.Y.
                           December 5, 19—

   In general, it's best not to use abbreviations of cities or
states, unless they are well-known and familiar like N.Y., N.J.,
Mass., etc. The name of the month should always be spelled
out in full. When in doubt as to whether or not to abbreviate

anything in a letter—*don't*. Even though abbreviations may be clear and understandable, they lack distinction. A letter in which all words are spelled out is always more dignified and attractive-looking.

Try to have the beginning of the date and the beginning of the complimentary close line up exactly, as that makes your letter look more evenly balanced on the page.

THE INSIDE ADDRESS

The inside address should be the same as the name and address on the envelope. It should be in line with the left-hand margin; and although it may be either in *step* or *block* form, the latter is preferred. The amount of space between the date and the inside address depends on the length of the letter. Commas may be used between lines or not, as your prefer; the tendency today is to omit punctuation at the ends of the lines.

All the following forms of inside address are correct and in general use:

1. To a specific individual in a firm

> Mr. Frederick B. Whalen
> Middletown Oil Company
> 416 Main Street
> Middletown, Oklahoma

2. To a specific individual, giving his title or position

> Mr. John Haley, Cashier
> Ajax Lumber Company
> 240 Broadway
> New York, N.Y.

3. To an anonymous official in the firm

> Advertising Manager
> Holton-Peet Company
> 50 State Street
> Chicago, Illinois

4. To the firm itself, to be opened by anyone

> Holton-Peet Company
> 50 State Street
> Chicago, Illinois

5. To the firm, attention of a specific individual

> Ajax Lumber Company
> 240 Broadway
> New York, N.Y.

> Attention of the Cashier
> *or*
> Attention of Mr. John Haley

The "attention" line should be centered above the body of the letter, and it may or may not be underscored.

As previously mentioned, the inside address is sometimes placed at the end of the letter instead of the beginning . . . especially in official correspondence. In this case, the correct position is about two to four lines below the signature, to the left, in line with the margin.

THE SALUTATION

The salutation immediately precedes the body of the letter and lines up evenly with the left-hand margin. There should be two spaces between the inside address and the salutation, and between the salutation and the body of the letter. The correct punctuation to use after the salutation is the colon (:).

In business correspondence, the forms of salutation most commonly used are:

> Dear Sir:
> Dear Madam:
> My dear Sir:
> My dear Madam:
> Dear Mr. Brown:
> My dear Mrs. Hartley:
> Gentlemen:

Whether married or unmarried, a woman is always addressed as "Dear Madam," *never* as "Dear Miss." "Gentlemen" is preferred to "Dear Sirs" and is more generally used, although both are correct. The plural form is used even when the firm name is a single individual, as:

> John Hayden, Inc.
> 20 Maiden Lane
> New York, N.Y.

> Gentlemen:

It is also good practice to use "Gentlemen" when writing to a firm that consists of both men and women, or even a firm consisting of women alone. (The form "Mesdames" is obsolete and should not be used.) "My dear Sir" or "My dear Madam" is more formal than "Dear Sir" or "Dear Madam"—although the use of "My" in the salutation is gradually dying out, especially in business letters. Note that when "My" *is* used, the word "dear" is not capitalized.

When writing to a personal business friend, it is permissible to use an informal salutation such as "Dear Fred" or "Dear Mary."

Form letters may be addressed to "Dear Reader," "Dear Doctor," "Dear Music Lover," "Dear Customer"—or to whatever group the subject of your letter is addressed. However, such salutations lack warmth and personality, and there is a growing tendency to omit salutations entirely from form and circular letters.

THE BODY OF THE LETTER

A business letter is always written for a specific purpose—and that purpose should be kept clearly in mind, from the first word to the last. Not a single sentence should be included that in any way obscures the basic purpose of the letter, or makes it any less swiftly and sharply understandable to the reader.

Before you begin the body of your letter, ask yourself: "What is my objective? What do I hope to accomplish by this letter, and what is the best way to go about it? What facts or ideas do I want to convey—what impression do I want to give my correspondent? How am I most likely to get the result or create the response I want?"

Then plan your letter, as a speaker plans his speech or a writer the chapter of a book. Think your letter through before you begin to write. *Know what you want to say;* and once you have decided on the BIG IDEA of your letter—stay with it! Don't ramble. Don't write about irrelevant or personal things (they don't belong in a business letter!). Stick to the facts. Tell your correspondent what he wants to know—or what you want him to know. Don't waste words on generalities—or on obvious and unnecessary remarks which merely clutter up your letter and cloud the main theme. Say what you have to say simply, clearly and to the point—making every sentence work toward the purpose for which the letter is written.

Bear in mind that business letters are often read under pressure, when people are busy and dozens of other interests compete for their attention. So streamline your letters to make them more effective. Keep them brief and fast-moving, with short sentences and short paragraphs. Start a new paragraph for each point you wish to stress, arranging the paragraphs in logical order so that your letter "reads easily" and moves, step by step, toward the aim or purpose you wish to achieve.

Both the opening and closing sentences of a business letter are very important. The opening sentence should indicate the subject or reason for the letter, and should compel the reader's interest and attention. The closing sentence should leave the reader with a single clear-cut thought or idea, and should inspire whatever action or response is desired.

THE COMPLIMENTARY CLOSE

The correct position for the complimentary close is two spaces below the body of the letter, to the right of the page, in line with the date block at the top.

There are a number of closings with varying degrees of intimacy and formality from which to choose. Your best choice, of course, is the phrase most appropriate for your purpose. For example, you wouldn't be likely to close a letter of complaint with "Very cordially yours,"—nor would it be suitable to write "Yours respectfully," to a clerk or a casual business acquaintance. "Yours truly," is the form most frequently used in general business correspondence, and is the best form to use when in doubt. But here are some others from which to choose:

> Yours very truly,
> Very truly yours,
> Yours sincerely,
> Sincerely yours,
> Very sincerely yours,
> Always sincerely yours,
> Faithfully yours,
> Yours faithfully,
> Very faithfully yours,
> Cordially yours,
> Yours cordially,
> Very cordially yours,
> Most cordially yours,

"Respectfully yours," is used, as a rule, only by a tradesman writing to a customer, or by an employee writing to an employer. It is also frequently used in letters to church dignitaries and high public officials, although "Faithfully yours," is now considered a more acceptable form for that purpose.

"Gratefully yours," should be used only when one has cause to be grateful—as, for example, when writing to thank a surgeon who has successfully performed a serious operation, or to a lawyer who has won a difficult case.

"Warmly yours," is an undesirable phrase and should be avoided. So should such closings as "Yours for more business," and "Yours for a better year." Abbreviations such as "Yrs." for "Yours" and "Tly" for "Truly" (you'd be amazed how many people use them!) make a letter look sloppy and hurried.

Try particularly to avoid the use of those familiar old participial phrases such as "Hoping to hear from you soon," and "Trusting this is satisfactory." They tend to make any letter sound stereotyped and dull. Avoid also the use of "I am" and "I remain" preceding the close of the letter, as they are equally out of date and serve no useful purpose.

THE SIGNATURE

Every business letter should be signed by hand, in ink—and whenever possible, by the person who has written it. A typed signature alone is not good form; the use of a rubber stamp is anything but effective; and a signature in pencil or crayon is a rudeness to the person who receives the letter.

The name should always be written out in full, as initials may be misleading or confusing. The signature should not vary from one letter to another. George F. Smith should remain George F. Smith in all his business correspondence. He should not sometimes become G. Smith, sometimes G. Ford Smith. Of course if a man is writing a business letter to someone who is also a personal friend, he may sign just his first name— George.

The signature should always be written clearly and legibly, especially when there is no typed version of it. It's very annoying to receive a letter signed with an indecipherable scrawl that might work out to be any one of half a dozen different names! Many a letter remains unanswered for no other reason than that the busy person who receives it has no time to solve the mystery of the signature. It doesn't take much more time to write your name clearly than to dash it off carelessly; and surely it's worth the little extra effort.

Most business letters, however, have the writer's name *typed* several lines below the complimentary close, leaving space between for the handwritten signature. This prevents the possibility of mistake or confusion, however illegible the written signature may be. For example:

Very truly yours,

John F. Martinson

John F. Martinson

Frequently the name of the firm represented is used in the signature, with the name of the person writing the letter immediately below it:

Very truly yours,
Dorrance Advertising Agency

Peter Halleck

Peter Halleck, Treasurer

The following forms are also correct, and their choice is merely a matter of personal preference:

Sincerely yours,
TheMason-Cortley Company

BY   *George C. Fraser*

George C. Fraser

Yours truly,

Wheeler Jones, Jr.

Wheeler Jones, Jr.
A. J. Harper Company

Sincerely yours,

Frederick B Prentice

Frederick B. Prentice, Editor
Trade Book Department

Cordially yours,

Leon R. Harris

Eastern Advertising Manager

Very truly yours,
R. H. Macy & Co., Inc.

Per   (Mrs.) *Mary Landis*

Estimating office

When a letter is dictated, it is customary to give the initials of the person who dictated the letter as well as the stenographer who typed it, for identifying purposes. The initials are placed below and to the left of the signature, in line with the left-hand margin. If Peter Halleck has dictated a letter to Margaret Foster, any one of these four methods of initialing may be used: PH/MF, PH:MF, PH-MF or PH/mf. Occasionally the full name of the person who dictated the letter is used, with the initials of the stenographer following, as for example: Peter Halleck/mf.

The following last paragraph, complimentary close and signature of a typical business letter are given to show how the identifying initials are used:

> I am sorry for the delay, and will see that you receive a complete set of proofs immediately.
>
> Very truly yours,
> Dorance Advertising Agency
>
> *Peter Halleck*
>
> Peter Halleck, Treasurer

PH/mf

If something is enclosed with the letter—such as a bill, check, proof or copy of another letter—attention should be called to it by writing "Enclosure" or "Enclosures" below the initials in the lower left-hand corner. For example:

PH/mf
Enclosures

The phrase "Dictated but not read" is a discourtesy and should not be used.

ADDRESSING THE ENVELOPE

All letters should be carefully addressed, otherwise they may be lost or delayed.* Be sure that the name of the firm, the name of the individual, the street number, city and state are all given correctly. Apart from the possibility of misdirection, remember that nobody likes to receive a letter in which his name is misspelled. It's one of the quickest ways possible to antagonize your correspondent.

* See pages 35 to 40 for detailed information concerning the addressing of envelopes.

Begin typing the address slightly below the middle of the envelope, a little toward the left—but leaving enough space to get even a long name or address in without crowding. Either straight block or indented step arrangement may be used. Postal authorities prefer the step arrangement as it's easier to read.

Special directions such as "Attention of" or "Personal" should be typed in the lower left corner of the envelope.

Mailing instructions such as "Air Mail" or "Special Delivery"—if they are not already stamped or printed on the envelope—should be typed at the upper right side, under the postage stamp or stamps.

SUGGESTIONS FOR WRITING
MORE EFFECTIVE BUSINESS LETTERS

John D. Rockefeller, Sr. once said: "The ability to deal with people is as purchasable a commodity as sugar or coffee. And I will pay more for that ability than for any other under the sun."

The ability to deal with people is greatly increased by the ability to write good letters. And anyone can write good letters by applying a few simple basic principles.

In the first place, make it a point to answer all business letters *promptly*. An answer long delayed is not, as a rule, well received—is in disfavor even before it arrives.

When you answer a letter, keep it in front of you. Check or underline the parts of the letter that require an answer. Get all the necessary data and information you will need to write a complete and intelligent reply. *Be sure of your facts before you write;* for no one can write a satisfactory letter without full command of the subject.

If it's a letter of inquiry, asking for specific information or seeking an adjustment, answer it fully and completely—leaving nothing to the imagination. Tell the reader exactly what he wants to know. Don't write vaguely, making alibis instead of stating facts. Don't make it necessary for your correspondent to write again, for more specific details. Make yourself thoroughly familiar with the matter under discussion . . . review any previous correspondence on file . . . and know exactly what you are going to say *before* you start to write or dictate. This may seem unimportant to you; but if you try *thinking through* your letters before you start to write, you will find that it helps you express yourself with greater ease and confidence . . . and keeps you from rambling, from becoming too wordy and involved.

WRITE YOUR LETTERS FROM
THE READER'S POINT OF VIEW

One reason why so many letters fail to achieve the purpose or secure the results for which they are written is simply this: They are self-centered, self-seeking, completely self-interested.

It's very important to adopt a "you" attitude in your correspondence—to project yourself to the other side of the fence and try to see things from the point of view of the person to whom you are writing. What are his needs and desires—his interests—his problems?

If there is any one great basic principle of success in the writing of business letters, it can be summed up as the ability to see things through the other fellow's eyes as well as your own.

So try to approach all business correspondence from the standpoint of the reader, subordinating your own interests or those of your firm. Whatever your objective—whether you are trying to sell something, secure information, clear up a misunderstanding, collect a bill, or build up confidence and goodwill—you can be sure your letter will be much more effective if it's written in terms of "you" instead of "we" or "I."

BE SURE IT SOUNDS SINCERE

Your letter won't carry weight unless it *sounds sincere*. You cannot win confidence with empty words. Your reader won't be impressed unless he believes what you say.

So when you sit down to write a business letter, no matter what kind of business letter it may be, try to feel a genuine interest in your correspondent and his problems. Don't make the mistake of thinking you can get by with mere flattery and pretense.

For no letter is a successful letter, however cleverly written, if it leaves an element of doubt in the reader's mind, if he feels he is being fooled, bluffed, patronized or exploited.

ENTHUSIASM IS CONTAGIOUS

In any business letter that has a selling job to do—whether you're selling a product, service or idea—*be enthusiastic*. Let your correspondent see that you believe what you say, that you yourself are sold completely on the product or idea. In other words, sound a positive note in your letters whenever you can.

Eliminate all negative thoughts. Don't even suggest that the reader may have any doubts or misgivings.

Take the advertising writer as an example! Every really good copy writer believes wholeheartedly in the products about which he is paid to write. He always uses them himself, if he can, and raves about them to his friends—insisting to everyone, including himself, that they are truly amazing and exceptional. He deliberately hypnotizes himself into believing that the product about which he happens to be writing at the moment is the best product of its kind in the world. For he cannot write enthusiastic copy unless he himself is sold on the product. And he knows he must write enthusiastic copy to be successful; for enthusiasm is contagious—it "catches on"—it makes people buy.

Bear that in mind when you are writing a letter that must sell, convince, impress, or in any way *win over* a correspondent to your way of thinking. If you write with enthusiasm, the reader will sense that you believe what you are saying—and your letter will be much more likely to get the response you want.

COURTESY COUNTS IN LETTER WRITING, TOO

It's not only in face-to-face contact with people that good manners are important. Courtesy counts in letter writing, too. Tact, kindness, consideration for the rights, feelings and sensibilities of others—all carry weight in business correspondence, and often make the difference between a successful letter and one that's a "flop." All other things being equal, it's the courteous and graciously written letter that usually wins out and gets the desired results.

So make a conscious effort to be well-mannered in your letters. Don't abuse, condemn, criticize or ridicule the person to whom you are writing, no matter what the circumstance. Say what you have to say tactfully, without giving offense. *You can be sure that an angry, impatient or sarcastic letter will not get you the results you want.* It may relieve your feelings to "get it off your chest"—but it won't do either you or your company any good.

On the other hand, it's often possible to win over the most stubborn or disgruntled individual by expressing yourself with dignity and restraint. It isn't necessary to be rude, curt or abrupt; you can say what needs to be said *courteously*. You'll find that it always pays to be tactful and polite, in business letters as surely as in your personal contacts.

HOW TO PREJUDGE THE
EFFECTIVENESS OF YOUR LETTER*

1. Does your letter *look neat?* Is it faultlessly typed, well spaced and balanced, free of noticeable erasures or errors?
2. Does it look *easy to read?* Is it concise, with short sentences and paragraphs?
3. Is the opening paragraph *pertinent* and *interesting* . . . does it refrain from "acknowledging" and "advising" . . . thus inviting further reading of the letter?
4. Is the letter *clear* and *forceful,* not involved or cluttered up with meaningless, stereotyped words and phrases?
5. Does it sound *natural* . . . not stilted, officious or affected?
6. Have you kept your *reader's point of view* . . . his desires, needs and requirements, well in mind? Approached him from *his* side of the fence, not yours?
7. Have you told your reader *what he wants to know?* Have you answered fully and completely all his questions, asked or implied?
8. Have you avoided saying anything that might be *misconstrued?*
9. Does your letter sound *sincere?* Does it sound as though you are really trying to be helpful and considerate of your reader's feelings, wishes and needs?
10. Have you said what you should say, *specifically and to the point?* Is your letter concise . . . brief without omitting important details, but not so brief that it appears curt?
11. Does each sentence and paragraph follow in natural sequence so your letter *reads easily—doesn't ramble?*
12. Have you made it as *easy as possible* for your reader to follow your bidding . . . are you sure you haven't asked him to do the impractical or unpleasant?
13. Have you used sound, logical *reasons why* your reader should do as you suggest or ask?
14. Are your closing lines *strong* and *forceful,* likely to cause your reader to react favorably to your suggestions or proposals?
15. Is the letter *friendly,* likely to build *good will,* as well as accomplish its purpose?
16. Is it the kind of letter *you yourself would like to receive* if you were in the reader's position? Is it fair and considerate, written in the right tone?

These are the points by which your reader will consciously or subconsciously accept or reject your message. If you can

* Courtesy of R. H. Morris Associates, Correspondence Consultants.

answer "Yes" to these questions when checking each letter you have written, you may be sure you have done a good job.

2. The Tone and Language of a Good Business Letter

No letter is a good letter if it fails to make friendly contact with the reader—if it fails to win his interest and hold his attention. Even letters of complaint, collection letters, routine letters of inquiry or adjustment—and above all letters that must sell products, services, ideas or good will—should be friendly in tone and spirit.

There is no reason why a business letter should sound stiff and formal, like a legal document . . . without life or sparkle. There is no reason why *any* letter, written for any purpose, should be cold, impersonal, forbidding. Yet so many letters are! For some reason the very atmosphere of a business office seems to induce the use of stilted, rubber-stamp words and phrases. Surely the difference between spoken and written language is at its worst in business correspondence!

I have on my desk before me right now a letter from one of the biggest department stores in New York. The signature on the letter is a familiar one to me. The person who wrote that letter is brilliant, witty, a wonderful after-dinner speaker. Yet here is the opening paragraph of the letter:

> Please be advised that your communication of recent date is at hand. We wish to state that the matter will be given our prompt attention. We regret that you have been put to an inconvenience, but assure you it was unavoidable.

Those sentences might have been lifted bodily from any typical business letter of 1900 or thereabouts! There's no life to the words, no freshness. There's no real feeling of interest or sincerity. It's just another routine letter, written in the routine way, without much thought . . . and certainly without any attempt to establish a warm, human, friendly contact with the reader.

The very best letters are conversational in tone. They are

interesting to read, cordial in spirit, sometimes witty and often imaginative . . . *and always natural.*

Imagine a salesman calling you on the telephone and saying: "I am in receipt of your letter of recent date concerning our new portable radio. I wish to state I am now in a position to demonstrate it at your earliest convenience." People just don't talk that way, and your letters shouldn't sound that way. Use the language of everyday conversation in your letters—the language in which people think, dream and talk. Use the words people themselves use in the streets, on the farms, in the shops and in their homes.

In a previous chapter we stressed the importance of sincerity. Your letter isn't likely to sound sincere if you use antiquated stock expressions that have long since lost all freshness and vitality. Hackneyed expressions like "assuring you of our interest," "yours of recent date" and "thanking you in advance," have no real meaning for the reader. They carry no vital message across—convey no clear image or picture. So avoid them like the plague! They only make a letter sound pompous and boring. They make a letter sound cold, impersonal and insincere.

If you do nothing more than eliminate the dull, stereotyped words and phrases that sprinkle most business correspondence —if you write with freshness, sparkle and originality—you are bound to write more successful letters. You don't need to use long "impressive" words; simple language is always the best —and an occasional word of slang, or even a coined word or phrase, adds color and life to your letter.

Always try to talk directly *to* your correspondent, not as though you were talking through a third person. Use his name now and then to maintain an intimate, friendly relationship. ("That's why, Mr. Peters, I think it would be best to . . .") Put a smile into your letter if you want to; there's no law that says business correspondence must be gloomy and solemn . . . must put the reader to sleep! *Smiles build good will.* Just be sure your letter is in good taste—that it is neither too flippant nor too familiar—and that it takes serious things seriously.

ABBREVIATIONS IN BUSINESS LETTERS

It is not advisable to use abbreviations in correspondence, unless they are very familiar and commonplace. There is less likelihood of mistakes and confusion if words are spelled out in full. The trend is more and more to avoid abbreviations entirely.

THE OPENING PARAGRAPH

The way you begin a letter is very important—unless, of course, it's just a routine matter-of-fact order or acknowledgment which doesn't need to win over or impress the reader. Because of its strategic position, the opening sentence is often the determining factor between success or failure. For upon it may depend the reader's *acceptance* of the letter: whether it is read with interest and attention, or merely scannd and thrown aside.

A good opening sentence is like the headline of an advertisement. It instantly attracts the reader's attention, stimulates his curiosity or desire, *makes him want to read on.*

A poor opening sentence "begs to acknowledge" or "wishes to state"—says what is obvious, unnecessary or trite—makes no bid whatever for the reader's attention.

Naturally, the opening differs with the various types of letters you write. If it's a simple letter of order, inquiry or acknowledgment, you don't need an especially interesting or original opening. In fact, the more direct and businesslike it is, the better. All that is required of it is that it state its purpose clearly, and (when appropriate) show a friendly interest in the reader's problems and needs. But not even the most simple routine letter need start out with an impersonal, stereotyped opening, like the following:

> Yours of the 15th regarding delay in shipment just received. We exceedingly regret this matter.

The same thing, expressed in a natural, conversational tone, puts the reader in a more receptive frame of mind:

> We are sorry to learn, from your letter of March 15th, that you have not yet received the chairs you ordered.

When a letter has a specific job to do . . . such as selling a subscription to a magazine or applying for a job . . . the opening paragraph must be more than merely warm and friendly in tone. *It must be interesting.* It must be exciting, provocative, newsy, imaginative—must instantly get under the skin of the reader—touch a life nerve—make him read on.

Here are a few of the more familiar ways of giving a letter an interesting start. There are many others. You'll find it stimulating and helpful to make a study of the letters you receive, and to keep a file of the opening sentences that impress you most.

Add others of your own to the list; and refer to it when you need help getting a letter off to a good start. But bear in mind that just compelling the reader's attention isn't enough; your opening paragraph must have direct bearing on the subject of the letter, must lead logically into what you want to say.

1. *Ask a Question*

A blunt statement of fact is never as provocative as a question. For example, if you were writing a letter to sell subscriptions to a weekly news magazine, you might start off with: "To be well-informed, you should know what is going on in all parts of the world today." But you will intrigue more readers and get better response if you put in the form of a question: "How would you like to be the most interesting, best-informed man in your community?"

2. *Make a Startling Statement*

Most people are intrigued by a startling or unusual statement of fact, something they didn't know before. They are likely to continue reading a letter that starts off with: "This may shock you, but it's true! Most people have had, or will some time have, anemia." You should be sure of your facts, of course; for an incorrect statement discredits your entire letter.

3. *Tell a Story or Anecdote*

When an anecdote is interesting or exciting, and ties in with the subject of the letter, it's an excellent way to get started. A good story always gives life and sparkle to a letter. For example, an ordinary run-of-the-mill letter on fire insurance might start off like this: "A recent national survey shows that property values have risen. If you haven't increased your fire insurance, you should do so at once." That's dull, "sleepy," uninspired. Compare it with this colorful opening paragraph:* "When Mrs. O'Leary's cow kicked over a lamp on the night of October 8, 1871, she set off the great Chicago fire. It was a *170 million dollar fire!* Many lives were lost and much property destroyed. However, that tragedy was the starting point of intensive safety measures and fire prevention programs that have steadily increased down through the years."

---

* From a letter sent to policyholders by the Hardware Mutual Insurance Company of Minnesota.

4. Quote an Authority

The opinion of a person of reputation carries weight, and makes an effective opening for many types of letters. If you were writing to the head of a department store, for example— explaining about a new system of inventory control—you might start off with: "According to Dr. John T. Hammond, noted economist, the most important single factor in successful merchandising is *inventory control.*"

5. Quote a Famous Saying of the Past

People are always interested in the great of the past, in their ideas and ideals . . . and their famous sayings. The lead for a letter sent out by a bank to encourage thrift might use as its opening sentence: " *'I shall study hard, save my money, become a great man!'* wrote Benjamin Franklin as a young lad."

6. Dramatize the Results of a Survey or Test

If you use the results of a survey or test for an opening paragraph, be sure to key it to the interests or problems of the reader. Give it a human, emotional appeal instead of expressing it coldly in terms of facts and figures. For example: "Do you realize the danger you are in, *right in your own home?* According to a survey conducted by the Council on Public Safety, more people die of accidents in their own homes than anywhere else."

7. Highlight a News Story

A tie-in with important news of the day gets your letter off to a good start, and makes it timely. A customer's man, writing to his client, might say: "I think you will agree with me that the recent Republican sweep foreshadows an era of greater freedom for business enterprise than has been possible in many years. As an investor, it is important that you know how this will affect your holdings."

EXAMPLES OF EFFECTIVE OFENINGS
FOR VARIOUS TYPES OF LETTERS

Do you know that only 2.3% of American families have incomes of $10,000 a year or more?

Sorry! It's our mistake and we apologize. Our driver will pick up the chairs tomorrow and deliver the ones you ordered.

We have good news for you! At last we have been able to match your Haviland china; and we now have six cups and saucers in the pattern you want.

Here's that old bill again! How about paying it, and keeping your credit good? Or if you can't pay it now, won't you let us know when we can at least expect some part of it?

I'm sorry you had to write me again about my bill. I know it's long overdue, and I shall make every effort to pay it before the end of the month.

I must say I am surprised by your letter of October 2. I thought we were being most generous and fair.

Our representative is heading your way—and he has some news for you! News that's *very important,* and that you must not miss.

I am happy to enclose my check for $150—which is little enough to pay for a boy as fine as Junior!

THE CLOSING PARAGRAPH

The closing paragraph of a business letter should leave the reader with a single clear-cut thought or idea—and should inspire whatever action or response is desired. It's here that you make your final bid for the reader's confidence and good will. It's here that you either get the order, sell the idea, win the reader over to your way of thinking, leave a good last impression, or do just the opposite . . . depending on what you say and the words you use in your closing paragraph.

Avoid weak, namby-pamby closings like "Hoping to hear from you soon" and "Trusting this meets with your approval." Avoid negative, uncertain closings like "We feel this is to your advantage" and "We hope you will find it satisfactory." If you aren't sure of yourself, your reader won't be. So make a strong exit! Use positive language. Ask for a direct course of action. Take it for granted that your correspondent will agree to the adjustment, accept the explanation, respond to the idea, send in the order, or make the payment that is long overdue. In other words, *push the button that animates your reader and gets quick response.*

A treacherous little word to avoid in closing paragraphs is the word *if*. Don't give your correspondent the choice between two decisions, unless either decision is a satisfactory one. Instead of "Please let me know if you can see me" write "Please let me know when you can see me." Instead of "If you will sign and return the enclosed card," make it positive, tell him what you want him to do, hurry him into action: "Sign and return the enclosed card to me now, today—before you forget!"

There are many types of business letters that do not necessarily strive for a particular response or course of action. The closings of such letters should strive to maintain confidence and good will. ("We hope you will enjoy your purchase for many years to come.") Or they should thank or compliment the reader. ("Thank you for sending your check so promptly," or "Congratulations on the fine job you have done!")

EXAMPLES OF EFFECTIVE CLOSINGS
FOR VARIOUS TYPES OF LETTERS

Please send a complete report, and we'll do everything we can to help.

Thank you for letting us know about it. We shall take care of it at once.

We are depending on you to help us in this undertaking. Please don't let us down!

You have been most patient and considerate and we are grateful.

We are always delighted to hear from our customers, and we hope you'll take the time to write us again.

Will you send confirmation of this order at once so that we can begin shipment?

May we have your check for $35.68 without further delay? Thank you.

I'll be looking for your check tomorrow morning. Don't disappoint me!

I'm enclosing a handy card for you to use. It requires no postage. Mail it right away, before you forget!

I hope this proves how eager we are to make amends, and to please you in every way we can.

Thank you for your order. We hope you and your family derive great pleasure from the use of your projector.

You can certainly pride yourself on your handling of this case!

THE USE OF POSTSCRIPTS
IN BUSINESS LETTERS

In social and personal correspondence, a postscript is just an afterthought, suggesting careless or disorganized thinking. It is usually unnecessary and often unsightly—and should be avoided.

But in business correspondence, a postscript is often purposely added to draw attention to some point or to emphasize a special offer. This is good practice, and is especially effective in sales letters. The postscript should be brief, and should contain only one clear-cut message. It may be used either with or without the "P.S." Here are some examples of typical business-letter postscripts:

Don't forget! June 10th is the deadline.

P.S. A discount of 2% will be given on all orders received on or before June 30th.

P.S. Be sure to use the enclosed card; it requires no postage.

P.S.: I can be reached any morning before 10 at Chesapeake 2-4500.

THE TEN COMMANDMENTS FOR WRITING
A GOOD BUSINESS LETTER*

1. *Write as You Would Talk:* Use plain, homespun, everyday English, which is more interesting and convincing than tongue-twisting, unfamiliar words.

2. *Be Courteous and Friendly:* Good manners always pay handsome dividends even in a letter. It's hard

---

* Courtesy of R. H. Morris Associates, Correspondence Consultants.

to resist someone who is trying to be sincerely friendly.

3. *Be Natural:* It has been wisely said: "The secret of writing a good letter requires the ability to put yourself in an envelope and seal the flap." This means, of course, that you should write as one human being to another. Do not take yourself or your position so seriously that your letters sound stilted, officious or superior to your readers.

4. *Learn to Visualize Your Readers and Be Helpful:* Acquire the knack of putting yourself in your readers' place. Base your appeal on how you are trying to help *them*—not yourself.

5. *Keep an Open Mind:* Appreciate your readers' point of view. Respect their rights, wishes and needs.

6. *Practice Real Diplomacy:* Don't assume a "teacher to pupil" tone. A true diplomat makes others feel how much they know—*not* how little; how important they are—*not* how unimportant.

7. *Be Willing to Admit Mistakes:* Don't argue or try to justify an error. The most effective way to disarm an irate person is to admit frankly any cause for complaint.

8. *Write Clearly and to the Point:* Use short, crisp sentences. Finish with one point before going on to another. Avoid long, involved paragraphs. Say what you have to say interestingly and completely —*then stop*. Be cordial—not curt.

9. *Tell Your Readers What They Want to Know:* It is so easy to be misunderstood, doubted or miscontrued. Therefore, don't be vague or evasive. Don't expect your readers to read between your lines or to interpret your intentions. Be specific and complete.

10. *Dramatize Your Letters: Don't* expect dry, stereotyped letters to produce results. Paint glowing word pictures of *how* your readers will benefit by follow-

ing your suggestions or proposals. Show them *reasons why* they should act for their own benefit.

3. Examples of Routine Business Letters

Dozens of different kinds of letters must be written every day, the letters of general business activity. Orders must be acknowledged, inquiries made, complaints answered. Letters must be written to customers, clients, lawyers, credit managers, buyers, representatives, manufacturers. . . .

Following are examples of various types of business letters, of the kind that are written every day in the week. For purposes of convenience, only the first letter is given in complete form, with date and inside address included. All other examples are given without date and inside address—it being understood, of course, that these should always be included.

LETTERS OF ORDER AND CONFIRMATION

All letters ordering merchandise should give explicit information, specifying a catalog or model number when available —and giving the shade, size, type, quantity or whatever other data is necessary to identify the merchandise. An incomplete or confusing order wastes time . . . and time is valuable in business.

April 14, 19—

The Upjohn Company,
Kalamazoo, Mich.

Gentlemen:

Please send the following as quickly as you can, and charge to our account:

6 bottles of 100 each of ferrated
liver concentrate tablets

6 bottles of 100 each of ferrated
liver concentrate capsules

12 bottles of 100 each of Unicaps

12 bottles of 4-oz. size of citrocarbonate

Yours very truly,

Gentlemen:

Please send samples and quotations on one million metal paper clips.

At the same time let us know if you can supply 50 Ace staplers, model 102—giving us a quotation on this also.

We would like to have the information by the end of this week if possible.

Very truly yours,

Gentlemen:

Please send me two pairs of men's striped broadcloth pajamas, at $7.50 a pair, as advertised in yesterday's *Times*. I would like one pair in blue and one in green, in size C.

Charge to my account.

Yours truly,

Dear Mr. Fredericks:

I have decided to accept the proposal submitted by you on April 12th for the construction of kitchen cabinets in my home. It is understood that the work is to commence no later than June 1st, and is to be completed within two weeks.

Mrs. Curtis and I like the revised plans very much, and we'd like you to know we appreciate your efforts to carry out our somewhat unusual ideas.

I enclose my check for $50 in accordance with the terms of your proposal.

Sincerely yours,

Dear Sir:

Will you please send me the floor plan and rates of the Royal Hawaiian, indicating the accommodations you can let me have for the month of February.

I require one double room with bath for my husband and myself; and a connecting room, if possible, for my young daughter.

We plan to arrive on January 30th and leave on February 28th.

Sincerely yours,

Dear Mr. Turner:

We have reserved a double room and bath in your name for the week of Sept. 7th to Sept. 14th. The rate is $10 a day.

We look forward to your visit and hope your stay will be a very pleasant one.

Sincerely yours,

Dear Mr. Hartley:

Many thanks for your order which has been forwarded to our plant for immediate manufacture.

I take pleasure in assuring you that I will personally follow through on your order, and see that each piece is made exactly according to specifications.

You can count on delivery on or before December 5th, as promised.

Sincerely yours,

Gentlemen:

Thank you for your order of February 10th. It is being shipped today.

We enclose an invoice and bill of lading.

Yours very truly,

Dear Mr. Peters:

This is in answer to your inquiry of March 4th.

We can ship immediately 1000 folders of the same size and quality as the sample enclosed. A price card is enclosed for your convenience.

We await your instructions, and will rush the folders to you as soon as your order arrives.

Sincerely yours,

Gentlemen:

We are sorry to have to tell you that we cannot fill your order for 200 pairs of black doeskin gloves.

We can send you all the white, tan or yellow gloves you want; but there is a temporary shortage of black due to difficulty with the dyes.

Thank you very much for your order—which we hope you'll give us an opportunity to fill when black doeskin gloves again become available.

Sincerely yours,

LETTERS OF COMPLAINT AND ADJUSTMENT

The purpose of the usual letter of complaint is to get better merchandise or service, or to effect a satisfactory adjustment of some kind. You are more likely to get what you want if you are *courteous* in your letter. Nothing is gained by being sarcastic or insulting. That only makes your correspondent want to double up his fists and fight back, though he *won't*, of course, if he values your good will above his own pride and feelings!

So just state your case . . . say what the trouble is and how you expect it to be corrected. Be specific and to the point, but be pleasant about it.

Gentlemen:

Many of our customers have been complaining about your ball-point pens. They are clearly not giving satisfaction, and we have had to refund the purchase price on many of them.

We have had trouble only with the last shipment. The pens received before were satisfactory and we had no complaints from customers.

Please check to see if there was an error in the making of these pens. We suggest that you check also to see if they are being packed with adequate protection for shipping.

We have 3½ gross of the pens left, and we'd like you to send a new shipment at once to replace them. We'll wait for instructions from you before returning the others.

Yours very truly,

Dear Mr. Perkins:

I cannot understand why there are so many mistakes in our billing recently. Is there any way this situation can be corrected?

I'm sure you'll agree that a little more care and accuracy on the part of your accounting department will benefit both of us.

Sincerely yours,

Gentlemen:

On December 12th I ordered a girl's raincoat with hood attached, red and green plaid, size 8, price $7.95.

Today I received a plain red raincoat, without a hood. Although it's the right size, and the same price as the one ordered, I cannot keep it as my daughter especially wants the one with the hood.

Please have your driver pick up this raincoat; and either deliver the one ordered or refund the money.

Yours truly,

The writing of adjustment letters, in answer to complaints, requires a very special technique. Such letters must be written without anger or impatience—must be written very skillfully and courteously to avoid *further antagonizing the complainant*. This holds true whether the complaint is a fair one or not. One of the most effective ways to disarm an irate person and win him over to your way of thinking is to admit freely a cause for complaint. Arguments and accusations only make things worse, as a rule. But "talking it over" in a friendly way—explaining how or why it happened, and being very reasonable and understanding about the whole thing—often settles the trouble pleasantly, and without loss of good will.

Dear Madam:

We can understand your annoyance at not having received the stationery you ordered on March 3rd.

Orders for printed stationery take three to four weeks for delivery; and our salesmen have been instructed to so inform customers. Apparently you were not told it would take that long; and we are certainly sorry for the oversight.

However, your stationery is now ready and will be sent to you at once. You should receive it about the same time as this letter.

We hope you will forgive us for the delay—and that you will thoroughly enjoy your purchase!

Sincerely yours,

Dear Madam:

Thank you for your very courteous letter.

We are sorry the plant stand arrived in poor condition. It was apparently damaged during shipment.

We are sending you another table at once—doubly well-packed, this time, to make sure it reaches you safely! The driver who delivers it will pick up the damaged table.

We hope that you have not been inconvenienced, and that you will enjoy your purchase for a long time to come.

Sincerely yours,

Dear Mr. Fraser:

We're sorry you found it necessary to return our last bill for correction.

You are right about the 10% discount, of course. But the $32 is not an error; it represents charges for air-express deliveries made at your request during the month of December.

We'll see that our billing department makes no mistake about the discount in the future.

Yours very truly,

LETTERS OF INQUIRY AND ACKNOWLEDGMENT

A letter of inquiry is written to obtain information or to make a request. It should be direct and specific; but most of all, it should be reasonable in its demands upon the time and effort of the person to whom it is addressed. Friendship should not be imposed upon. An inquiry requiring clerical help should be accompanied by an offer to pay for the expenses involved. Anyone seeking personal or confidential information should make his purpose clear and show himself to be a person of responsibility.

Always enclose a stamped addressed envelope when writing to a stranger for information. This isn't necessary, of course, if you are writing for information about a trip you expect to make, or books you expect to buy—and the company to which you are writing stands to benefit by the correspondence. But if you are writing for information that is of importance *only to you*—if you want to know how to pronounce a certain word, what to do or say under certain circumstances, or perhaps what to do about certain personal problems or difficulties— you should enclose a stamp or a stamped addressed envelope.

All letters of inquiry should be acknowledged, except those obviously written by a crank. The reply should be courteous and friendly, whether it grants the request or not. If information is withheld, the reason should be given as tactfully as possible. A simple statement of company policy is often the best way out. The refusal to give information or grant a request is always more gracious if another more likely source is suggested.

Dear Mr. Tavis:

We are making a survey of the buying habits of the American public.

Could you let me know whether you have sold more *modern* furniture this year than *period* furniture? Or was it the other way around?

We will be grateful for your answer and will, of course, keep it in strictest confidence.

Sincerely yours,

Gentlemen:

Do you have a booklet on interior decorating?

I am interested in doing over two rooms in my house, using plywood for the walls and built-in book-cases.

I thought you might have a booklet available showing interesting or unusual use of plywood in the home. If so, I'll be very pleased to receive a copy.

Yours very truly,

Gentlemen:

I am writing for permission to reprint a letter which appears on page 179 of *Northern Nurse* by Elliot Merrick, published by Scribner's in 1942.

I should like to use it in a book on letter writing, to be published by Prentice-Hall in October. It illustrates perfectly a point I wish to make: that to *receive* interesting letters one must *write* interesting letters.

I'll be glad to make any payment required for reprint permission; and of course adequate acknowledgment will be given both to Scribner's and to the author.

Yours very truly,

Dear Mrs. Miller:

Thank you for your inquiry about the *Betty Parnell* dress shown in the advertisement in the September Vogue.

Clark & Company of Middletown is the store nearest you that carries this dress.

Should you decide to buy it, I take this opportunity to wish you many happy moments as you wear it!

　　　　　　　　　　Cordially yours,

Dear Mr. Hoyt:

I'm so sorry I cannot accept your invitation to speak at the school on Thursday evening, May 1. I should like to very much indeed, but I have a previous commitment for that evening.

However, I am passing your request on to the American Association of Advertising Agencies as they usually have speakers available. You will no doubt hear from them in a few days.

　　　　　　　　　　Sincerely yours,

Dear Mrs. Watson:

Thank you for your letter and your interest in our work.

We enclose copies of the material you wish to use from our Correspondence Manuals, and which you have our permission to reprint.

There will be no charge for the use of this material, and the credit line you suggest is satisfactory.

Best wishes for the success of your new book!

　　　　　　　　　　Cordially yours,

LETTERS ABOUT CREDIT

Much of the business of the world is conducted on a credit basis. This involves a great deal of correspondence: letters applying for credit, investigating credit rating, extending or refusing credit and so forth.

Letters giving credit information should be straightforward and truthful, based only on fact. Letters refusing credit should be tactfully written, the emphasis being on some broad general principle or on company policy rather than anything personal.

Gentlemen:

We enclose a check for the merchandise ordered on May 12.

We should like our name put on your books as a charge customer, being billed once a month instead of each time we send an order.

If you will let us know what information you require, we'll be glad to send it.

Yours very truly,

Gentlemen:

I'd like to open a charge account with your store.

I have accounts with Lord & Taylor, Altman's, Best & Company and Bonwit Teller.

Yours truly,

Dear Madam:

We are delighted to welcome you as a charge customer. Your name is now on our books, and you may feel free to order merchandise at any time.

To complete our records, will you please fill out the enclosed forms and return them to us?

We hope you will enjoy your association with this store; and we shall, of course, make every effort to serve you courteously and well.

Sincerely yours,

Gentlemen:

Thank you very much for your order, which has received our careful attention.

As your name is not on our books, we are enclosing a credit application. Please fill it out and return it to us at once so that shipment will not be held up.

We hope this marks the beginning of a long and pleasant association between us.

Cordially yours,

Gentlemen:

Thank you for your courteous letter. I understand the need for credit references and am glad to give them.

Two firms with which I have accounts and to whom you may refer are Smith, Emmett & Co., Inc. and Arnold & Dupree—both of Dallas.

I'd appreciate a quick checkup on these references, as I'd like to receive the order in time for our Easter sale.

Yours very truly,

Dear Mr. Burton:

Thank you for your letter giving references in connection with your application for credit.

It's embarrassing to us to realize we did not make ourselves entirely clear in our last letter. Our house policy requires *trade references*—that is, the names of firms who have supplied you with goods on credit terms.

Will you please send us two such references; and in the meantime you may order what you like, as your name has been entered on our books as a credit customer.

Sincerely yours,

Dear Mr. Haskins:

We have received a request from Mr. William Turner, of Dallas, to be placed on our books as a charge customer. Mr. Turner asks credit up to $3000 for a period of three months.

Will you tell us what you can about Mr. Turner? We would like to know his financial standing, the extent of his business, and his reputation for meeting obligations. Your reply will be kept in strict confidence.

We shall be very grateful indeed for your help.

Sincerely yours,

Gentlemen:

We are glad to give you a reference for the Ray Bolton Company.

This firm is well known to us, and we have had considerable business dealings with them through the years.

Ray Bolton is a highly reputable and trustworthy firm, sound financially and prompt in the payment of bills. You should have no hesitancy about extending credit to them.

Sincerely yours,

Gentlemen:

The firm mentioned in your letter of April 8th is not well known to us.

As far as we know, this is a respectable and trustworthy firm; but as we have had little business dealing with them in recent years, we cannot vouch for their credit standing.

We're sorry that we are not able to be more helpful.

Sincerely yours,

Gentlemen:

We are sorry to say that we cannot vouch for the reliability of the Spencer-Crane Company. Our own experience with them has not been satisfactory.

During the three years Spencer-Crane have been on our books, they have repeatedly failed to meet their obligations on time; and they have caused us much trouble with regard to payments. Right now they owe us $318.55 for purchases made over a period of six months.

We give you this information in confidence, in the hope it will be of help to you.

Cordially yours,

COLLECTION LETTERS

Collection letters are generally written in a series, one letter following the other at periodic intervals, with increasing degrees of urgency and insistence.

The best collection letters do not bully, threaten, call names. They are firm, but *tactful*. They assume that the debtor wants to pay, give him a chance to explain why he does not or cannot pay, stress the advantages of maintaining good credit rating . . . make it possible for him to pay graciously and without resentment.

Often the first collection letter fails to get results; but the second or third one may. Therefore *persistence is important*. But it isn't necessary to write a long series of angry, threatening letters. If three or four letters have been sent and ignored, it's reasonable to assume that the firm or individual either can't or won't pay the bill. In that case, a last brief letter may be written giving the correspondent "fair warning" that other steps are about to be taken. This should be in the nature of a *notice*, not a *threat*.

Following are examples of collection letters in varying degrees of insistence. The first four represent a series:

Dear Mrs. Franklin:

In checking our accounts, we find there is a balance of $42.50 due us for purchases made in September.

As you have no doubt overlooked this bill, we are bringing it to your attention.

Will you please send your check at once so we can clear this indebtedness from our books and bring your account up to date.

Yours very truly,

Dear Mrs. Franklin:

As you are usually very prompt in paying your bills, we wonder why you have overlooked your September account.

Is there some reason why you are not paying this bill? Would you like to come in and talk it over with us?

The amount is for $42.50, and it is now more than three months overdue.

We'll be looking for your check in the next day or two; or for a letter telling us when we may expect at least part of the amount due us.

Yours very truly,

Dear Mrs. Franklin:

We are disappointed not to have received any word from you in answer to our letters concerning the bill of $42.50 which you owe us.

As you know, the terms of our agreement extend credit for one month only. This bill is now four months overdue. Surely you don't want to lose your credit standing with us and with other stores—nor do we want to lose you as a customer.

We therefore urge you to send a check at once. We urge you to keep your account on the same friendly and pleasant basis it has always been in the past.

Of course if there is some reason why you cannot pay this bill, or can pay only part of it now, we'd be very happy to talk it over with you . . . and perhaps we could be helpful.

Yours very truly,

Dear Mrs. Franklin:

We can't tell you how sorry we are you haven't answered any of our letters about the $42.50 you owe us. We must now regretfully assume you do not want to pay, and we have no other choice than to turn the matter over to our collection attorneys.

This is most distasteful to us, especially in your case —and we are therefore making *one last request* for your check, or for a letter of explanation.

We are holding up proceedings for five days in the hope of hearing from you. Please don't disappoint us!

Yours very truly,

Dear Mr. Ellis:

We don't like to remind a good customer like you that a bill is overdue.

However you have probably overlooked the balance of $32 due on January 15; and we know you would want us to bring it to your attention.

If your check is already in the mail, Mr. Ellis, just forget this letter—and forgive us for writing it!

Sincerely yours,

Gentlemen:

This is to remind you that the amount of $325 was due on your account on January 1.

We know that reminders like this are annoying, and we certainly don't like to send them. But we cannot function efficiently unless our accounts are kept up to date. We hope you understand.

And we hope there's a check from you for the full amount in the next day or two!

> Sincerely yours,

ACKNOWLEDGING COLLECTION LETTERS

If you are unable to meet a bill on the day it is due—or if you are waiting for a change or correction to be made in a bill before you pay it—*write and say so*. Explain the circumstances fully and courteously. You will find your creditor much more reasonable, much more willing to co-operate with you and give you an extension of time, if you tell him exactly what the situation is.

Gentlemen:

We are placed in a most uncomfortable position! We are obliged to ask for an extension of time on your bill for $921.45.

We had depended on a check from a client to take care of this bill. But we have just been informed that this check will not arrive until April 15th.

We must therefore ask for a two weeks' extension of time on your bill. We are sorry for the delay and hope it will not inconvenience you.

> Sincerely yours,

Gentlemen:

The reason we have not paid your bill of August 15 is because of an overcharge of $60, which we pointed out to you in a previous letter.

As soon as you send a corrected bill, we shall be glad to send payment in full.

> Yours truly,

Dear Mr. Richards:

I'm sorry you had to write me again about my bill.
I know it's long overdue, and I shall make every effort
to pay it before the end of the month.

You have been most patient and considerate, and I
am grateful.

Sincerely yours,

MISCELLANEOUS BUSINESS LETTERS

Gentlemen:

Thank you for your letter of May 20.

We have already placed an order for summer sports-
wear, but we are interested in carrying your line for
the Florida season.

Will you have your salesman drop in to see us when
he is in this territory?

Very truly yours,

Gentlemen:

We have given your letter of June 12th very careful
consideration.

As we have done business with each other so pleasantly for many years, we should like to comply with
your request for lower prices.

However, our own overhead has increased sharply in
recent months and we cannot reduce prices 15% without lowering our standards of quality . . . and that
we are not prepared to do.

We suggest an overall reduction of 5% in price,
throughout the line.

We hope this is satisfactory, and that we can continue our long and friendly association.

Sincerely yours,

Dear Mrs. Watson:

This note is to thank you for your valuable assistance. Yours is a most interesting story, and I am sure it will fit nicely into the pattern of my article.

The forms will be open for another two or three weeks, so if you think of anything we didn't discuss which would make interesting reading—I'll be glad to have it.

I'm returning the pictures and clippings you let me use.

I hope you know how grateful I am to you for your courtesy and help.

Sincerely yours,

Dear Mr. Crosley:

Mr. Rogers is in Des Moines and expects to be there until at least May 15.

I have sent him your letter, and no doubt he will answer it from there.

Sincerely yours,

Marchant Condon

Secretary to Mr. Rogers

4. Letters That Sell

A good sales letter is like a good advertisement. It compels the reader's attention—makes him stop, look, read and *buy*.

If you will study and analyze all the really *good* sales letters you receive, the letters that convince and persuade you almost against your own will, you will find that they are keyed to what I call "The 7 Basics of Mass Selling." Every good sales letter you write, whatever its nature or purpose, should conform to this 7-point structure. The body of the letter, the wording.

the approach, the strategy of appeal, may all be as original and different as you like; but the structure should be basically this:

1. *Compel attention!* Make contact with the reader— attract his interest or curiosity with your very first sentence.

2. *Offer a definite promise!* Make it imperative for the person to read on, to find out more about the service, product or idea that can mean so much to him or to his family.

3. *Aim at some simple fundamental human instinct!* Never mind how the product is made or how many people bought it last year. The reader wants to know, "What does it mean to *me?*"

4. *Feature the "plus" value of your product or idea!* Find the point of difference between your product and others of a similar nature—and show that difference to be an advantage.

5. *Prove what you say!* Back up your claim or claims with facts. Sell fast with fast-selling sentences! Make the reader say "Yes! Yes!" in his mind. (If he says "Yes, that's true!" three times in the course of reading your letter, he's *sold.*)

6. *Persuade the reader to grasp the opportunity or advantage you offer!* The effect of a good sales letter on a prospect should be . . . *not* "What a wonderful letter!"—but "What a wonderful opportunity! I mustn't miss it!"

7. *Close with an urgent request for action!* Give the reader something to do—give specific directions or instructions. An order blank or return post card enclosed with the letter helps get action.

Of these seven basics, Number 3 is by far the most important. Your letter must appeal to some deep-rooted human instinct or emotion.

Give a man a pen to try, and what does he write? His own name!

Give a man a group picture in which he appears, and what does he look for? His own face!

It's as simple as that. People buy a product or subscribe to an idea because it offers something they want or need for *their own* profit, pleasure, success or well-being.

Bear that in mind when writing a sales letter. Remember that people are interested in your product only in terms of what it means to them or their loved ones.

Here is an advertising expert's check-list guide to what people want, the advantages they are most interested in gaining. One of these should be the basic appeal of your sales letter, whether you are selling a bar of soap or a Steinway piano.

1. Better health
2. More money
3. Greater popularity
4. Improved appearance
5. Security in old age
6. Praise from others
7. More comfort
8. More leisure
9. Pride of accomplishment
10. Business advancement
11. Social advancement
12. Increased enjoyment (from food, drink, entertainment, etc.)

According to the same excellent source, people also want to:

Be good parents
Have influence over others
Be sociable, hospitable
Be gregarious
Express their personalities
Resist domination by others
Satisfy their curiosity
Be up-to-date
Emulate the admirable
Appreciate beauty
Be proud of their possessions
Be creative
Acquire or collect things
Be efficient
Win others' affection
Be "first" in things
Improve themselves mentally
Be recognized as authorities

And people also want to save money, time, work, discomfort, worry, doubts, risks, embarrassment, offense to others, boredom, personal self-respect and prestige.

EXAMPLES OF EFFECTIVE SALES LETTERS

Dear Sir:

How would you like to be one of the most interesting and best-informed men in your community?

How would you like to be in a position to discuss the important social, economic, political, national and international affairs of the day—not by reading more, but *by reading less!*

You can, so easily, just by reading WORLD NEWS MAGAZINE! This fascinating digest of world events brings you all the vital and significant news stories of the week. It tells you about people, places, things—everything that's going on—in condensed, quick-reading form.

You cannot really grasp the shape of our times unless you get the story *whole*—unless you know everything that's happening, here and abroad. You should not only know what statesmen, scientists, world leaders in all fields are doing, saying and planning to help shape the world's future. You should also know what *plain people* everywhere in the world are doing, saying and thinking,

And that's what WORLD NEWS brings you: *all* the news, about *all* people, *all* over the world! Issue after issue brings you the news of treaties, agreements, international meetings, conferences, discoveries, inventions . . . news as sharp and clear and true as experienced on-the-spot reporters and journalists can make it.

But side by side with these big stories of the week, WORLD NEWS brings you the little *human* stories that never break into the headlines. WORLD NEWS brings you stories of people in every part of the world working, fighting, dreaming, laughing, loving—people at work and people at play—intimate, dramatic stories to enrich your knowledge of humanity and make you a more brilliant, well-informed conversationalist.

WORLD NEWS is the favorite magazine of doctors, bankers, lawyers, architects, engineers, business executives. It's the favorite magazine of nearly *two million* alert, intelligent families like yours from coast to coast!

We know it will be *your* favorite magazine, too— once you start reading it. We know you'll wait for it eagerly, week after week, read it from cover to cover, mark things to remember, clip items to save. . . .

Try WORLD NEWS at the Special Introductory Rate that brings you a whole year's subscription for only $5. That's a real saving—$2.80 less than the 52 copies would cost you on the newsstand!

Remember: *Even if you don't read anything else all week*, WORLD NEWS *will make you one of the most interesting and best-informed persons in your community!*

The special saving is available for a limited time only. So please sign the enclosed postage-paid card and *air mail it back to us today!*

Sincerely yours,

Dear Sir:

There's a chill in the air. . . . Have you noticed it? And that chill spells *danger* to your car!

Don't wait for signs of trouble. Come in and give your car the cold weather servicing it needs—*right now!*

Servicing at this time of the year keeps your car in sound, smooth-running condition . . . protects its trade-in value. But even more important, expert servicing now means safer driving all winter for you and your family.

We'd like you to know we have improved service facilities, skilled mechanics, up-to-date equipment, time-saving tools, genuine parts—everything for making your car perform at its best.

So drive in some time during the next day or two, and let us look over your car. We'll see if it has any dangerous symptoms of neglect. We'll tell you what it needs in the way of a winter pick-up or tonic. *Be smart!* A check-up and servicing now may save you a lot of time and money later when the real cold weather comes around!

Drive in today or tomorrow. . . . Hand the enclosed card of introduction to one of our attendants, and he'll see that you get special, personal attention.

Don't put it off—*you may be sorry!* It pays in every way to *act now* and beat the cold!

Sincerely yours,

Dear Subscriber:

"Parting is such sweet sorrow. . . ." according to Shakespeare.

But is it? Perhaps there was some sweetness in Juliet's sorrow as she stood whispering good-by to her beloved. But there's no sweetness in *our* parting! We're filled with sadness at the thought of losing you as a subscriber.

And lose you we must, unless you renew your subscription *at once* to MODERN HOME MAGAZINE! As much as we hate to part with you, we must remove your name from our lists . . . unless you say: "Wait! Stop! I'm staying to enjoy all the good things you are planning for the coming year!"

So we are writing you *just this once more* in the hope you will change your mind. We are writing to say, "Please don't go! Stay on with us. . . . Renew your subscription for another year. . . ."

A renewal form and return envelope are enclosed. Decide right now there'll be no parting for good old friends like us! Fill in the renewal form and rush it back to us *today*.

Sincerely yours,

LETTERS THAT SELL GOOD WILL

Strictly speaking, the letters in this section are not sales letters. They are written to establish or strengthen friendly relations, and to build good will.

Dear Doctor:

Here's another handy timesaver for you! It's designed to fill a real need in the practice of a busy doctor.

This pad of leaflets contains 50 copies of *The Hygiene of Pregnancy*. You'll find it very convenient to keep on your desk, pulling off one leaflet at a time as you need it.

The leaflet answers the most frequently asked questions of an expectant mother concerning personal hygiene during the prenatal period. You can save time by giving her one of these leaflets instead of answering all her routine questions in the routine way.

The leaflet has been carefully checked and approved by well-known obstetricians. The instructions are *general*, containing nothing to take the place of diagnosis. There is space at the bottom of each leaflet for any special instructions you may wish to add.

Initial and return the enclosed card for your pad of leaflets today. They will be sent to you with the compliments and good wishes of Blank Baby Soap.

Sincerely yours,

Dear Mr. Thompson:

This is to tell you how very much I appreciate the cordial reception you gave me on my first visit to Dallas.

As a new salesman in your territory, it was especially gratifying to me to be received so well—and treated so kindly.

Thank you very much, not only for the order but for your friendly interest. I appreciate more than I can say your helpful advice about local conditions and problems.

I shall do my best to repay you by any "extras" of service that are within my power to provide.

I look forward with great pleasure to seeing you again in April.

Cordially yours,

Dear Mrs. Harkness:

We were flattered and pleased by your choice of Bingham Inn for your vacation.

We sincerely hope you enjoyed your three weeks here, and that the Inn lived up to your expectations in every way.

We look forward to greeting you again some day, and to the pleasure of extending once more the full hospitality of Bingham Inn.

Sincerely yours,

5. Letters of Application

"We are all salesmen, every day of our lives," said the late Charles M. Schwab. "We are selling our ideas, our plans, our energies, our enthusiasm to those with whom we come in contact."

The purpose of a letter of application is to help you *sell yourself*. It should state clearly the job you want, and should tell what your abilities are and what you have to offer. It should give a quick, clear picture of your qualifications, your accomplishments and your aims. It should present you to possible employers in the best light.

A well-written letter of application does not necessarily guarantee a position; but it does insure *consideration* and a better chance of an interview. You cannot hope to get your whole story into a letter, but you should cover enough ground to intrigue the prospective employer and make him want to see you, speak to you and find out more about you. It takes more than a good letter to land a good job; it takes ability, specific experience and good character. But the letter *opens the door for you* and gives you the chance to sell yourself.

Your letter of application should be simple, human, personal —and brief without omitting any essential or pertinent facts. It should be as carefully prepared as an advertisement, since, like an advertisement, it is intended to attract attention, create interest, impel action.

Try not to write a dull, stereotyped letter of application. Make it *interesting*. A letter can reveal character and personality in many unexpected ways. It's not easy to write a good letter of application, but it's worth all the effort you put into it. For a good letter almost always receives careful consideration from a prospective employer. *Good letters are rare.*

The appearance of your letter is extremely important. Remember that the purpose of a letter of application is to *impress* the prospective employer, to win his interest and confidence. You cannot hope to do a good job of selling yourself with a letter that is sloppy, untidy, poorly written, hard to read, or full of finger marks, erasures or blots.

A letter of application is usually discarded at once if it's written:

> —in pencil, crayon or red ink
> —on wrinkled or dirty paper
> —on hotel stationery
> —on stationery with a business letter-
>   head that has been crossed out
> —on odd-sized or odd-shaped stationery
> —on perfumed stationery
> —on brightly colored stationery
> —on a post card

Type your letter of application if possible, for a typed letter is easier to read than a handwritten one. Use standard business-size stationery of good quality, plain white and unlined. If you are applying for a job in an executive capacity, it's helpful to have your own personal letterheads. Otherwise, type your address in the upper right corner above the date.

If you can neither type your letter nor have it typed by someone, write it out very neatly and legibly. No busy employer is going to waste his time and his eyesight trying to decipher what you have written. Use letter-size stationery of good quality, plain white or very pale buff or gray and *black ink only*. Never send out a letter that discredits you by its appearance.

When writing a letter of application, use simple, familiar words that express your meaning clearly. Watch your spelling; be sure your punctuation and grammar are correct; avoid the misuse of words; avoid long, involved, confusing sentences.

There may be some excuse for lack of training and education, or even for lack of originality in your letter; but there can be no excuse for grammatical errors, misspelled words, trite phrases or poor punctuation. In these respects at least, let your letter be perfect. One sure way to mark your letter for the wastebasket is to misspell the name of the firm or the name of the individual to whom your letter is addressed.

The opening paragraph of your letter is perhaps the most important part of it. For if the first few sentences fail to win the reader's attention, the rest of the letter may not be read at all. Try to key your opening remarks to the needs or interests of the prospective employer—not to your own needs or desires. *Offer* something instead of asking for something. Right at the start, in the very first sentence if you can, make it clear that you have a *giving* attitude rather than a *getting* attitude. Put yourself in the reader's place; try to imagine the questions he would ask if he were seated across the table from you; try to capture his attention by showing a knowledge of, or a special interest in, his particular business.

For example, instead of opening your letter with some such trite, worn-out statement as, "I saw your advertisement in today's paper," plan your first sentence to arouse interest at once. You might say, "I have made a careful study of your advertising during the past six months," or, "I have made a survey in my neighborhood to find out how many housewives use your product and why they like it."

If there is nothing interesting or different in the first sentence or two of your letter, there is no incentive for a busy employer to read on. But if you can capture his attention at the beginning of your letter, hold it through your list of qualifications and experience, and close with specific information that makes it easy for him to get in touch with you for an interview . . . your letter has at least done a workmanlike job.

A very long letter that rambles on and on—long-winded and disorganized—makes no hit with busy executives. So try to keep your letter as brief and concise as you can. However be sure you tell everything about yourself that you think is necessary for getting the job. To avoid any essential facts concerning experience, training or education is to create a feeling of *evasion*, which, of course, does you more harm than good. Look upon your letter as an "interview on paper" in which you anticipate all likely questions and answer them clearly, to the point.

In writing a letter of application, bear in mind that the things a prospective employer is most likely to want to know about you are:

> Your age
> Your education
> Your domestic status (married or single)
> Your personality (how you get along with others)
> Your training
> Your experience
> Your abilities (what can you do?)
> Your record (what have you done?)
> Your work habits
> Your character
> Your aims or ambition

Try to avoid generalities in your letter of application. *Be specific.* Tell exactly which college you graduated from; give the names of the firms you worked for; be precise about kinds of jobs you have held. Above all, *be specific about the kind of job for which you are now applying.* Do not make the mistake of saying, "I'll do anything!" That's a sure way to rule yourself out. Ask for the *exact* job you want, and give the reasons why you feel you have something of special interest and value to bring to such a job.

If possible, avoid any mention of salary in your letter— unless the employer has requested it in his advertisement or in previous communication with you. It's always best not to give a specific figure, as the difference of a small amount may keep you from making a good connection. Rather than avoid the subject entirely, you might say: "As to salary, may we talk it over?" or "I'll be glad to discuss salary in a personal interview."

College graduates looking for their first positions often ask, "What can I offer in a letter? Employers want experience— which, naturally, no beginner has."

The answer is that *everything you've ever done is experience.* Were you ever on a debating team? Have you ever taken part in amateur theatricals? Did you ever sell subscriptions to magazines? Sift out all your experiences, whatever their nature, and see exactly what you have of value to offer the business world. If you have been president of your school literary club, won a prize for domestic science, edited the school paper, or even

been voted first in a popularity contest, say so. A good mixer is
an asset to any organization. So is the ability to write good
English. So is a knowledge of food, a knack for selling or a
talent for acting or directing. Any evidence of initiative, dependability, originality, perseverance or skill is well worth
mentioning in your letter of application if you have no previous
business experience to offer. Refuse to be discouraged or dis-
mayed by that lack; *dramatize what you have.*

It's important to write a good strong closing for your letter.
Avoid such colorless phrases as "awaiting a favorable reply" or
"hoping to hear from you soon." Make a specific request for an
interview such as, "May I telephone you on Thursday morning
to arrange for an interview?" Or give the prospective employer
something definite to do or expect, such as, "I'll telephone
tomorrow at ten o'clock to arrange for an interview" or, "If
your secretary will telephone me at Jamiston 4-6700, I'll be
happy to arrange for an interview any time to suit your convenience."

An excellent idea is to enclose a stamped, self-addressed envelope with your letter of application. That makes it easier and
more convenient for a prospective employer to get in touch
with you . . . and at the same time shows that you have
initiative and confidence in yourself. Another good idea is to
enclose a post card addressed to yourself and asking you to call
for an interview—leaving a blank space for the date and hour
to be filled in by the employer. It may be just some such simple
device that turns the tide in your favor when a busy employer
is going over scores of letters and does not know which to
choose.

Be *different* in your letter of application. Be original. But be
careful not to make yourself appear eccentric or bizarre. Stunt
or "trick" letters attract attention—and sometimes compel the
interest of the reader where a more familiar or commonplace
approach might fail to do so. But such devices should be used
only when applying for a job where promotional, imaginative,
creative or dramatic abilities are required. In general, freakish
or stunt letters are received with skepticism and distaste in the
average business office.

Always sign your name very carefully. We suggest that you
type or print out your name under the written signature so that
the prospective employer won't have to study it to make out the
proper spelling. Many an excellent job opportunity has been
lost because of an illegible signature.

If you send a photograph with your application, be sure it's
not too informal. For example, do not send a picture of yourself in a bathing suit on the beach, or romping with your dog or
posing in front of the family car. The picture should be of *you*

and nothing else. Don't send a passport photograph that makes
you look like an ex-convict. Don't send a group picture with a
circle drawn around yourself. Such pictures lack dignity and
do not help your cause. A small full-face photograph showing
your general appearance is best.

DON'TS IN PREPARING YOUR LETTER OF APPLICATION

Don't give details of your childhood and early school-
ing.

Don't relate your experiences in the war unless they
have some direct bearing on the job for which you are
applying.

Don't brag or boast; if you have some outstanding
ability, simply state the facts and let the employer
draw his own conclusions.

Don't be a bore; when you've said what you have to
say, close the letter. Don't add postscripts.

Don't refer to yourself as "the writer." It is not the
best form to say, "The writer has had five years' experience." Say, "I have had five years' experience."

Don't ask for a job because you need it . . . because
your father died . . . or your sister is an invalid.
Never base your appeal for work on sympathy, but
only on ability and what you have to offer.

Don't offer to work for very little "to get experience."
It's unwise to sell yourself as a bargain. People take
you at your own estimate of yourself; and if you don't
think you are worth much, no one else will.

Don't say you are not interested in salary; that makes
it sound as though you *are.*

Don't discuss "secret" ambitions or pet peeves. Concentrate on selling your abilities and qualifications.

Don't use the vague and ambiguous *"etc."* For example, don't say "I can typewrite, operate a switch-
board, etc." Enumerate *all* your capabilities.

Don't complain about, or criticize, a former employer. That hurts your chances more than it helps them.

Don't apply for a job for which you are unsuited, or for which you have inadequate qualifications. Go after the kind of job *you know you can do well.*

Don't use bookish, unfamiliar words in an effort to make an impression. Business men like terse, to-the-point language.

Don't waste space on unrelated subjects. If a man is looking for a copy writer, he is not interested in the fact that you were a marbles champion or won a waltz contest. He might, however, be very much interested in the fact that you won a prize for a short story.

Don't make demands. Don't write in an aggrieved tone, as though the world owes you a job and you are determined to get it. Employers are quick to perceive and to resent such an attitude.

Don't emphasize *your* needs, *your* hopes, *your* plans . . . what *you* expect or want from the job. Keep the employer's interests foremost. . . . Tell him what *he* will get and how *he* will benefit.

Don't be satisfied until you have written a letter you feel is original, interesting and forceful enough to stand apart from others, attract attention, *win you a hearing.*

It pays to take pains with your letter of application, to write and *rewrite* it until you are sure it shows you to best advantage.

EXAMPLES OF GOOD LETTERS OF APPLICATION

The following examples should help you prepare an effective, well-integrated letter. But use these examples as guides only, not as exact forms to follow. Use your own ideas and express your own personality—even though it may mean violating one or two of the points listed above. You needn't accept these points as absolute "musts"—though, in general, it's best to be guided by them, and by the examples that follow, unless you have good reasons to the contrary.

Dear Sir:

According to this morning's *Times,* you want an experienced, efficient secretary.

During the past 12 years I have served in that capacity to three prominent executives, all three of whom will vouch for my efficiency and dependability. They are:

Mr. Matthew Borden, Hollins-Borden Company, Trenton, N. J. (Hospital supplies) 19— - 19—.

Mr. Curtis Thompson, Worden Associates, New York. (Manufacturers of surgical instruments) 19— - 19—.

Mr. John Peterson, Billings, Holt & Company, New York. (Advertising agency) 19— - 19—.

Following the recent reorganization of Billings, Holt & Company, Mr. Peterson was transferred to Chicago—which is the reason I am now looking for another connection.

I am 29 years of age, a high school graduate, unmarried, living at home with my family. I am in excellent health, and am told that I make an especially good appearance for a secretary.

My former associates will tell you I am neat, accurate and painstaking in my work; that I am tactful and courteous; resourceful; loyal to the job; and of pleasing personality.

I am well-trained and experienced in all the many duties and responsibilities of a good secretary; and I should like the opportunity of coming in and talking with you personally. May I?

The self-addressed card is for your convenience. Just write on it when you would like me to come for an interview.

                                        Sincerely yours,

Dear Sir:

I am a typist, but not an ordinary one! I *like* typing. I thoroughly *enjoy* it. I take pride in turning out clean, attractive, well-spaced copy.

Your advertisement in this morning's *Transcript* appeals to me because I know I'd especially enjoy typing radio scripts. I offer my qualifications in the hope you will consider me for the job.

I am 24 years of age, a high school graduate and a graduate of the National Business Institute where I studied stenography as well as typing. I can take dictation when required, and I can operate a teletype machine; but I specialize in typing.

For two years I typed manuscripts for Mrs. Charles Weston, writer of mystery stories.

When Mr. Weston went to Hollywood, I joined the typing staff of Fred Olcott Associates, where I typed play scripts, synopses and reports. I was there for three years, then accepted the job I now hold with Lehn and Fisher, attorneys, where I am required to do the most exacting kind of legal typing.

It would be fascinating to type scripts again after a year of nothing but dull legal documents. I'd bring more than speed and efficiency to the job. I would bring a delightful new interest and enthusiasm—and that, of course, would mean more and better work for *you*.

Please check my former employers, including Lehn and Fisher who know about this letter. They will tell you I am conscientious, that I have an agreeable personality and appearance and that I get along well with everyone.

My telephone number is Lincoln 2046. I can start at once, if you like, as my present employers have known for some time that I plan to make a change.

Sincerely yours,

Dear Sir:

Your advertisement offers a most tempting job to a young man just out of college. I can't think of any job I'd like better than consumer research for a famous organization like yours. I look upon it as a wonderful opportunity, and here is what I can offer you in return:

I am 22 years of age, make a good appearance and get along exceedingly well with people.

I have an inquisitive and analytical mind—I enjoy finding out about things—I have tact and good humor—and the ability to draw people out.

Perhaps you will agree that these qualities—plus enthusiasm, persistence, and the willingness to work hard and long—make me acceptable for the job you offer as a beginner on your research staff.

I specialized in advertising and merchandising at New York University, from which I graduated in June—and I have unusual letters of recommendation from my instructors in these subjects. I should like the opportunity of showing them to you.

Although I have had no actual experience in consumer research, I am familiar with the procedure, and fully understand its significance in charting buying habits and trends.

I enclose a card addressed to myself, in the hope you will use it to tell me when to come for an interview. Or if you prefer calling, my telephone number is Plaza 6-3454.

                                        Sincerely yours,

Dear Mr. Bolton:

I understand from Mr. James Harris that there is an opening for a reporter on the staff of the New York *Sun*.

Four years' experience on the Middletown *Star*—writing a daily sports column as well as covering a regular news beat—gives me the confidence to apply for this desirable post.

I decided five years ago, when I graduated from Princeton, that reporting the news was my love—and my life's work. My first job was a sort of combination copy boy and rewrite man on the Middletown Press, where I learned the ropes . . . and got the idea for my somewhat unusual sports column. On the strength of this idea, I got a job on the regular staff of the *Star*, where I have been ever since.

I like my job. It has been a lot of fun. And Mr. Philip Jennings, the managing editor, will tell you I've been more than moderately successful; I've proved myself a good reporter and an alert, dependable newspaper man.

The reason for wanting to make a change at this time is an exciting reason to any young and ambitious reporter: *there's an opening on the New York Sun!* That's opportunity knocking with both fists. What intelligent newspaper man wouldn't welcome the broader opportunities of a big metropolitan daily like the *Sun!*

So I'm putting in my bid for the job, Mr. Bolton. I'm 26 years old, of good appearance and personality, married and have a year-old son. I like hard work. and I don't care how long my hours are. I'm told that I have a flair for quick and easy writing, a sense of the dramatic—and the well-known "nose for news."

I'll be in New York next Thursday, and will take the liberty of telephoning your secretary at 10 o'clock for an appointment sometime during the day. In the meantime, I enclose clippings of my columns and a few of my news stories to give you an idea of the kind of writing I can do.

I look forward to the pleasure of a personal interview.

                                        Sincerely yours,

Dear Mr. Winslow:

The Lowen Placement Agency informs me there will soon be an opening in your organization for an art director . . . and I ask you to consider my qualifications.

I am 43 years old, a graduate of Columbia University and the New York School of Fine and Applied Arts, and I have 20 years of successful experience behind me.

My first job was in the Bureau of Engravings, where I got a good basic training.

After a year I moved on to Frederick's Department Store where I was in full charge of all layouts and art work for newspaper advertising, booklets, mailing pieces and catalogs.

Two years later, having learned all I could from this job, I accepted an offer from Benton-Curt & Co. as art director on food accounts. Here I received the best training and experience of all, learning to know and practice all art and layout forms and techniques, how to organize and efficient staff, how to work constructively and well with others. Here I learned to be a good advertising executive as well as a good art director.

From Benton-Curt I went on to the Preston Agency, where I am now employed. I am director of the entire art department here; but as the emphasis is on radio rather than printed word advertising, the scope of my job is somewhat limited. That is my reason for wanting to make a change.

I have always admired your organization and should welcome the opportunity of becoming associated with it. My previous employers will tell you I am thoroughly competent and dependable, and that I have no undesirable traits of character or personality.

I enclose a card addressed to myself. Please fill in the day and hour you would like me to come, and I'll bring along some examples of my own art work, as

well as proofs of the many varied types of campaigns
I have supervised and directed.

Sincerely yours,

LETTERS OF REFERENCE

Dear Mr. Jones:

I am very glad of this opportunity to give Miss
Helen Fraser a reference.

She was my secretary at the New York office of the
Kenyon, Day Company; and I was certainly sorry to
lose her when I was transferred to the Chicago office.

Miss Fraser is an excellent secretary. She is efficient
and conscientious, always pleasant to everyone, tactful
and intelligent.

I recommend her without reservation, as I know you
will find her a most helpful and responsible secretary.

Sincerely yours,

Dear Mr. Burke:

I find it rather awkward to answer your letter about
Mr. Alan Roberts. I like him personally, but I cannot in
all fairness recommend him to you.

Roberts is unquestionably a talented young man,
with a flair for the dramatic and a real sense of show-
manship. He was program director of two of our day-
time shows for about a year; and he certainly knows his
business and can do a good job if he wants to.

But that's just the trouble: *he doesn't always want
to*. Sometimes he wants to drink instead, and then you
can't depend on him. He'll walk out on the job for a
couple of days and let somebody else take over. . . .
That's why he isn't here any more.

I'm sorry to have to tell you this, because Roberts has
great talent and ability, and he could probably become
the best program director in radio if he didn't drink.

Perhaps if you talked the situation over with him, and gave him the job on the understanding that he'd be fired the first time he took a drink, it might make a difference. I think it would be well worth trying, because he has so much to offer.

Sincerely yours,

LETTERS OF INTRODUCTION
AND REFERENCE

Dear Mr. Brown:

The bearer of this letter, Richard Collins, was my son's roommate at Exeter, and is a recent graduate of Harvard Law School. He is looking for a job in a law office where he can get sound basic training and experience, and he has asked me to give him a letter to you.

I have known young Collins for more than 10 years, and I can truthfully say I have never met a more likable, intelligent and ambitious young man. I only wish he had studied architecture instead of law—I'd take him on as an assistant without thinking twice about it!

I hope you can find room for Collins in your office, and start him on the way to the brilliant career I feel certain is ahead of him. If not, I know he'll appreciate just meeting and talking with you, as he has always had the greatest admiration for you and your work.

I'll be glad to return the compliment any time you want to send an ambitious young architect to see me!

Cordially yours,

LETTERS REQUESTING INFORMATION
FROM REFERENCES

Dear Sir:

Mr. James Merrill has given us your name as reference. He tells us he was credit manager of your store for three years, and that he left of his own accord to make another connection.

We should like to know whether you think Mr. Merrill is capable of handling the credit department of a large organization like ours. We shall appreciate any information you can give us about his personality, reliability, judgment . . . and especially his ability to work well with others.

We will, of course, keep your reply strictly confidential.

Very truly yours,

Gentlemen:

We are considering the application of Mr. John H. Payne for the position of accountant.

We understand that Mr. Payne was employed by you in that capacity from 19— to 19—.

It would be very helpful to us to have a statement from you as to his character, personality and ability. Can you tell us why he left your employ? He seems somewhat vague on that point.

Thank you very much for your help. You can be sure that any information you give us will be kept confidential.

Sincerely yours,

"THANK YOU" LETTER FOR HELP IN GETTING A JOB

Dear Mr. Butler:

I am now credit manager of Lambert, Strauss and Company—and very happy about it!

I know that the fine letter about me which you sent Mr. Strauss had a lot to do with getting me the job. I'm deeply grateful to you, not only for this particular reference but for the help and encouragement you have always given me.

I shall certainly make every effort to do an outstanding job here and justify your faith in me.

Sincerely yours,

6. Your Club Correspondence

In your club correspondence, simply follow the same general rules as in business correspondence. Keep in mind the *reason why* the letter is being written, and say what you have to say briefly, to the point—without rambling or writing of other things.

A great deal of club correspondence is about membership and dues. The following letters are offered as helpful suggestions.

Dear Mrs. Richmond:

I would like to present Mrs. Thomas Young for membership in the Century Club.

Mrs. Young has recently moved to Concord from New York. She has long been interested in civic improvement, and through her lectures has encouraged many clubs to undertake important projects for town and city betterment.

I am sure Mrs. Young would be a real addition to our membership.

Yours sincerely,

Dear Mrs. Carelton:

The Monmouth Garden Club takes great pleasure in inviting you to become a member.

We have sent you a folder containing all the information about our club. As you have already visited us several times, you know how charming the clubhouse and grounds are; and we know you will find the members interesting and congenial.

Our annual autumn flower show is scheduled for September 25, and is to be followed by a dinner and dance at the clubhouse. We hope you will be a member by that time and we look forward to having you with us.

Please let us know this week, if possible, whether you accept our invitation and will share our club activities.

Sincerely yours,

Dear Mr. Clark:

You have been suggested to me as a man who might like to take part in the very important work we are doing here at the Civic Center.

I am sure you are familiar with the work of this organization. I am enclosing booklets which tell about our aims and purposes, and some of our accomplishments. I am also enclosing our current program of events in the hope that you will find time to attend some of them—and see for yourself the work we are doing and its great value to the community.

I should like the privilege of proposing your name for membership. Will you be my guest at the next regular meeting, October 3rd, at eight o'clock? I'd like to meet you personally and answer any questions you may have about the organization.

Cordially yours,

Dear Mr. Esmond:

I am pleased to report that at the meeting of the Stamp Society, held on January 10th, you were elected to membership.

There will be a meeting at the home of Mr. Peter Crane, 46 Lake Drive, on Tuesday, January 28th, at eight o'clock.

We hope you will be with us at that time, and we look forward to greeting you as a member.

Sincerely yours,

Dear Mrs. Harkins:

It gives me great pleasure to accept your invitation to join the Ladies' Club.

I have long been interested in the programs and activities of the Club, and am delighted to become a member.

Sincerely yours,

Dear Mr. Pratt:

I appreciate the honor and courtesy of being nominated for membership in the Oakdale Council.

I am sorry I am unable to accept, but I am leaving for Manila at the end of this month to open a branch office of the Telecast Company—and I'll probably be gone for a year or more.

Please express my sincere thanks to the nominating Committee. I hope I shall again be given the opportunity to join on my return from Manila.

Sincerely yours,

Dear Mr. Manton:

In totaling and closing the Club's books for the year, I find that your dues have not been paid.

I'm sure this is just an oversight on your part, and that you will take care of the matter at once.

As soon as I receive your dues, I shall be able to close the books for the year and prepare my annual financial report.

Sincerely yours,

NOTIFICATION OF ELECTION TO OFFICE

Dear Mr. Crosby:

The Executive Committee of the Camden Sky Club has instructed me to notify you that you have been unanimously elected president for the coming year.

Your election is a great source of satisfaction to the members of the club. We look forward to a happy and successful year under your leadership and guidance.

Sincerely yours,

Dear Mr. Harrison:

Thank you for your letter confirming my election as president of the Historical Society.

I am happy and proud to receive this great honor, and shall do everything I can to make my term of office a pleasant and successful one for the Society.

Sincerely yours,

LETTERS OF RESIGNATION

Dear Mrs. Leslie:

Illness and unexpected duties at home make it impossible for me to continue my Club interests and activities. I am compelled to offer my resignation, effective at once.

I am sure you must know I do this with regret, for I have always enjoyed the Club and my association with the fine group of women who make up its membership.

I send my very best wishes for the continued success of the Club.

Sincerely yours,

Dear Mrs. Blanding:

Your letter of resignation was read at a meeting of the Ladies Club yesterday.

We are all sorry to hear you are moving to another part of the country and that you will no longer be with us. We accept your resignation only because we must.

We hope that you and your family will be happy and successful in California.

Cordially yours,

REQUESTS TO SPEAK OR ENTERTAIN
AT A CLUB

Dear Mrs. Hubbard:

The members of the Music League enjoyed your concert at the Town Hall so much last week that they are eager to have you give it this winter at one of our club meetings.

Will you let me know whether you would consider playing for us, and if so, what your terms are?

We would like you to give your concert here at the clubhouse on the evening of January 3rd, 10th or 17th —whichever is most convenient for you.

Sincerely yours,

Dear Mr. Stratford:

The Yacht Club is entertaining Mr. Robert Yorke at dinner on July 23rd.

As you know, Mr. Yorke is a world-famous yachtsman who has won many prizes here and abroad.

We should like to have you act as toastmaster at this dinner, as we know your witty remarks would add much to the success and enjoyment of the occasion.

May we hear from you soon—and *favorably?* I speak for all the members of the club when I say it would give us all great pleasure to have you act as official toastmaster of the evening.

Cordially yours,

Dear Mr. Grasslands:

The members of the Artists' Club are most interested in your lecture on "Modern American Painting."

Would it be possible for you to give this lecture on Tuesday, May 12th, at eight o'clock? We meet in the Art Exhibits Building, 92 Center Street, in Auditorium B. There are always at least 125 members at each meeting; and we usually pay $100 for feature lectures like yours.

We hope to have the pleasure of welcoming you on the twelfth and hearing your lecture.

Sincerely yours,

Dear Mr. Crile:

Bob Lanson has told me of your recent visit to Russia, and of the fascinating collection of color slides you brought back with you.

At the next regular meeting of our Town Forum, on September 20th, we plan to discuss Russia; and it would certainly be interesting and helpful if someone who was actually there could tell us about it.

Would you be willing to come to this meeting as our guest of honor to tell us what you saw in Russia and show us some of your pictures. It would be of tremendous interest to the members, and I'm sure they would greatly appreciate your courtesy and kindness.

We can supply a slide projector and screen unless you prefer using your own.

Sincerely yours,

ANSWERS TO INVITATIONS
FROM CLUBS

Dear Mrs. Colwell:

I shall be delighted to speak on "Modern Homemaking" before your Mother's Group on Wednesday, August 6th.

No, I don't require any props or equipment. I'll bring along everything I need for the lecture.

I understand I am to speak from 8:30 to 9:30 P.M., and then answer questions for about half an hour. I plan to get there about eight so that I can meet you and talk with you for a few minutes before the lecture.

Sincerely yours,

Dear Mrs. Brown:

I am happy to accept your invitation to play before the Music League on Tuesday evening, January 10th.

In addition to the Beethoven and Tchaikovsky selections you heard at my Town Hall concert, I'd like to play Brahms' *Rhapsodie* and Schumann's *Carnival*. I shall arrange the numbers and send you a complete program in a few days.

My fee is $200 for a two-hour recital.

Thank you for your interest, and for your most gracious invitation.

Sincerely yours,

Dear Mrs. King:

I'd love to come and sing for the Choral Club on April 4th, but I'll be in Washington on that day.

From Washington I go to Philadelphia, and then to New York, for a series of concerts. I won't be back here until May 30th, and therefore cannot make any engagements until after that date.

Please tell the members of the Club how sorry I am, and how deeply I appreciate the honor of their invitation. I hope they'll ask me again some day—and that the next time I'll be able to accept.

Sincerely yours,

LETTERS OF THANKS FOR SPEAKING OR ENTERTAINING AT A CLUB

When an invited guest speaks before a club or an organization—or sings, plays or otherwise entertains the members—a letter of appreciation should be written. This may be either a formal note of thanks in the name of the club secretary; or it may be a friendly, informal note written by the person who was responsible for the invitation.

Here is the way a formal note of thanks is generally expressed:

Dear Mr. Perkins:

The Program Committee of the Mothers' Club wishes to thank you for your lecture on March 10th.

We appreciate your interest in the Club, and your fine spirit of co-operation.

We'd like you to know that the members were unanimous in their praise of your most interesting and helpful talk.

Sincerely yours,

Informal notes are on a more friendly basis, expressing not only the thanks of the club but the personal appreciation of the member who issued the invitation. Frequently a gift accompanies the letter of thanks.

Dear Mrs. Emmett:

It was gracious of you to come all the way to Middletown to sing at the luncheon of the Professional Women's Club. I hope you know how much we appreciate it!

I speak for the entire membership when I thank you for giving so generously of your time and talent. We owe you a real debt of gratitude for one of the most delightful and enjoyable meetings of the year.

We hope you like the little gift we are sending with this letter to say, "Thank you for a wonderful concert!"

Cordially yours,

If the secretary of an organization writes to thank you for making an address or giving a concert, no acknowledgment is necessary. But a personal and complimentary note, telling you how well you spoke or played—and how much everyone enjoyed it—deserves a brief note of acknowledgment. For example:

Dear Mrs. Mason:

How nice of you to write me such a flattering letter!

I thoroughly enjoyed singing at the Community Club, and I'm glad the members liked me. I liked *them,* too! It's always gratifying to have such an attentive and appreciative audience.

It was a real pleasure to meet you and Mr. Mason, and I hope our paths will cross again.

Sincerely yours,

Book V

*

Children's Correspondence

* * *

1. The Letters All Children Must Learn to Write

The ability to express oneself easily and well on paper is an important asset, of ever-increasing usefulness throughout life ... and children cannot be trained too early to acquire it. One way is to encourage them, from a very early age, to write their own letters.

This does not mean composing letters for children to copy in their own sprawling, uncertain handwriting—dictating word for word what they should say. While that may help give the child a sense of responsibility toward letter writing, it won't do much to help develop the ability of self-expression.

Youngsters should be permitted to compose their own little social notes, their own personal letters to members of the family, as soon as they are able to guide a pen across paper and express themselves in understandable language. Grownups may make tactful suggestions, if they like; but they should not dictate. And they should not be too critical of a child's first efforts; for praise does far more than criticism toward encouraging a better effort next time.

So let the child express himself in his own words, however quaintly misused those words may be. A letter that clearly conveys the personality of the child and expresses his own thoughts and ideas has far greater charm and appeal than any precisely expressed letter in a child's handwriting but a grownup's words.

Children may hate to write letters, and may bitterly resent any obligation which makes letter writing necessary. Nevertheless there are certain letters every well-bred child *must* write. These include letters of thanks for gifts, favors and hospitality ... letters of congratulations to young relatives and friends

. . . letters of invitation and acknowledgment. And most important of all, perhaps—because they are the most eagerly awaited—are the letters children away at school or camp are expected to write to their doting parents back home.

Even very young children should be taught to recognize their responsibilities and write the letters expected of them *without waiting to be told.* They should grow up with an awareness of their obligation to those who are kind to them, who give them presents or entertain them in their homes. They should not be permitted to take such kindnesses or courtesies for granted, to let them go unnoticed. They should be taught that it's bad manners not to write the letters expected of them, and *especially* letters of thanks. Surely the aunt, uncle, grandparent or friend who sends a gift deserves a note of appreciation. And the more enthusiastic the note is, the more natural and spontaneous—and characteristic of the child's own personality—the more pleasure it is bound to give.

CHILDREN'S THANK-YOU NOTES
FOR GIFTS

Children should be trained to write their notes of thanks while the glow is still with them—while they are excited and happy about the gift. They should get their gratitude down on paper while it's still gurgling inside them, not wait until it's worn off.

Here are some examples of letters of thanks to guide the young beginner. The first few are presumably the letters of very young tots, just learning how to express themselves; the others are those of somewhat older children:

Dear Uncle Jim:

I always wanted a train. Thank you for sending me a train for Christmas. It is wonderful. It lights up and whistles like a real train.

I got a drum and a wagon, too. But I like my train best of all. I like to make it go through the tunnel.

I hope you will come and see us soon.

With love,
Peter

Dear Aunt Jean:

That's a wonderful dollhouse you sent me. It's so big and beautiful. Thank you very, very much. All my friends say I am lucky to have such a nice aunt.

When you come to see me, I'll show you how I fixed up the house with furniture. I make believe it's a real house. Mother is making curtains for the windows.

I didn't have a party this year because Ginny was sick. But she is better now. This morning she got out of bed to see my dollhouse.

I almost forgot to tell you—Dad gave me a little black kitten for my birthday. He's the cutest thing! He has white feet, and his name is Jinx. You must come and see him.

Thanks again for the beautiful dollhouse.

> With love,
> Patsy

Dear Peggy:

I'm sorry you couldn't come to my party. I hope your cold is better now.

Thank you for the books. I'm reading *Heidi* now, and I love it.

Can you come and see me when you are better? I have a new game I'd like to play with you. It's called "Monopoly" and it's lots of fun.

Guess what? My dad promised me a puppy! We're going to pick it out on Saturday. I'm so excited about it I can hardly wait.

Thanks again for the books, Peggy—and hurry and get well!

> Your Friend,
> Anita

Dear Mrs. Cranston:

I was so surprised to receive your gift. It was sweet of you to remember me at Christmas.

I like the scrap book very, very much. I think it's beautiful. I'm going to save it just for very special clippings, and keep it always.

Thank you, Mrs. Cranston—and I hope you and Mr. Cranston have a very happy New Year.

Affectionately,
Rosalind

Dear Aunt Ruth:

I just can't think of *anything* I'd have liked more than "The Treasury of Stephen Foster"! I love the songs and I'll enjoy playing them. The pictures are so beautiful, too. It's a simply wonderful graduation gift, and I'm delighted with it.

Thank you so much, Aunt Ruth! I hope you'll come and see us soon so that I can play some of the songs for you and hear you sing them. I wish I had a voice like yours!

The graduation exercises were very nice. I'm sorry you couldn't come. I got the silver Music Medal and two honor certificates.

Mother and Dad send their love. Thanks again. . . .

Affectionately,
Janice

Dear Grandma:

I am sorry you were too ill to come to my confirmation. Everybody was disappointed not to see you there. I hope you are all better now.

Thanks for the brief case. I like it a lot. I'll have good use of it in high school.

Dad gave me a watch just like Jerry's. It's shock-proof and waterproof. I like the watch and your brief case best of all the gifts I received.

Hurry and get well, Grandma. We don't like you to be ill. Love from all of us,

Dick

CHILDREN'S THANK-YOU NOTES FOR HOSPITALITY

When a child is entertained as a house or week-end guest at the home of a friend, a note of thanks should be written to the young host or hostess. The mother also should be thanked, either in the same letter or in a separate one.

Dear Mrs. Watson:

I want to thank you for the lovely time I had at your house. It was one of the best times I ever had. I enjoyed the movies so much; and I just loved the buffet supper in the garden.

I hope you will let Anita come and spend a week end with us soon.

Mother and Dad send best regards.

Sincerely yours,
Patsy

A note like that, in a child's round scrawl, certainly makes one want to invite her again! And even though an occasional word is misspelled, one doesn't mind; for it shows that the note was written by the little girl herself, without grown-up help.

Here are some examples of thank-you notes from children to young friends who entertained them:

Dear Fred:

I had a wonderful time at your house. It was lots of fun to go ice skating on the pond. I wish we had a pond like that near *our* house!

Please tell your mother I enjoyed the barbecue very much. I think it was swell of her to go to so much trouble for me.

Don't forget! You promised to come here for a week end real soon. Mother says she'll get tickets for the Music Hall as soon as she knows when you are coming. Thanks for everything.

Your pal,
Eddie

Dear Sandra:

Thank you for the lovely time I had at your house.

I've just been telling Mother what fun I had. You always dream up the most unusual ideas! I think I enjoyed the Treasure Hunt most of all—especially the nice prize I won.

Be sure and thank your mother for me. That was a wonderful dinner party she gave us on Saturday; and the beach picnic was simply *super*. Wasn't Claire funny in the charades? I still giggle every time I think of her trying to act out *The Egg and I!*

Remember—we expect you here on July 15th. Let us know what train you are taking and we'll meet you at the station. I'm not as clever as you are, but I promise you a good time anyway!

Your loving friend,
Lenore

CHILDREN'S PERSONAL CORRESPONDENCE

In their correspondence with family and friends, youngsters should be encouraged to write as they speak, without self-consciousness or constraint. This is more easily accomplished by *suggestion* than by scolding or faultfinding.

For example, a child going away to school or camp is generally warned to "write as soon as you get there!" He is reminded half a dozen times "now don't you forget!" As a result, his letters home are usually brief and hurried . . . and sadly inadequate. They sound something like this:

Dear Mom:

I am fine. How are you? Please send me some cookies.

Love,
Johnny

Then, perhaps, the disappointed parent writes back . . . and
scolds . . . "Why don't you write me a nice long letter? You
know how I miss you!"

But instead of warning or scolding, the youngster should be
encouraged by *helpful suggestion*. He should be told what is
expected of him in a letter home—what he should write about.
Not "Why don't you write me a nice long letter"—but this:

I met Charlie's mother today and she says he has
learned how to swim. Imagine! Only two weeks at
camp and he can swim. How about you, Johnny? Can
you swim yet? What else have you learned to do at
camp? Be sure and write me all about it in your next
letter so I can tell Charlie's mother what *you* can do.

Don't expect too much of a very young child away from
home for the first time. The newness and excitement of strange
surroundings often make it difficult for a child to write. Just
give the youngster some stamped, addressed stationery (to
make it as easy as possible) and suggest that you would be
interested to know:

— how he enjoyed the trip to camp or school
— how he likes his new surroundings
— how he likes his new young friends
— what he did the first day or two
— what he likes most about school or camp
— whether there's anything he wants or needs

Remember: Don't scold, criticize or find fault—*make suggestions* instead. Children can be encouraged and drawn out in
their letters the same as in conversation. The following examples, read to children before they go away to school or camp,
may prove helpful. They start with the uncertain letters of a
seven-year-old, away for the first time—and progress through
various stages of childish development to the confident letters
of a teenager.

Dear Mother:

I like it very much at camp. It is fun. We play games and go swimming. I am learning how to swim. On the train I sat with Peter, and he let me look at his comic books.

Peter is in my bunk. His bed is next to mine. There is another boy whose name is Tommy. I like him.

Are you coming to see me soon? Mothers can come on Sunday.

Love,
Tommy

Dear Mother:

It is nice here. The lake is right near my bunk. There is a little house with rabbits, snakes and turtles. There are some ducks, too. The nature teacher takes care of them, but he lets us watch when they eat dinner.

I like shop best of all. We make things in shop. I am going to make a tray for you.

We had chicken for lunch today. It was very good. We had ice cream for dessert. After lunch we all marched out singing camp songs.

I must say good-by now. We are going swimming. Don't forget to come and see me.

With love,
Dick

Dear Dad:

Jasper Camp is swell. I like it a lot. The lake is even bigger than Pinecrest; and the fellows say there is good fishing.

All the boys in my bunk have been here before. They know one another from last year. But I made friends with them right away, as you said I should . . . and we get along fine.

We have two teams—the yellow and the green. The teams have tournaments and swimming meets. The good swimmers are allowed to go out in canoes for the boat races. At the end of the year the team that wins gets a prize. I am on the yellow team.

Do you know what? I forgot to take my flashlight along. Will you tell mother to send it, please? I need it at night when we walk back from the Recreation Hall. That's where they show the movies. We are going to see *Meeting at Midnight* tomorrow after dinner.

It's raining today, so we can't go swimming. Isn't that a shame? I guess I like swimming best of all, dad. I'm going to learn how to dive this summer.

How is Mother? I hope everything at home is all right. I miss you both very much.

With love,
Peter

Dear Mom and Dad:

Well, another week is over and the days are speeding by. Soon I'll be coming home for Christmas. I can hardly wait. It seems *ages* since I saw you!

Everything here is fine. The tests weren't too hard, and I'm sure I passed with high marks. I expect honors in history and math—and maybe in Spanish, too.

I saw the perfect Christmas gift for Judy in a little shop here. I'm not going to tell you what it is because she may see this letter. How is Judy-braids getting along? Is she still having so much trouble with her spelling? I wouldn't know, of course, because she never writes to me. I guess big sisters just don't count with the pigtail crowd!

I got a box of cookies from Aunt Alice last week. They were delicious. Barbara and I had a real picnic in our room. I wrote to Aunt Alice and told her how good they were and how much I enjoyed them. She's so sweet—she's always sending me things. I must get her a real nice Christmas gift this year.

By the way, I went to the Exeter game last Thursday. Exeter beat Andover 17 to 6. It was awfully cold but I wore my beaver coat and my stadium boots and I felt nice and snug. We all had hot chocolates before we went back to school.

I hope you are well and that everything at home is fine. Don't forget to send me my plane ticket. I'd like to take the two-o'clock plane from Boston; there's a train out of here at 11:15 and that would get me to Boston in plenty of time.

My, it's exciting to be going home! I'm counting the days, darlings. Love to you both—and to that little imp, Judy.

> Your devoted
> Suzanne

2. Children's Invitations and Acknowledgments

Children's party invitations are usually in the form of gaily decorated cards with blank spaces for filling in the date, place, hour, occasion and so on. Even very young children should be permitted to fill in and address their own party invitations, as it gives them a sense of social responsibility. But it's wise to check on the time, date and other essential data to make sure it's entirely correct.

When printed cards of invitation are not used, notes are written—either by the child or by his mother. Naturally a child of three or four needs to have his invitations written for him.

NOTES OF INVITATION

Dear Mrs. Davis:

Jimmy will be four years old on Saturday, June 10th, and I'm having a little birthday party for him.

I know he won't be happy unless his pal, Ronnie, is at the party; so I hope you will let him come.

If you bring Ronnie about three, he'll be just in time for the fun. I'd like you to stay and have tea with the other mothers at five. But if you can't stay, I'll see that Ronnie is safely delivered to your door no later than six o'clock.

Sincerely yours,
Ethel B. Hubbard

Ronnie's mother promptly writes a friendly note of acceptance or regret. If her little boy cannot attend the party, she explains why in her letter.

Dear Mrs. Hubbard:

Ronnie is thrilled and excited about Jimmy's birthday party. Of course he'll be there—with his best party manners, I hope!

I'll bring him at three and call for him about six, so you won't need to bother about getting him home.

I'd like very much to stay and have tea with the other mothers, but I have a previous appointment for the afternoon and I can't very well get out of it. Thanks for asking me.

Sincerely yours,
Martha P. Davis

Dear Mrs. Hubbard:

I haven't told Ronnie about the birthday party because I know how disappointed he would be not to go. But he is scheduled to take a series of allergy tests on June 10th and unfortunately the date cannot be changed.

I am sure you understand, and that you and Jimmy will forgive Ronnie for not being there.

Thank you for Ronnie and myself for your gracious invitation. And many happy returns of the day!

Sincerely yours,
Martha P. Davis

As soon as a child is old enough to write his own invitations, he should be permitted to do so. Don't tell him the *exact words* to write; just make whatever helpful suggestions you think are necessary. Let the invitation be natural and childish.

Dear Marian:

Next Sunday is my birthday. I will be eight years old. I am going to have a cake with eight candles. Can you come to my party? It starts at two o'clock. Good-by, but don't forget to come.

Judy

Dear Peggy:

Will you come to my house on Wednesday, February 12th, at one o'clock? It's Lincoln's birthday, and there's no school.

Mother's letting me have a real grown-up luncheon party. So come at one, and bring your appetite along! We'll play games in the afternoon, and there's a special surprise . . . but I'm not going to tell you what it is.

I hope you can come. You know most of the girls I've invited and I'm sure you'll have a good time.

Love,
Annette

NOTES OF ACCEPTANCE

Children's party invitations are not, as a rule, as conscientiously acknowledged as adult invitations. They don't need to be. Sometimes the mother telephones to say the young guest will be there. Sometimes the child's presence on the day of the party is the only acknowledgment. It's always more gracious, of course, to write a note of acceptance . . . and youngsters should be encouraged to do so. But there's no question about the need for acknowledgment when a child *cannot* attend. In that case a note of regret must be sent at once, explaining why the invitation cannot be accepted.

Following are specimen letters of acceptance and regret to guide the young beginner in his social duties:

Dear Joseph:

Thank you for inviting me to your party. I am very glad to come. The movies sound wonderful. I'll see you on Saturday.

Your pal,
Richard

Dear Mrs. Collins:

I want to thank you for inviting me to spend the week end with Joan. I'll be glad to come, and I know I'll have a wonderful time. I always do with Joan!

Dad will drive me to Hawthorne Saturday morning and call for me Sunday evening—but thanks very much for offering to call for me.

I'm looking forward to seeing you this week end.

Sincerely yours,
Phyllis

NOTES OF REGRET

Dear Tom:

Mother says to tell you I can't come on Friday because my Dad's coming back from England, and she wants me to be here.

I hate to miss your party. But I'm sure excited about seeing my Dad.

Happy birthday, Tom—and thanks a lot for inviting me.

Larry

Appendix

Forms of Address

Forms of salutation beginning with *"My dear"* are not included in the chart. In all cases, *"My dear"* may be used instead of *"Dear"* for greater formality. (This applies to the United States only, as in Great Britain the reverse is true.)

The words *"honor"* and *honorable"* are spelled according to the residence of the person addressed. In the United States, *"honor"* and *"honorable"* are preferred; in Great Britain *"honour"* and *"honourable"* are the preferred forms.

Social invitations to a married man of title or rank are addressed to the man *and* his wife. For example:

> Senator and Mrs. James Blank
> The President and Mrs. Blank
> Lord and Lady Blank
> Their Excellencies, The French Ambassador and
>   Mrs. Blank

When the wife is the person of title or rank, the husband's name is still written first on the envelope and inside address. For example:

> Mr. John and the Honorable Mary Smith
> Mr. Frank and Dr. Margaret Symonds
> Mr. George and Lady Mary Blakely

The use of the word *to*—as in "To his Grace, the Duke of York"—is optional. There is no hard and fast rule about it; you may use it or not, as you prefer. Our own choice is for the simpler form: "His Grace, the Duke of York."

Old feudal phrases of courtesy like "My Lord" and "Your Lordship" are not used in the United States. But they should be used by an American writing to dignitaries of foreign countries entitled by tradition to such forms of address.

RANK OR TITLE   ABBOT

Address the Envelope   *Begin the Letter*

The Lord Abbot of Fieldston   Dear Father Abbot:
          or   My Lord Abbot:
The Right Reverend Abbot Blank

AIR FORCE OFFICERS

Like Army and Naval Officers

ALDERMAN

Alderman John Smith   Dear Sir:
                                 Dear Mr. Smith:

AMBASSADOR (American)

His Excellency the American   Sir:
    Ambassador to Great Britain Your Excellency:
American Embassy   Dear Mr. Ambassador:
London, England
          or
The Honorable John D. Smith
American Ambassador to Great Britain
American Embassy
London, England

AMBASSADOR (British and other foreign countries)

His Excellency the Ambassador of Sir:
    Great Britain   Excellency:
British Embassy   Your Excellency:
Washington, D.C.   Dear Mr. Ambassador:
          or
His Excellency John Farbish
Ambassador of Great Britain
British Embassy
Washington, D.C.

ARCHBISHOP (Anglican)

His Grace the Lord Archbishop   My Lord Archbishop:
    of London   Your Grace:

RANK OR TITLE   ARCHBISHOP (Catholic)

Address the Envelope	*Begin the Letter*

The Most Reverend John Smith   Most Reverend Sir:
Archbishop of St. Louis   Most Reverend Arch-
       or   bishop:
The Most Reverend Archbishop   (In England:)
   Smith   Your Grace:
(Followed by postal address)   My Lord:
                                My Lord Archbishop:

ARCHDEACON

The Venerable John Falten   Venerable Sir:
Archdeacon of New Orleans

ARMY OFFICERS

Always address letters to army officers   Sir: (formal)
in accordance with their exact rank.   Dear General Fiske:
(In the salutation, however, you   Dear Colonel Pryor:
drop the qualifying adjective—such   Dear Sgt. Blank:
as the "Lieutenant" in "Lieutenant   Dear Corporal Smith:
Colonel." In other words, letters to
both "Lieutenant Colonel Phillips"
and "Colonel Pryor" would begin
"Dear Colonel ——") A retired
army officer is addressed by his title,
with "U.S.A., Ret." following his
name. A doctor, dentist or clergyman may be addressed either by his
professional degree or his army
rank, unless he is in an administrative capacity—in which case the
army rank is always used.

Lieutenant General John Fiske
Commanding Officer
Army of the United States
3rd Corps Area
(Followed by postal address)

Major General John Crane, U.S.A.
Commanding Officer, 2nd Tank
   Corps

RANK OR TITLE   ARMY OFFICERS

Address the Envelope   *Begin the Letter*

Colonel Arthur Pryor
Medical Corps, U.S.A.

Major Thomas Quinn, U.S.A., Ret.
(Postal address only)

Captain James T. Ballard
Field Artillery, U.S.A.

Lieutenant Peter Adams
Coast Artillery, U.S.A.
              or
Peter Adams
Lieutenant, Coast Artillery, U.S.A.

Corporal Henry T. Smith
5th Quartermaster Corps, U.S.A.
              or
Henry T. Smith
Corporal, 5th Quartermaster Corps,
    U.S.A.

ASSEMBLYMAN

The Honorable John B. Rogers   Sir:
Member of Assembly   Dear Sir:
Albany, New York   Dear Mr. Rogers:
              or
Assemblyman John B. Rogers
The State Capitol
Albany, New York

ASSISTANT SECRETARY (Assistant to a cabinet officer)

Washington, D.C.   Sir:
The Assistant Secretary of Commerce   Dear Sir:
              or   Dear Mr. Hansen:
Honorable John B. Hansen
Assistant Secretary of Commerce
Washington, D.C.

RANK OR TITLE

ASSOCIATE JUDGE OF A COURT OF APPEALS

Address the Envelope	*Begin the Letter*
The Honorable John Clearly	Sir:
Associate Judge of the Court of Appeals	Dear Sir:
peals	Your Honor:
Albany, New York	Dear Mr. Justice:

ASSOCIATE JUSTICE OF A STATE SUPREME COURT

The Honorable Frank Parsons	Sir:
Associate Justice of the Supreme Court	Dear Sir:
Court	Your Honor:
Albany, New York	Dear Mr. Justice:

ASSOCIATE JUSTICE OF THE SUPREME COURT OF THE UNITED STATES

The Honorable Edward Brent	Dear Sir:
Associate Justice of the Supreme Court	Dear Mr. Justice:
Court	Dear Justice Brent:
Washington, D.C.	

or

The Honorable Edward Brent
Justice, Supreme Court of the United
States
Washington, D.C.

or

Mr. Justice Brent
Supreme Court of the United States
Washingon, D.C.

ATTORNEY GENERAL

The Honorable	Sir:
The Attorney General of the United States	Dear Sir:
States	Dear Mr. Attorney
Washington, D.C.	General:

or

The Honorable John Lane
Attorney General of the United States
Washington, D.C.

RANK OR TITLE

BARON

Address the Envelope   *Begin the Letter*

The Right Honourable Lord Blakely   My Lord:
          or
The Lord Blakely

BARONESS

The Right Honourable the Baroness   Madam:
    Cleve
          or
The Lady Cleve

BARONET

Sir John Holt, Bt. (or Bart.)   Sir:

BISHOP (Anglican)

The Right Reverend the Lord Bishop   My Lord Bishop:
    of Sussex   My Lord:
          or
The Lord Bishop of Sussex

BISHOP (Catholic)

The Most Reverend Thomas Hall   Your Excellency:
Bishop of Chicago   Dear Bishop Hall:
          or
The Right Reverend Bishop Hall

BISHOP (Methodist)

The Reverend Bishop John Smith   Dear Bishop Smith:

Bishop (Protestant Episcopal)

The Right Reverend Michael Vale   Right Reverend and
Bishop of Cleveland   Dear Sir:
                                        Dear Bishop Vale:

CARDINAL

His Eminence John, Cardinal Blank   Your Eminence:

RANK OR TITLE

CHIEF JUDGE OF A COURT OF APPEALS

Address the Envelope	*Begin the Letter*
The Chief Judge of the Court of Appeals	Sir:
	Dear Sir:
Albany, New York	Dear Judge Brown:
or	
The Honorable Myron F. Brown	
Chief Judge of the Court of Appeals	
Albany, New York	

CHIEF JUSTICE OF A STATE SUPREME COURT

The Chief Justice	Sir:
Supreme Court of the State of New York	Dear Sir:
	Dear Mr. Chief Justice:
Albany, New York	Dear Mr. Justice Gilmore:
or	
Honorable Patrick Gilmore	
Chief Justice of the Supreme Court	
Albany, New York	

CHIEF JUSTICE OF THE UNITED STATES

The Chief Justice of the United States	Sir:
	Dear Sir:
Washington, D. C.	Dear Mr. Chief Justice:
or	Dear Mr. Justice Blank:
The Honorable John Blank	
Chief Justice of the Supreme Court of the United States	
Washington, D. C.	
or	
The Chief Justice	
Washington, D. C.	

CLERGYMAN

The Reverend Frank Hall	Dear Sir:
or	Reverend Sir:
Reverend and Mrs. Frank Hall	Dear Mr. and Mrs. Hall:
or (if a doctor of divinity)	
Reverend Dr. Frank Hall	Dear Dr. Hall

RANK OR TITLE
COMMISSIONER OF A GOVERNMENT BUREAU

Address the Envelope	*Begin the Letter*

The Commissioner of the Bureau of
    Education   Sir:
Department of the Interior   Dear Sir:
Washington, D. C.   Dear Mr. Commis-
           or   sioner:
The Honorable Dwight Kelley   Dear Mr. Kelley:
Commissioner of the Bureau of
    Education
Department of the Interior
Washington, D. C.

CONGRESSMAN

See Representative in Congress

CONSUL

The American Consul at London   Sir:
London, England   Dear Sir:
       or   Dear Mr. Smith:
Mr. John Smith
American Consul at London
London, England

COUNTESS

The Right Honourable the   Madam:
    Countess of Blank   Dear Lady Greystone:
       or
The Countess Greystone

DEACON

The Reverend Deacon Black   Reverend Sir

DEAN (Ecclesiastic)

The Very Reverend the Dean of   Very Reverend Sir:
    Barth   Sir:

RANK OR TITLE

DEAN OF A COLLEGE OR UNIVERSITY

Address the Envelope	*Begin the Letter*
Dean Albert S. Frank School of Business Columbia University New York, N. Y. <center>*or*</center>Albert S. Frank, Ph.D. Dean of the School of Business Columbia University New York, N. Y. <center>*or*</center>Dr. Albert S. Frank Dean of the School of Business Columbia University New York, N. Y.	Dear Sir: Dear Dean Frank: Dear Dr. Frank: Dear Mr. Frank: (if he does not hold a doctor's degree)

DELEGATE (Member of the House of Delegates of a State Legislature)

The Honorable John F. Weylin The House of Delegates Charleston, West Virginia	Sir: Dear Sir: Dear Mr. Weylin:

DUCHESS

Her Grace, the Duchess of Blank	Madam: Your Grace:

DUCHESS OF THE ROYAL BLOOD

Her Royal Highness the Duchess of Kent	Madam: May it please your Royal Highness:

DUKE

His Grace, the Duke of Blank	My Lord Duke: Your Grace:

DUKE OF THE ROYAL BLOOD

His Royal Highness the Duke of Kent	Sir: May it please your Royal Highness:

RANK OR TITLE
EARL

Address the Envelope	*Begin the Letter*
The Right Honourable the Earl of Blank	My Lord:
	Sir:
or	Dear Lord Grayson:
The Earl of Blank	

EARL'S WIFE

See "Countess" above

GOVERNOR OF A STATE

The Honorable the Governor of Michigan	Dear Sir:
Lansing, Michigan	Your Excellency:
or	Dear Governor Tarr:
His Excellency	
The Governor of Michigan	
Lansing, Michigan	
or	
His Excellency, John E. Tarr	
Governor of Michigan	
Lansing, Michigan	
or	
The Honorable John E. Tarr	
Governor of Michigan	
Lansing, Michigan	

HEAD OF A STATE DEPARTMENT

The Secretary of State*	Sir:
The State Capitol	Dear Sir:
Topeka, Kansas	Dear Mr. Blank:
or	
The Secretary of State	
State of Kansas	
Topeka, Kansas	
or	
The Honorable John C. Blank	
Secretary of State	
The State Capitol	
Topeka, Kansas	

* Some states (like Pennsylvania and Massachusetts) use the term "Commonwealth" instead of "State." The first line in that case would read: "The Secretary of the Commonwealth."

RANK OR TITLE

INSTRUCTOR IN A COLLEGE OR UNIVERSITY

Address the Envelope	*Begin the Letter*

John T. Rice, Ph.D.
Department of Economics*
Harvard University
Cambridge, Massachusetts
or
Dr. John T. Rice
Department of Economics
Harvard University
Cambridge, Massachusetts
or
(if the instructor does not hold a
doctor's degree)
Mr. John T. Rice
Department of Economics
Harvard University
Cambridge, Massachusetts

Dear Sir:
Dear Dr. Rice
Dear Mr. Rice: (if he
holds no doctor's de-
gree)

JUDGE OF A FEDERAL DISTRICT COURT

The Honorable Frank Preston
United States District Judge
Eastern District of New York
Brooklyn, New York

Sir:
Dear Sir:
Dear Judge Preston:

JUSTICE OF THE SUPREME COURT

See Associate Justice of the Supreme Court of the United States

KING

The King's Most Excellent Majesty
or
His Most Gracious Majesty, King
George

Sir:
May it please your
Majesty:

---

* If the word "Instructor" is substituted for "Department" the word "in" is
used instead of "of." For example: "Instructor in Economics" (but "Department *of*
Economics").

RANK OR TITLE
LADY

Address the Envelope	*Begin the Letter*
The title "Lady" is held by all peeresses under the rank of Duchess. It is also held by all daughters of dukes, marquises and earls—and by the wives of baronets, knights and lords of session.	Madam: My Lady: Your Ladyship:

The envelope is addressed:
> Lady Florence Heath
>> *or*
>
> Lady Heath
>> *or*
>
> The Honourable Lady Florence

LEGISLATOR

The Honorable Arthur James The State Legislature Albany, New York *or* The Honorable Arthur James Member of Legislature The State Capitol Albany, New York	Sir: Dear Sir: Dear Mr. James:

LIEUTENANT GOVERNOR OF A STATE

The Lieutenant Governor State of Wisconsin Madison, Wisconsin *or* The Honorable Edward Doyle Lieutenant Governor of Wisconsin Madison, Wisconsin	Sir: Dear Sir: Dear Mr. Doyle:

LORD OF SESSION

Honourable Lord Overton	My Lord:

MARCHIONESS

The Most Honourable the Marchioness of Blankton	Madam:

RANK OR TITLE

MARINE OFFICERS

Address the Envelope	*Begin the Letter*

Like Army and Naval Officers. The appropriate designation—U.S.M.C. (United States Marine Corps)— should follow the branch of the service in which the person addressed is engaged. For example:

    Colonel Roy Tait
    Medical Corps, U.S.M.C.

MARQUIS

The Most Honourable the Marquis of Blank	My Lord Blank:
or	
The Marquis of Blank	

MAYOR OF A CITY

The Mayor of the City of Chicago	Sir:
City Hall	Dear Sir:
Chicago, Illinois	Dear Mayor Blank:
or	Dear Mr. Mayor:
The Honorable John F. Blank	
Mayor of the City of Chicago	
City Hall	
Chicago, Illinois	

MINISTER (Diplomatic) *American*

His Excellency	Sir:
The American Minister	Your Excellency:
Stockholm, Sweden	Dear Mr. Minister:
or	Dear Sir:
His Excellency Carl Hawks	
American Minister	
Stockholm, Sweden	
or	
The Honorable Carl Hawks	
American Minister	
Stockholm, Sweden	

RANK OR TITLE
MINISTER (Diplomatic) *Foreign*

Address the Envelope	*Begin the Letter*
His Excellency	Sir:
The Swedish Minister	Your Excellency:
The Swedish Legation	Dear Mr. Minister:
Washington, D.C.	Dear Sir:
or	
The Honorable James Fount	
Minister of Sweden	
The Swedish Legation	
Washington, D.C.	

MINISTER OF RELIGION

See Clergyman, Priest, Rabbi

MONSIGNOR

The Right Reverend Monsignor	Right Reverend Sir:
Blank	Dear Monsignor:

MOTHER SUPERIOR OF A SISTERHOOD

Reverend Mother Superior	Reverend Mother:
or	Dear Reverend Mother:
Reverend Mother Mary (followed by initials designating the order)	
or	
Reverend Mother Superior Mary (without the initials designating the order)	
or	
Mother Mary, Superior	
Convent of the Blessed Virgin	

NAVAL OFFICERS

Always address letters to naval officers in accordance with their exact rank. (In the salutation, however, you drop the qualifying adjective —such as the "Rear" in "Rear Admiral." In other words, letters to both "Admiral Bailey" and "Rear Admiral Shannon" would begin "Dear Admiral ———") A doctor,	Sir: (formal)
	Dear Admiral Bailey:
	Dear Captain Blank:
	Dear Cadet Holt:

dentist or clergyman may be addressed either by his professional degree or his naval rank, unless he is in an administrative capacity—in which case the rank is always used.

Admiral James K. Bailey
Chief of Naval Operations
Navy Department
Washington, D.C.

Rear Admiral Thomas Shannon
New London Submarine Base
New London, Connecticut

Captain John Blank, U.S.N.
U.S.S. Missouri
Pensacola, Florida

Lieutenant Commander John Wagner
Medical Corps, U.S.N.
Philadelphia Navy Yard
Philadelphia, Pennsylvania

NUN

See Sister of a Religious Order

POPE

His Holiness the Pope	Your Holiness:
His Holiness, Pope Pius XII	Most Holy Father:

POSTMASTER GENERAL

The Honorable the Postmaster General	Sir:
	Dear Sir:
Washington, D.C.	Dear Mr. Postmaster
or	General:
The Honorable William Kane	Dear Mr. Kane:
The Postmaster General	
Washington, D.C.	

RANK OR TITLE
PRESIDENT OF A COLLEGE OR UNIVERSITY

Address the Envelope   *Begin the Letter*

John Smith, LL.D. (or Lit.D.,   Dear President Smith:
    D.Sc., etc.)
President of Dartmouth College
Hanover, New Hampshire
         or
Dr. John Smith
President of Dartmouth College
Hanover, New Hampshire
    or (if he holds no doctor's degree)
President John Smith
Dartmouth College
Hanover, New Hampshire

PRESIDENT OF A THEOLOGICAL SEMINARY

The Reverend President John K.   Dear Sir:
    Hancock   Dear President Han-
Western Theological Seminary   cock:
Austin, Texas

PRESIDENT OF STATE SENATE

The Honorable Richard Daly   Sir:
President of the State Senate of Kansas
The State Capitol
Topeka, Kansas

PRESIDENT OF THE SENATE OF THE UNITED STATES

The Honorable   Sir:
The President of the Senate of the
    United States
Washington, D.C.
         or
The Honorable Thomas Fenton
President of the Senate
Washington, D.C.

RANK OR TITLE

PRESIDENT OF THE UNITED STATES

Address the Envelope	*Begin the Letter*

The President
The White House
Washington, D.C.

or

The President of the United States
The White House
Washington, D.C.

or

The President
Washington, D.C.

or

President John Blank
Washington, D.C.

or

His Excellency
The President of the United States
Washington, D.C.

Sir:
Dear Mr. President:

PRESIDENT'S WIFE

Mrs. John Blank
The White House
Washington, D.C.

Dear Mrs. Blank:

PRIEST

Reverend James E. Murphy
or
Reverend Father Murphy

Dear Father:
Reverend Father:
Dear Father Murphy:

PRINCE OF THE ROYAL BLOOD

His Royal Highness Prince Charles   Sir:

PRINCESS OF THE ROYAL BLOOD

Her Royal Highness the Princess
  Mary

Madam:

RANK OR TITLE

PROFESSOR IN A COLLEGE OR UNIVERSITY

Address the Envelope	*Begin the Letter*
Professor John Smith Department of Mathematics Northwestern University Evanston, Illinois	Dear Sir: Dear Professor Smith: Dear Dr. Smith:

or

John Smith, Ph.D
Professor of Mathematics
Northwestern University
Evanston, Illinois

or

Dr. John Smith
Department of Mathematics
Northwestern University
Evanston, Illinois

QUEEN

The Queen's Most Excellent Majesty	Madam:
or	May it please your
Her Gracious Majesty, the Queen	Majesty:

RABBI

Rabbi Kenneth Bogen Temple Emanu-el Fifth Avenue New York, N.Y.	Reverend Sir: Dear Sir: Dear Rabbi Bogen: Dear Dr. Bogen: (if he
or	holds a doctor's de-
Reverend Kenneth Bogen	gree)
or	
Reverend Kenneth Bogen, D.D.	
or	
Dr. Kenneth Bogen	

RANK OR TITLE

REPRESENTATIVE OF CONGRESS

Address the Envelope	*Begin the Letter*

The Honorable John Smith
The House of Representatives
Washington, D.C.

or

Representative John Smith
The House of Representatives
Washington, D.C.
   or (if sent to his home)
The Honorable John Smith
Representative in Congress
(Followed by postal address)

Sir:
Dear Sir:
Dear Congressman
   Smith:
Dear Representative
   Smith:
Dear Mr. Smith:

SECRETARY OF AGRICULTURE (Secretary of Commerce, Interior, Labor, Navy, State, Treasury or War)

The Honorable
The Secretary of . . . .
Washington, D.C.

or

The Honorable John Smith
Secretary of . . . .
Washington, D.C.

Sir:
Dear Sir:
Dear Mr. Secretary:

SENATOR

The Honorable John Blank
United States Senate
Washington, D.C.

or

Senator John Blank
The United States Senate
Washington, D.C.
   or (if sent to a home address)
The Honorable John Blank
United States Senator
(Followed by home address)

Sir:
Dear Sir:
Dear Senator Blank:

RANK OR TITLE
SISTER OF A RELIGIOUS ORDER

| *Address the Envelope* | *Begin the Letter* |

Sister Mary Angela   Dear Sister Angela:
          or   Dear Sister:
The Reverend Sister Angela

SPEAKER OF THE HOUSE OF REPRESENTATIVES

The Honorable   Sir:
The Speaker of the House **of**   Dear Sir:
  Representatives   Dear Mr. Speaker:
Washington, D.C.
          or
The Speaker of the House of Repre-
  sentatives
Washington, D.C.
          or
The Honorable Frederick Knight
Speaker of the House of Representa-
  tives
Washington, D.C.

STATE REPRESENTATIVE

The Honorable Peter Blank   Sir:
The House of Representatives   Dear Sir:
The State Capitol   Dear Mr. Blank:
Jefferson City, Missouri

STATE SENATOR

The Honorable John Smith   Sir:
The State Senate   Dear Sir:
Trenton, New Jersey   Dear Senator Smith:
          or
Senator John Smith
The State Capitol
Trenton, New Jersey

RANK OR TITLE

UNDERSECRETARY OF STATE

Address the Envelope	*Begin the Letter*

The Undersecretary of State
Washington, D.C.

Sir:
Dear Sir:
Dear Mr. Corey:

or

The Honorable Robert Corey
Undersecretary of State
Washington, D.C.

VICE PRESIDENT OF THE UNITED STATES

The Honorable
The Vice President of the United
  States
Washington, D.C.

Sir:
Dear Sir:
Dear Mr. Vice President:

or

The Vice President
Washington, D.C.

or

The Honorable Michael Brent
Vice President of the United States
Washington, D.C.

COMMISSIONED RANKS IN THE ARMY AND NAVY

The Army	*The Navy*
2nd Lieutenant	Ensign
Lieutenant	Lieutenant Junior Grade
Captain	Lieutenant
Major	Lieutenant Commander
Lieutenant Colonel	Commander
Colonel	Captain
Brigadier General	Commodore
Major General	Rear Admiral
Lieutenant General	Vice Admiral
General	Admiral
General of the Army	Admiral of the Fleet

SPECIAL
MONEY SAVING
OFFER

Now you can have an up-to-date listing of Bantam's hundreds of titles plus take advantage of our unique and exciting bonus book offer. A special offer which gives you the opportunity to purchase a Bantam book for only 50¢. Here's how!

By ordering any five books at the regular price per order, you can also choose any other single book listed (up to a $4.95 value) for just 50¢. Some restrictions do apply, but for further details why not send for Bantam's listing of titles today!

Just send us your name and address plus 50¢ to defray the postage and handling costs.